Praise for
*Human Permaculture*

In the times of rapid and deep transition that we find ourselves in, we need the right tools at our disposal. We need to be imaginative, playful, effective, resourceful, and we need to roll our sleeves up and do stuff. But at the same time, we need templates, principles, and a lens through which to see the possibilities before us. *Human Permaculture* provides that — a distilled crash course in how to think in a way the future needs us to think. Vital reading.

— Rob Hopkins, author, *From What Is to What If,*
founder, Transition movement

I am encouraged that so many permaculture practitioners, designers, teachers and activists are finding their voices in writing about permaculture and I am sure your book will make a contribution in that process and I personally wish you well with the book.

— Dr. David Holmgren, Permaculture co-originator

By closely examining the second directive of permaculture — people care — this beautifully illustrated book applies design science to one of the oldest questions ever asked: what makes a good life? The younger you are, the sooner you need to read this.

— Albert Bates, author, *The Biochar Solution* and *Burn*

This is an outstanding book bringing together the theory and the practice of the most enlightened way of growing food, harvesting energy, and living in harmony with our precious planet Earth. It is an inspirational, as well as a practical, book. It celebrates the soil, nourishes the soul, and sustains the human spirit.

— Satish Kumar, author, *Elegant Simplicity*, founder, Schumacher College

This book could not have arrived at a more crucial time. The coronavirus pandemic has upended our food system, requiring us to rethink it quickly and in broad strokes. The principles for doing so, to the benefit of people and planet, are all contained herein. Accessible, well-grounded, and profound.

— Richard Heinberg, author, *The End of Growth*,
Senior Fellow, Post Carbon Institute

We know *how* to bring massive change for the better to the whole world and its environments. It is the human element that blocks that progress. This book helps unlock that block so we can bring meaningful change for the good of this planet.

—Stefan Sobkowiak, MSc, MLA,
teacher, presenter, and orchardist at Miracle Farms,
featured in the film *The Permaculture Orchard: Beyond Organic*

*Human Permaculture* expands the goal of creating self-sustaining agricultural systems towards the vision of creating regenerative human ecosystems. This book serves as a guide for anyone wanting to create a more sustainable lifestyle for their family, business, or community. Rather than working alone on self-sufficient homesteads, *Human Permaculture* outlines tools to bring people together towards collaborative solutions for all.

— Thomas J. Elpel, author, *Botany in a Day* and *Green Prosperity*

*Human Permaculture* invites each of us to deliberately design our lives so we can more fully realize our own potential, while also contributing to greater collective abundance, and working with all other life forms to co-create regenerative ecosystems. People who understand the importance of the "human angle" and have been thirsting for more works along the lines of Looby Macnamara's *People & Permaculture*, will find *Human Permaculture* a welcome addition to their bookshelves.

— Jenny Nazak, author, *Deep Green,* blogger, www.jennynazak.com

*Human Permaculture* opens up our minds — with humour, well researched facts, fascinating examples of real-life permaculture projects, and interesting graphics — to the idea that designing an environmentally respectful life is within our reach. We find out that permaculture is not just practised in agriculture, but that it is a set of life-principles we can learn to use, in order to become "artisans of change," for the recovery of the planet. I highly recommend this book.

— Elizabeth Serreau, head librarian, French American International School

*Human Permaculture* is the book that so many have been waiting for. It widens the territory of permaculture to more fully include the need to not just redesign what we manage in the environment but, more foundationally, ourselves and our ways of understanding and living in the world. This is an essential resource for all who want to make a meaningful, equitable, nurturing, and ecologically sustainable contributions to our shared future.

— Stuart B Hill, Emeritus Professor, Western Sydney University, NSW, Australia

At last! This book establishes the design of the individual and collective human "system" firmly as a priority in permaculture! It also shows us many examples of how humans can learn and have learned from nature's elegant solutions to systemic problems.

— Jessie Darlington, permaculture trainer and designer

A must read for anyone exploring permaculture, looking to reconnect with their deep relationship with Mother Nature, and how we can transform ourselves and society with Her benevolence.

— Krishna McKenzie, Solitude Farm, www.krishnamckenzie.com

I loved the part on diet, especially the summary of the many adaptations that other species have made, as guidance for our own dietary choices. This is vital information for our species, we now have such choice of what to eat that we seem to be lost at best, or worse still, engaged in our own destruction, via soil loss biodiversity loss and pollution of air, land, and sea.

— Andrew Darlington, permaculture trainer and designer

This is the book for people who want to apply permaculture in their personal lives. It will join the canon of social permaculture together with Looby MacNamara's *People & Permaculture*.

— Rosemary Morrow, Blue Mountains Permaculture Institute, author, *Earth User's Guide to Permaculture*

# Human Permaculture

## Life Design for Resilient Living

Bernard Alonso and Cécile Guiochon

**Illustrated by Marie Quilvin**
**English translation by Scott Irving**

new society
PUBLISHERS

Les Éditions Écosociété, 2016, from the original French edition, *Permaculture Humaine: Des clés pour vivre la Transition.* www.ecosociete.org

Cover design by Diane McIntosh. Cover image © Marie Quilvin.

English translation by Scott Irving.

Illustrations by Marie Quilvin.

Printed in Canada. First printing June, 2020.

Inquiries regarding requests to reprint all or part of *Human Permaculture* should be addressed to New Society Publishers at the address below. To order directly from the publishers, please call toll-free (North America) 1-800-567-6772, or order online at newsociety.com

Any other inquiries can be directed by mail to:
New Society Publishers
P.O. Box 189, Gabriola Island, BC V0R 1X0, Canada
(250) 247-9737

LIBRARY AND ARCHIVES CANADA CATALOGUING IN PUBLICATION

Title: Human permaculture : life design for resilient living / Bernard Alonso and Cécile Guiochon ; illustrated by Marie Quilvin.

Other titles: Permaculture humaine. English

Names: Alonso, Bernard, 1953- author. | Guiochon, Cécile, author. | Quilvin, Marie, illustrator. | Irving, Scott, 1986- translator.

Description: Translation of: Permaculture humaine. | Translated by Scott Irving. | Includes bibliographical references and index.

Identifiers: Canadiana (print) 20200213571 | Canadiana (ebook) 2020021358X | ISBN 9780865719316 (softcover) | ISBN 9781550927245 (PDF) | ISBN 9781771423205 (EPUB)

Subjects: LCSH: Sustainable living. | LCSH: Human ecology. | LCSH: Permaculture.

Classification: LCC GE196 .A4613 2020 | DDC 304.2—dc23

Funded by the Government of Canada    Financé par le gouvernement du Canada

New Society Publishers' mission is to publish books that contribute in fundamental ways to building an ecologically sustainable and just society, and to do so with the least possible impact on the environment, in a manner that models this vision.

AMAZING DATA

FOCUS ON WATER

KEYS TO SUCCESS

PIONEERS

INSPIRING EXAMPLES

TIPS AND TRICKS

TO FIND OUT MORE

# Contents

# Preface:
# Building the World of Tomorrow, Today

*In November 2013, Jean-Marie Pelt warmly welcomed us into his office at the European Institute of Ecology in Metz, France, an organization he created in 1971 to "promote initiatives to improve quality of life, the environment, and relationships among people." He was excited about our book project and agreed to write the preface, which he did in March 2015. Months later, in December, he died at age 82. All of his life, as a pharmacist, researcher, professor and enthusiast of botany, and author of some sixty books, he generously shared his love of living things with the public.*

BEFORE I CAME ACROSS THIS BOOK, all I knew about permaculture was its name. I pictured it as a sort of "agroecology plus," a field that encompassed broader factors by marrying the discipline even more closely than usual with the general values of ecology. But the notion of human permaculture lay beyond my imagining.

What does *permaculture* mean, exactly? The *perma-* is from *permanent*, which is synonymous with "sustainable." And *-culture* implies both senses of the word: agriculture and human culture.

The chief benefit of permaculture is that it draws inspiration from the models we find in nature to promote a more ethical and less predatory lifestyle. It does so in a way that bridges the laws of nature and those governing human societies. (I try to point out these areas of close overlap with every book I write.) Human beings, like animals and plants, are subject to the laws that reign over all living beings. In short, the natural sciences and the human sciences agree over the core principles of permaculture — and that's saying quite a lot.

*Jean-Marie Pelt*

Take the laws of evolution, for example, which apply to the biological world and human societies alike. In both cases, the same mechanisms are at work: mutation, hybridization, migration, isolation, speciation, and so on. It is valid to draw comparisons between social species (companies, labor unions, political parties, religions, etc.) and biological species; both evolve and are acted upon by the mechanisms mentioned above. It follows that nature can be reasonably viewed as a matrix for understanding social evolutionary changes in humanity — and that permaculture as practiced in fields and gardens can be seen through the same lens and according to the same criteria as permaculture employed within human groups.

The permaculture approach is profoundly innovative. For centuries, and especially in modern times, we separated and cloistered knowledge into disciplines, each consigned to its own corner. Disciplines cordoned off in this way are much less likely to "hybridize" with each other. Permaculture, by contrast, explodes boundaries. In my view, this cross-cutting approach is its best feature. After reading this book, I think it heralds a promising trend that foreshadows fruitful innovations in many domains.

The authors begin by defining permaculture as "a systemic approach that makes it possible to create viable ecosystems inspired by the laws of nature.... It seeks to care for human beings and the environment while generating life and fostering abundance and sharing." The human species is both natural and cultural; we are thus included in biological nature by virtue of our bodies, but we emerge from it with our minds. We are individuals imbued with the ability to choose and to assume responsibility. We cannot be seen as existing outside of nature, as its "masters and possessors" (to use Descartes's dubious terms), bringing it under our dominion and predation.

We are conditioned by the dominant culture of our era: producing and consuming ever more stuff, we are swept along with the progress of science, technology, and industry, even to the point of neglecting and suffocating our core identity. Hence the existential malaise that is so noticeable today. In conditions such as these, how do we regain our sense? How do we avoid burning ourselves out? How can we cope without reference points, without bearings, without an ideal, without hope? The often cruel need to adapt to outer constraints ultimately serves to kill our inner selves. But when those inner selves bounce back, when spiritual experiences are sparked, a new world that arises from the depths of us impels us, on our modest scale, to transform the world around us. We recall the famous adage, often attributed to Gandhi: "Be the change you wish to see in the world." Humanity teeters precariously between our most deeply held aspirations and the dominant economic model imposed upon us by the never-ending media stream that threatens to drown us. Thus, we seek another model — and this is where permaculture holds the keys.

Those who are attuned to the language of nature, so precious in the eyes of our preindustrial ancestors, are familiar with the many artful examples it offers up. Nature has solved problems for plants and animals alike — problems we too face. Did nature not supply the template for hook-and-loop fasteners (better known under the brand name Velcro) in the tiny hooks of the burdock plant? Or for self-cleaning glass in the drop of water that trickles over the lotus leaf without wetting it? Or for flying machines in birds, or for helicopters in the hovering insects of the Syrphidae family? We emulate all these examples in our technologies, a process known as biomimicry.

Nature also provides us with the model of ecosystem functioning — the whole web of species existing in relation to each other, exchanging services that form the very basis of the delicate balances that support them. The same goes for human societies — vast ecosystems where each individual, each group, each profession, each institution contributes to the balance of the whole. This is the balance we must aim to achieve, one in which nature, living beings, people, and human groups all attain their full potential. This is the key objective of human permaculture. In this book, the authors elaborate on several subjects that help create and maintain these balances. They propose 12 methods for building unified and functional teams, also known as collective intelligence. After all: "If you want to go fast, go alone; if you want to go far, go together." This is a favorite saying among permaculturists. I also enjoy this quotation attributed to Charles Darwin: "It is not the strongest of the species that survives, nor the most intelligent that survives. It is the one that is most adaptable to change." We also know that the adaptation process will be a smoother ride if it is based on the principle of cooperation; indeed, in nature as in society, living beings exist not only in competition with each other but also in cooperation with each other, a fact that biological research underscores every day.

I greatly enjoyed the authors' vision of striking the proper balance between the right brain and the left brain. In our modern age, the left brain is king. It analyzes, deduces, and is perfectly suited to the world of information and communication technology, in which we act out logical and linear sequences on our devices: keystroke 1, keystroke 2, and so on. This is completely unlike the operation of the right brain, the seat of our emotions, intuitions, sensations, and affects — the brain of creativity and spiritual drive. Education must allow both sides to develop in tandem. School will no longer just be a venue for gaining knowledge; it will be a place that fosters the creative expression of a society on the path towards qualitative growth. Permaculture represents another way to see the world, a transition towards another model of society, a different manner of feeling and acting. It is a path that so-called transition towns and cities are already on.

The book lays out the different steps involved in creating a design, which the authors define as "a set of practices for conceiving, planning, arranging, and structuring a space, project, group, relationship, or organization to make it fertile, abundant, and sustainable." Such designs are always inspired by the laws of nature and are meant to include the best strategies for ensuring the system's functionality: producing energy, protecting biodiversity, using resources optimally, recycling, reducing the environmental impact of human activities, etc. A design may apply to a person, group, or community (including urban collectives and rural folks).

With these foundations in place, the body of the book goes on to discuss the practices needed to care for the Earth and human beings, especially by finding alternative ways to fulfill their basic needs. A set of practices and behaviors are listed, each inspired by examples that have yielded results that work. This makes it a precious source of information, offering successful existing models that can be used to inspire future action. Even just reading about these developments, one gets the sense that the world of tomorrow is nigh.

The authors have chosen a suitable form for their book. The writing is perfectly structured, and their editorial opinions and elaboration of ideas and proposals are easy to follow. The language is clear, the style flowing. As I read this book, I was struck by how pleasant the potentially dry material was to read. The authors write persuasively, and the reader will be persuaded. We ultimately reach an understanding that everything ultimately boils down to love — including the love humans have for nature and for each other. Reading between the lines, one discovers a work brimming with fraternity, solidarity, and conviviality.

I am convinced that you, dear reader, will feel as I do when you see the richness and vast potential of this conception of permaculture for yourself. I wish you all the pleasure I experienced myself in making this discovery. I have no doubt that this book will be the success it deserves to be. *Bon voyage* as you journey through the world of permaculture, a world so different from our own and yet so easily within reach of anyone who, like us, wishes to help bring about the emergence of a new world.

*Jean-Marie Pelt*

Author of these recently published books:
- *Cessons de tuer la terre pour nourrir l'homme! Pour en finir avec les pesticides,* with Franck Steffan (Paris, Fayard, 2012).
- *Héros d'humanité* (Paris, Flammarion, 2013).
- *Le monde a-t-il un sens?* with Pierre Rabhi (Paris, Fayard, 2014).

*Pour ce qui est de l'avenir,*
*il ne s'agit pas de le prévoir mais de le rendre possible.*

*It is not for us to foresee the future*
*It is only necessary that we make it possible.*

— Antoine de Saint-Exupéry

**Introduction**

# Guiding Individuals and Groups through the Transition

## GROWING AWARENESS OF A WORLD REACHING AN END-OF-CYCLE PHASE

A GREAT TRANSITION encompassing both humanity and the environment is already underway. In a world of fluctuating oil prices, worldwide economic crises, and worry about climate-related disasters, our living habits are in upheaval. Individualism, born of the euphoria of industrial growth and unfettered consumption, is on the wane: people are thinking twice before hopping into their cars, reading labels before making purchases, paying attention to the energy efficiency of their homes, and engaging in all kinds of other such shifts. Collective-minded behaviors are becoming commonplace: carpooling, community gardens, educational work bees, and bartering are springing up everywhere. People are questioning how we organize ourselves socially and economically when it comes to food, health, education, agriculture, energy, finance, governance, access to natural resources, and other concerns. All human activities are being re-examined in the light of our new reality: the awareness of a finite and fragile world. Urgent changes are required, a fact that is worrying to many citizens. As our old benchmarks fade away, our new reference points remain only vaguely defined.

## THE URGENCY TO ACT

The urgency of seeing this transition through is being felt all the more strongly as demographic pressure mounts: the global population is expected to rise from seven and a half billion in 2020 to nine billion by 2050. Currently, one out of every two human beings is a city dweller. By 2050, three out of every four of us will live in an urban environment—most in huge cities. The limits of today's urban models are becoming apparent: the world's largest cities currently occupy two percent of the world's surface yet consume 75 percent of the available energy, emitting 80 percent of human-generated $CO_2$ in the process. What will this picture look like with two billion more people bustling about our cities?

We know that our fundamental human needs aren't going to change. To live peacefully, to flourish, and to lead creative and productive lives, humans must count on having food, housing, clothing, transportation, communication, etc. We are a long way off from that point today, with millions still unable to have these vital needs met. How will humanity withstand the demographic explosion that is playing out on our bounded planet? The need to rethink our economic and sociocultural models, already obsolete, is inevitable.

## PREPARING TO LIVE WITHOUT FOSSIL ENERGY

If we do not act, true disruption lies in wait. Who today is prepared, either personally or collectively, to cope with a power outage lasting several days or — worse — several weeks? How about a major break in the energy supply resulting from an earthquake, storm, tsunami, nuclear accident, or attack? This is not the stuff of science fiction: each of these scenarios has played out in one country or another in the last few years. Picture this — suddenly, no lights in your home (thankfully, candles and matches still work!), no streetlights, no drinking water from the tap (city water is distributed by electric pumps), no stovetop for cooking, no heating other than woodstoves (almost all heating systems rely on electricity, including pellet stoves), no hot water to shower with, no gas for the car, no delivery to stores (supermarkets have only three days' worth of food), no more newspapers, no more radio or television, no more telephones, no more computers, no more Internet, no more emails! No more elevator to carry you down from the office after a day's work. No more credit or debit card payments, no more ATMs. Pretty much *everything* runs on electricity or oil!

One ripple in the supply and all of society enters a state of paralysis, with a domino effect that is hard to imagine on a large scale. Apart from a few countries like Canada, where 60 percent of the grid runs on a hydroelectricity (96 percent in the province of Quebec), most of our societies rely heavily on fossil energy for electrical power.

Even France, whose leaders proudly tout its energy production independence thanks to nuclear power, is 100 percent reliant on imported uranium to supply its reactors. Uranium, a strategic (and therefore fragile) fossil resource, is a nonrenewable material that powers an industry in which hazards and radioactive waste pose major threats that remain unsolved.

## TAKING CHARGE OF THE ENERGY IN YOUR LIFE

The precariousness of the situation is a wake-up call encouraging us to reduce our dependence on fossil energy, to limit our greenhouse gas emissions (which threaten the climate), and to engage concretely in the transition to renewable energies in all dimensions of our lives: our water and food supply, our housing, our transportation methods, and our social, professional, and cultural activities. The priority today is to bring our lifestyles — as individuals, families, and collectives — into harmony with the available resources on the planet.

## HUMAN PERMACULTURE AS A RESPONSE TO THIS DELICATE PERIOD OF TRANSITION

To rise to the challenge and help build the newly emerging world, the field of human permaculture proposes an innovative, holistic, creative, and interactive approach. It maps the foundations of classic permaculture — a concept born over four decades ago — onto human pursuits. Permaculture, the natural practice of agriculture defined by Australians Bill Mollison and David

Holmgren, has seen burgeoning success throughout the world in recent decades. Permaculture training opportunities are widespread and festivals are thriving, attracting masses of youth, not to mention adults of all ages, looking to delve into this approach. Yet the human-focused dimension of the discipline remains much less well known — and the time has come to fill this gap!

The originality of the "human permaculture" approach is considering the discipline in its broadest scope. It's about building (or rebuilding) human ecosystems using the models provided by nature: generating more interactions between people rather than having everyone working solo in urban silos, producing more energy than we consume, and opting for simple tools over high-tech solutions — they are so much easier to maintain and repair, after all!

This approach is in keeping with the aims of the growing number of people who want to work together to design solutions in the face of current and future uncertainty.

## BUILDING THE CHANGE RATHER THAN ENDURING IT

Because we know that "another world is possible," because we are helping build it around us, we are writing this book to offer readers the chance to master the keys to human permaculture (Part 1). Through a design process (Part 2), we invite readers to ask the right questions in order to find appropriate responses for their specific situations, rather than defaulting to ready-made solutions.

This book invites readers to reconcile with nature (on which we are totally reliant given that we form an integral part of it), to discover or rediscover the ways in which they are vitally linked to the water, the soil, and the forest (Part 3), and to "permacultivate" their food in a way that's in line with today's issues (Part 4).

This book gives informed readers the tools they will need for the transition. Each reader can adapt these tools to suit their own pace and their own preferences, and for whatever situation — be it their family, neighborhood, school, business, and so on. Armed with an understanding of the global issues connected to their everyday actions, and inspired by pioneers and examples of workable alternatives, readers will be equipped to design their daily lives. They will be able to reorganize their activities sustainably and harmoniously to create viable and fertile ecosystems around them, freely and fully consciously. Most will likely have to work to overcome the inevitable "resistance to change." But overcoming these sticking points is easier when one can see how others have made the leap and landed on their feet!

Enthusiastic permaculturists may gather new perspectives and be tempted to bore their friends and family with tedious exhortations. But remember, our only power resides in changing ourselves. There is no point in trying to change others! The example we set will either give people the urge to commit to undergoing a transformation in their own time, or it won't. Such choices are strictly personal — though extremely contagious!

# What Is Your Impact on the Planet?

HERE ARE A FEW FUN TESTS designed to calculate the impact of your personal and collective activities on the planet. The point, of course, is to become aware of these impacts so that you can try to limit them.

## 1) CALCULATING YOUR CARBON ACCOUNTING AND YOUR ECOLOGICAL FOOTPRINT

**What is the surface area of your home?** How many kilowatt-hours of electricity do you consume each year? How old is your refrigerator?

**How many kilometers** do you clock in your car each year? How many on public transportation?

**How many times per week do you eat meat?** Fish? How much butter and cheese? What volume of locally grown vs. out-of-season fruits and vegetables do you consume? Do you drink bottled water or tap water?

**How much household waste** do you take out every week?

**What is your annual budget** for computers and other electronic devices? How much do you spend on shoes and clothes?

**How much meat or pet food** do your pets eat?

**How many weeks per year** do you spend on vacation in sunny climes?

Answering these questions about your housing, transportation, diet, and consumer products yields a wealth of information. Developing a consciousness of the impact our lifestyles have on the planet and on global warming is a precondition for reducing our *carbon accounting* and our *ecological footprint*. What does this mean?

### Carbon accounting

Carbon accounting is a way to assess the volume of greenhouse gas (especially $CO_2$) emitted by a person or group in the course of their everyday activities, with the goal of reducing their impact on the climate. Knowing the type (fossil or renewable) and amount of energy people consume indicates how dependent they are on fossil energy — and how vulnerable they are in the event of a (potential) energy crisis. These facts are good to know!

We encourage you to do your carbon accounting test online! For example, try this calculator: carbonfootprint.com/calculator.aspx

Much more complex calculators are available for companies and communities: ghg protocol.org/companies-and-organizations

### Ecological footprint

The notion of the ecological footprint, first developed by William E. Rees and Mathis Wackernagel in 1992, gained widespread public attention during the 1990s.

The ecological footprint reveals the influence human activities have on natural resources (the exploitation of soil, water, forests, terrestrial and aquatic wildlife, and so on); unlike carbon accounting, which deals "only" with the effect of human activities on the climate. The ecological footprint compares the pressure from human activities to the Earth's "biocapacity" to restore itself (i.e., to regenerate its resources and absorb the waste produced by humans). The planet's resources are limited, while the population is increasing. If I consume more than my share of natural resources that I am entitled to mathematically, if I consume resources faster than nature can replace them, and if I produce more waste than the planet can absorb, then I am monopolizing the public good; I am infringing on the share that belongs to my fellow human beings and that of future generations. The ecological footprint applies at all levels: individuals, cities, countries, and humanity as a whole. It can be expressed in equivalent "hectares" and equivalent "planets," as in, "How many planets would we need if everyone lived like I do?"

The Global Footprint Network maintains the most current and complete footprint calculator: footprintcalculator.org.

### 2) REDUCING YOUR CARBON ACCOUNTING BOTTOM LINE AND YOUR ECOLOGICAL FOOTPRINT

This entire book will help you pursue this goal! People often find the results of carbon accounting and ecological footprint tests surprising — and motivating. By pointing out which parts of our lifestyle make up the biggest pieces of the ecological pie, these tests encourage us to find ways to improve our results.

We recommend that you take both tests *before* reading this book — and then take them again a *few months later,* once you have begun your transition and absorbed some of the basics of energy sobriety and resource sharing. The difference will surprise you!

## We are consuming the resources of one and a half planets: spot the error!

After you subtract the global surface area of oceans, deserts, and mountains, and once you have accounted for the space needed by other animal species, what remains is an average of one and a half hectares of biologically productive land, or three soccer (football) fields for each of the roughly seven billion individuals alive today. That's not much to meet a person's needs from cradle to grave (water, food, living space, materials to manufacture all the equipment they will need, clothing, transportation, etc.). Especially when you consider that this area is shrinking as the population increases. China, the United States, India, Brazil, and Russia alone represent 50 percent of the world's ecological footprint.

If we do nothing to change our lifestyles (though we are starting to!), by the year 2050 humanity will need the equivalent of three planets to meet our needs, process our waste, and absorb our pollution. The interest owing on this ecological debt will be a significant drain on our grandchildren's food, health, and pocketbooks. Adopting a lifestyle compatible with the planet's limited resources is an urgent matter.

For a deeper dive into our ecological footprint and one planet living, check the Global Footprint Network: footprintnetwork.org/

# Part 1

## The Keys to Human Permaculture

**Chapter 1**

# Definitions and Foundations of Classic Permaculture

*I hold it equally impossible to know the parts*
*without knowing the whole,*
*and to know the whole*
*without knowing the parts in detail.*

— Blaise Pascal (1623–62)

HUMAN PERMACULTURE takes the principles of permaculture as defined in the 1970s by its founders, Bill Mollison and David Holmgren, and applies them specifically to the human domain. In Part 1 we will explore a few keys to understanding the meaning of this transposition and performing it successfully.

Those new to permaculture will no doubt appreciate a simple definition of the concept of permaculture. However, it would be very limiting to box permaculture into just one definition since it encompasses such varied practices and domains. For starters, we can say that permaculture is a systemic approach that makes it possible to create viable ecosystems inspired by the laws of nature. Although the term permaculture was applied to agriculture when initially conceived, it has since evolved to deal with human culture more broadly, including its social and economic dimensions. It is a mix of ancestral wisdom and common sense, enriched by scientific understanding. Permaculture combines a holistic approach with local solutions that seek to limit the negative impacts of human activities on the planet.

Permaculture is inspired by the functioning of natural ecosystems, the dynamic matrix of living organisms interacting with each other and with their environment, exchanging energy and matter to maintain and develop life. Every ecosystem is bound to evolve, transform, and adjust to outside changes through a process of adaptation. Otherwise, it is doomed to vanish! The interrelation of all ecosystems overlapping with each other since the dawn of time has continuously allowed life to sustain and renew itself. This is how the immense puzzle that forms our planet Earth, each piece of that puzzle a complex ecosystem unto itself, has played out for the last 4.5 billion years. These ecosystems have formed, matured, and refined themselves, allowing for the propagation of species and their continued existence. The

*Permaculture is a systemic approach that makes it possible to create viable ecosystems inspired by the laws of nature.*

ecosystems are all the more dynamic and fertile by virtue of their being connected to a wide diversity of species, each stimulating and reinforcing the others through positive interactions.

Being modelled after the laws that govern natural ecosystems, permaculture organizes human activities as harmoniously as possible. The approach provides viable and sustainable designs that take into account all strata of the ecosphere and increase the number of interactions between the systems created. Permaculturists are encouraged to pay attention to natural resources — wild plants and animals, water, soil, wind, and sun — but also to the economy, agriculture, urban planning, and the relationships and exchanges among individuals. The spirit of permaculture is summed up by its founders as follows: it seeks to care for human beings and the environment

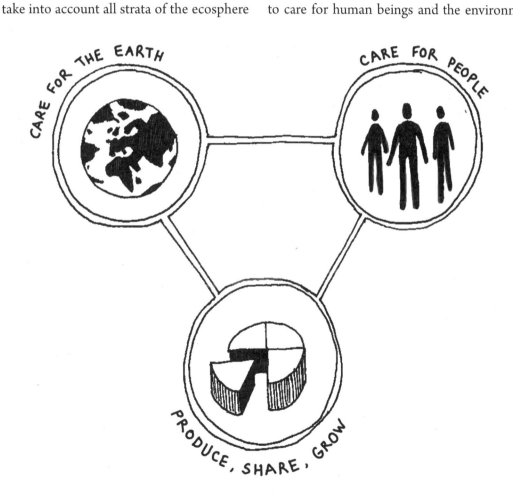

while regenerating life and fostering abundance and sharing.

## DESIGN: AN EFFECTIVE DEVELOPMENT TOOL

The word *design* appears frequently in permaculture jargon. In this context, design refers to a set of practices for conceiving, planning, laying out, and structuring a space, project, group, relationship, or organization to make it fertile and sustainable.

In nature, species adapt to their environment. With humans, this plays out somewhat differently. In the industrial world, which is based on the idea that economic growth is infinite, education has given itself the mission of making people efficient at producing and consuming. Schools and universities teach working methods, techniques, and pedagogical content geared toward this objective. Diplomas reward the students who fit into this mold, sidelining the rest. Similarly, human beings exert influence on the environment to make it respond to the needs identified by society — even if it means defying the fundamental laws of nature. We fashion landscapes as we please, often with little regard for the living things that already occupy them, neither knowing nor worrying about the long-term consequences of our actions.

By contrast, permaculture encourages people to account for the fundamental needs of both humans and the environment with a view to achieving long-term overall well-being. In this model, human intervention consists of creating systems that exist synergistically and harmoniously with each other, respecting the laws of nature and the original features of the site in question. Permaculturists endeavor to intervene as little as possible in the ecosystems in which they work, and strive to enhance all life-giving elements. They transform what can be transformed and bring in as little as possible from outside the system. This means every design is by definition unique. Acquired knowledge or past success can be incorporated, but each design remains particular to its own situation.

## PHILOSOPHICAL FOUNDATIONS

Permaculture rests on the idea that nature is spontaneously abundant — that life begets life indefinitely through the interrelation of all its existing forms. Thus, a forest destroyed by fire is able to build itself up again through interaction with other living systems that contribute to its rebirth. Like all living species, the human species has a special role to play; human beings are endowed with a singular capacity to create and to act in a deliberate, planned fashion — for better and for worse. This liberty comes with great responsibility for the species. Using freedom for good requires a great deal of wisdom and intelligence. *Homo sapiens*, which came on the scene just 200,000 years ago on a 4.5-billion-year-old planet, has committed some serious follies of youth in recent decades: by exploiting human

*Permaculture rests on the idea that nature is spontaneously abundant — that life begets life indefinitely through the interrelation of all its existing forms.*

and natural resources to satisfy certain short-term interests, "*Homo industrialis*" threatens the equilibrium and preservation of the Earth system. Permaculture is a summons — one among others — to help modern humans rediscover wisdom. Nature and the effectiveness of its mechanisms of regeneration provide the template: that is what biomimicry is all about. By restoring equilibrium in natural ecosystems using the tools of permaculture, humanity may gradually regain its rightful place in the universe.

## ORIGIN AND EVOLUTION OF THE WORD *PERMACULTURE*

The concept of permaculture was developed in Australia in the 1970s in response to the major climate crisis that was already rearing its head. The word is a contraction of *permanent* and

# The founders' legacy

Two Australians, considered the cofounders of permaculture, helped spread the movement around the world.

**Bill Mollison** (1928–2016). It is with gratitude that we salute the memory of this founder of permaculture, whose death we learned of in late September 2016, just as we were finishing up the first French edition of this book. He taught in the unit of Environmental Psychology at the University of Tasmania, where he met the young David Holmgren. In 1978, together they published, *Permaculture One: A Perennial Agriculture for Human Settlements*. The book was the outcome of their discussions on the relationships between agriculture, landscape architecture, and ecology, a vision that Mollison had begun to encapsulate in the term *permaculture* in 1974. In 1978, Mollison founded the Tagari community in

Stanley, Tasmania, a 70-acre establishment that achieved self-sustainability. In 1979, he created the first permaculture training institute and published *Permaculture Two: Practical Design for Town and Country in Permanent Agriculture*.[1] In 1988, Mollison published *Permaculture: A Designer's Manual* and, in 1991, *Introduction to Permaculture* (revised in 1997).[2]

Mollison also spread permaculture by delivering intensive 72 hour training courses around the world. These became the international standard for permaculture design courses. He laid out a number of principles used in the design process, some of which have become slogans among permaculturists:

– Work with nature rather than against it.
– Plan for energy efficiency.
– We are limited only by our imagination.
– Diversity is the basis of resilience.

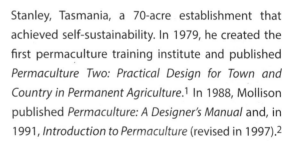

– Each element performs multiple functions.
– Every function is performed by multiple elements.
– Use the least effort for the maximum effect.
– The problem of one element is the solution to another element.
– Take responsibility for your life — now.

Mollison showed that the robustness and effectiveness of a system are the result of both the quality and the quantity of its interconnections: for example, if one element weakens or malfunctions, it is usually because another element is missing. In such situations, Mollison therefore proposed the introduction of a new element into the system to regulate the disturbance. He received the Right Livelihood Award, the "Alternative Nobel Prize," in 1981.

**David Holmgren** (1955–) In 1978, he published *Permaculture One* with Bill Mollison. He experimented with and refined the permaculture approach on his mother's farm and later on his own farm. In 2002, he defined 12 principles that underpin a sustainable society and published *Permaculture: Principles and Pathways Beyond Sustainability*,[3] a work based on a quarter-century of experience. Holmgren wagered that energy consumption would decrease after peak oil. His vision inspired Rob Hopkins and the transition town movement. Holmgren has been giving "certified Permaculture Design Courses" since 1991. He helped found the Australian ecovillage Fryers Forest, home to 11 families. Through the application of permaculture principles, this 300-acre site (once devastated by the operation of a gold mine) has been rehabilitated, in particular by developing the forest and by stocking water in reserves. Holmgren also works on retrofitting suburbs.

 **TO FIND OUT MORE:** Holmgren Design: Permaculture Vision and Innovation, holmgren.com.au.

*culture.* In this context, *permanent* connotes sustainability rather than mere continuation over time. *Culture* evokes both cultivating the soil and the cultural dimension in itself. In this book, we use the word *culture* in its broadest sense, with reference to cultivating the soil, cultivation of the self, and human cultures. Similarly, we use *nature* to speak about the physical and biological environment, but also "human nature" as well.

Permaculture did not invent anything new! From time immemorial, well before the word "permaculture" existed, Indigenous people have been "caring for people and the environment by generating abundance in a spirit of sharing." For many decades and in many parts of the world, knowledgeable people and groups have kept the flame alive, bringing new life and credit to ancestral practices that all but disappeared as they were eclipsed by the industrial era. Today, these approaches are being built upon with the application of more recent scientific discoveries. And with the intention to advance a long-term vision that blends respect for human beings and for the environment, they share the same goal as permaculture. Depending on the field to which they are applied, these approaches go by such names as agroecology, agroforestry, biodynamics, biomimicry, sociocracy, alternative economies, citizen alliances, vernacular architecture, bioelectronics, talking circles, and so on.

In this book, the word *permaculture* includes all activities that apply and imitate the natural

## Permaculture ethics

In adhering to the ethics of permaculture, permaculturists commit to:

### Care for the Earth

Here, caring means protecting, it means paying attention, and offering respect and gratitude. "Earth care" applies to living things in all strata of the ecosphere. These include the life of the soil and subsoil, microorganisms, the world invisible to the naked eye (the most populous and oft-forgotten world); water in all its forms, marine and other aquatic life; the atmosphere, the air, and the gaseous components needed for life; and the other planets that influence life on Earth, as well as invisible realities (depending on individuals' beliefs).

### Care for humans

"People care" means ensuring that every person, starting in childhood, is given the proper conditions to live, grow, develop consciousness, achieve their potential in all dimensions, and do what they were born to do. It means ensuring that every individual has access to the abundance that is an inherent principle of life. It means organizing work to ensure human beings struggle as little as possible to produce the goods they need.

### Share resources fairly and redistribute the surplus

Given that our planet has limited resources and is home to a rapidly growing human population, permaculture encourages sobriety in production and consumption. It calls for the "fair share" of natural resources and goods. It encourages people to strike a just balance between the needs of each person — present and future — and those of other living organisms (human, animal, and plant).

proclivity of ecosystems to create a dynamic of life, regardless of the field of application.

In fact, these three pillars of permaculture interact in a virtuous circle: if we care for the Earth, humans benefit from higher quality of life. If we care for the Earth and people, the abundance thus generated can be shared equitably. Equality will motivate people to care for other people and for the Earth, and so on.

All living species evolve and participate in the action of life. These permaculture ethics highlight human beings' place in creation and their role in co-constructing the world. They help clarify the meaning of our presence on Earth.

### PERMACULTURE PRINCIPLES AS DEFINED BY DAVID HOLMGREN

The illustration "house person" (page 15) is inspired by a drawing featured on David Holmgren's website, representing the appropriate position of humans within the universe. Each person and their habitat are harmoniously connected to the environment. In Holmgren's view, it is incumbent upon each person to become a responsible citizen and to do their part in building a sustainable world, without waiting for ready-made solutions to arrive from on high.

The 12 principles of permaculture.

1. Observe and interact
2. Catch and store energy
3. Obtain a yield
4. Apply self-regulation and accept feedback
5. Use and value renewable resources and services
6. Produce no waste
7. Design from patterns to details
8. Integrate rather than segregate
9. Use small and slow solutions
10. Use and value diversity
11. Use edges and value the marginal
12. Creatively use and respond to change

## DEFINING HUMAN PERMACULTURE

"Human permaculture" is created by the *interaction* of individuals within a "team." Teammates organize their work around projects in which each person has the opportunity to express their particular skills (their "niche") by reaching for a common objective, all while applying the three foundational ethics proposed by permaculture: earth care, people care, and fair share.

The term we created, human permaculture, is intended to go much further than social human *interrelations*: communication, caring, and functioning around societal rules, etc. Human permaculture projects are built around the human qualities and capabilities that are present (rather than those that aren't), which stimulates the creation of enhanced exchange zones — a well-known concept ("edge effect" or "border effect") in the world of permaculture for those regions of greater diversity of life where ecosystems meet and overlap.

- Social permaculture is about human inter*relation*.
- Human permaculture is about the inter*action* of human talents, which are woven together in teams to create Life in all its forms.

The two approaches are complementary. Human permaculture contributes:

- The idea of the individual life design, also known as the life plan.
- The expression of niche profiles that belong to each individual.
- The exchange zone (border effect), i.e., the stimulation of talents that merge within a team to spark collective intelligence and genius.

This functioning can be observed in the wild in a number of social species such as termites, bees, and lions. It also seems to appear in the complex construction of our modern societies — which have nevertheless forgotten an elementary principle: that every life is imbued with its own function, its own niche, flowing from the fact that it possesses the biological tools required to express itself.

## Chapter 2

# The Contribution of Human Permaculture

LIKE ALL "LIVING" THINGS, permaculture evolves. Today's pioneers of change seek to transform all dimensions of their lives, not just how they work the land. They are on the lookout for possible solutions. Things have changed since permaculture first emerged in the 1970s. The movement is adapting to today's needs, feeding the new emerging consciousness to facilitate our transition to the dawning new humanity. This means we must extend our thinking to integrate the human factor into the design process. We carry within us the creative energy that animates all strata of life. The time has come to permacultivate our whole lives! Bill Mollison himself ended his book *Permaculture Two* by affirming that "the only security lies within ourselves, the only safety in having friends, good neighbors, and a meaningful society of man."

This book contains the keys to taking our first steps in the transformation process. Other steps will appear as experiences and needs come to light.

### PRACTICING PERMACULTURE

Changing the world begins with changing ourselves. All outward changes in our behaviors and actions are the product of inner transformation. To integrate with the surrounding ecosystem, the permaculturist first endeavors to determine the role that belongs to them: in other words, to find their "niche," according to the definition first advanced by the biologist George Evelyn Hutchinson in the late 1950s and now used in permaculture. Each human being is a full participant in the activity of creation. Thus, each person has a specific role to play in the great puzzle of humanity. Determining what this role is gives people meaning in their lives, a feeling of being in their rightful place and connected with the never-ending creation of the world. To make this discovery, we must remain flexible and open-minded in our approach, profoundly transform our modes of thinking, and gradually unlearn our habits — and that can take some time! The design steps we present in this book will help you transform your life across different dimensions so you can fit into your ecosystem in a productive and joyful way.

One major contribution of "human permaculture" is the conviction that a life can be planned! As they would do in any company or project, each person should take the time to put together a life plan to reach their most deeply held goals. Teammates working on a common project should be able to explain their life design to the rest of the team (see Part 2, Design: A How-To Guide). Each person should present their niche, their raison d'être, their aspirations, and their vision of what they wish to accomplish, along with the experience they have acquired and the career path typically found in a resume. In this way, it is possible to confirm whether the shared objectives have been set in a manner consistent with each person's niche and aspirations. Human permaculture contributes this fresh angle, which sees the life design as an opportunity for participants to flourish through the expression of their innermost abilities.

Once each person's life design is understood by the teammates of the common project, each person's intrinsic talents can be appreciated and valued and the optimal result obtained. Becoming a permaculturist makes it possible to delve much deeper than simply "making a living" or earning enough money to maintain a fleeting illusion of happiness.

Informed permaculturists will spot a thousand opportunities to refine their personal transformation and to use their talents in service to their environment: this includes developing the creative potential of the right hemisphere of their brain; improving and enriching their surroundings simply by being present; limiting their consumption and exercising moderation in their use of resources; insulating their homes properly and opting for local and biodegradable building materials; spearheading group and shared housing initiatives; providing open access to drinking water while ensuring it returns to the environment in a pure state after use; fostering the production of healthful and local food; ensuring access to nature, land, and care for basic needs; protecting farmland threatened by urban sprawl and development; promoting renewable energy; limiting waste production and encouraging recycling; supporting the development of alternative currencies; giving themselves permission to express their role in a job that suits who they are; promoting social equality; adapting their city, neighborhood, or village to the transition; encouraging teamwork; promoting and using "soft" (environmentally friendly) and collective modes of transportation; encouraging intergenerational interactions to take place; exercising their right to be different and to think and act freely; preserving areas untouched by human activities; promoting biodiversity; fostering plurality at all levels to improve the effectiveness of systems; favoring interdependence over self-sufficiency; appreciating that all living species have an intrinsic value and role; creating harmony and cooperation; avoiding competition; educating children by helping them be their authentic selves; adopting a sane and joyful lifestyle oriented towards being rather than having; and more.

No matter what field they are applied to, the permaculture principles make systems more effective. They generate a dynamic abundance of

> **Language note: permaculture.** Permaculture is a vision, a philosophy, an approach applied to living within an ecosystem — it is not a technique. Thus, we speak of "applying the vision or principles of permaculture" to a garden or to a business, or "taking a permacultural approach" to urban design. There is a widespread idea that permaculture is just a collection of agricultural techniques. This is a reductive view which deprives the concept of its deep meaning.

wealth, including human wealth. When the right hemisphere of the brain (the seat of creativity and intuition) is stimulated, right action arises spontaneously, illuminated by our profound nature, which is itself intimately related to the whole.

In this book, we present — by no means exhaustively — a number of facets of permaculture. In so doing, we hope to reveal a fertile and creative approach that each person can build upon, based on their goals and priorities.

One of the key insights of human permaculture is the acknowledgement that a human life is something that can be planned! Every person should take the time to develop their personal life design (and tweak it over time) in order to reach their most deeply held goals. In a group project setting, you should be able to articulate your personal life design to your teammates. Your design sums up your niche, your raison d'être, your aspirations, and your vision of what you want to accomplish — in addition to the experience and career path that would be outlined in a typical resume. Human permaculture provides a fresh lens. Through this lens, life design is seen as an opportunity for teammates who articulate theirs to attain fulfilment beyond reaching the project's objectives (see Part 2, Design: A How-To Guide).

More than anything else, becoming a permaculturist means leading a "purposeful" life — one with a raison d'être and one which, like all other lives around us, has a "niche" that helps keep the surrounding ecosystem functional. It means going beyond the reductive need to hold down a job merely to "make a living" and/or make enough money to maintain a passing illusion of happiness. By living your life as opposed to making a living, you are sure to set yourself up for fulfilment—a sense of being where you belong—as well as abundance. Like an obvious truth, a life mission is something that reveals itself with time.

**Chapter 3**

# Change the World, Starting with Yourself

HOW CAN WE CHANGE the outside world without first (or at the same time) transforming our inner landscape? There's more to the human factor than just "other people"; it includes ourselves. To change yourself — what an adventure! Usually change is something imposed on us by the events of our lives. But making the decision to change yourself is an act of courage. It is a case of mobilizing both hemispheres of your brain to guide you to the right attitude — a more personal one.

Sustainable, profound, and conscious change only moves in one direction: from interior to exterior. Such change roots us in our deepest dimension, in our relationship with that which is "bigger than ourselves" and in our relationships with other people and with society.

How do we start this inner change? By activating our "Zone 00" (pronounced "double zero")! Zone 00 is a recent "invention" in the history of permaculture. To save travel in their everyday activities, the first permaculturists originally devised five concentric zones, from their personal habitat (Zone 0) out to the wilderness (Zone 5). As time went on, it became unavoidable to consider the uniqueness of the inhabitants themselves: their niche, their sensitivity, their deep needs. Thus was born Zone 00, which represents the most intimate reality of each person. This zone was inspired by observations of Zone 5, which remains untouched or given over to nature. Zone 5 can inspire the attitude we adopt in all domains, from how we build our habitats, to what food choices we make, to what projects we undertake, and so on. It is from Zone 00 that the seeds of change germinate, allowing us once more to blend harmoniously with the flow of the world and become fully actualized as humans.

## CHANGE CAN BE CONTAGIOUS

The legend of the hummingbird and the wildfire, an originally Amazonian story popularized by Kenyan environmental activist and Nobel Peace Prize Laureate Wangari Maathai, reminds us that

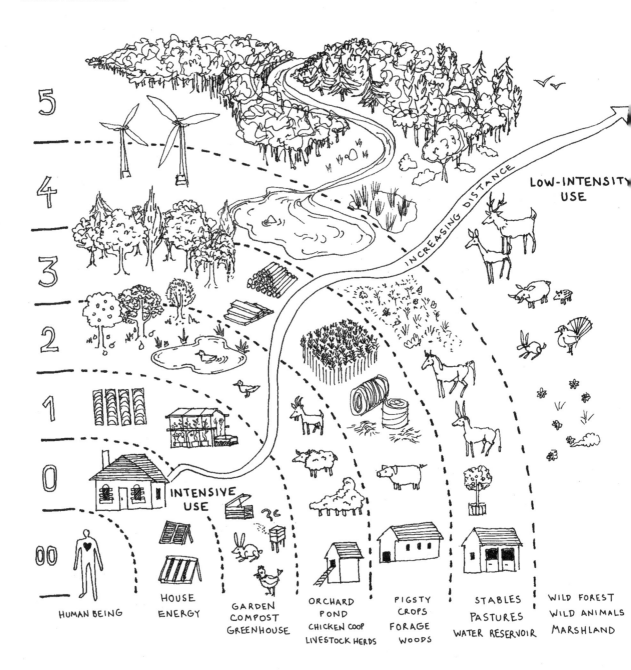

5
4
3
2
1
0
00

LOW-INTENSITY USE

INCREASING DISTANCE

INTENSIVE USE

| HUMAN BEING | HOUSE ENERGY | GARDEN COMPOST GREENHOUSE | ORCHARD POND CHICKEN COOP LIVESTOCK HERDS | PIGSTY CROPS FORAGE WOODS | STABLES PASTURES WATER RESERVOIR | WILD FOREST WILD ANIMALS MARSHLAND |

*Zones.*

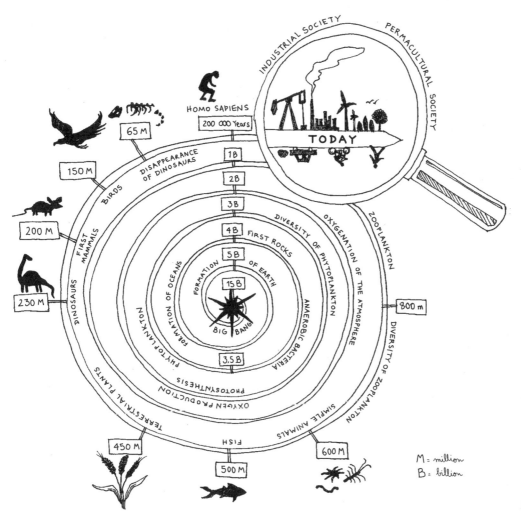

INDUSTRIAL SOCIETY

PERMACULTURAL SOCIETY

HOMO SAPIENS
200 000 Years

TODAY

65 M

150 M

DISAPPEARANCE OF DINOSAURS

BIRDS

1B

2B

3B

4B  FIRST ROCKS

5B

DIVERSITY OF PHYTOPLANKTON

OXYGENATION OF THE ATMOSPHERE

ZOOPLANKTON

200 M

FIRST MAMMALS

DINOSAURS

15 B

FORMATION OF OCEANS

FORMATION OF EARTH

BIG BANG

ANAEROBIC BACTERIA

230 M

800 m

DIVERSITY OF ZOOPLANKTON

PHYTOPLANKTON

3.5 B

OXYGEN PRODUCTION

PHOTOSYNTHESIS

SIMPLE ANIMALS

TERRESTRIAL PLANTS

FISH

450 M

500 M

600 M

M = million
B = billion

*Spiral of evolution.*

change is contagious: from individual to individual, example spreads to a group and from there to the entire society.

Men and women have always innovated by introducing new methods in art, architecture, technology, resources management, etc. Such innovations have impacted all of humanity, often reaching far beyond their initial geographical location. By working on our personal development, we contribute to a global evolution. Once again, we become part of the whole, in connection with the rest of humanity.

## The legend of the hummingbird

One day, a huge fire was raging through the forest. Terrified, the animals fled the disaster. Only the hummingbird, the smallest bird in the forest, flitted into action. Back and forth, back and forth it flew, darting between the pond and the blaze, carrying a few drops of water in its tiny beak with every trip. Bothered by this pitiful effort, the armadillo called out, "Hummingbird! How foolish you are! You can't possibly believe you will extinguish the fire one drop at a time! Flee with us!"

The hummingbird replied, "I won't put the fire out all by myself, but I'm doing my part."

### WHAT SHOULD I TRANSFORM – AND HOW?

If your situation predisposes you to inaction (often the case for people who live in safe, comfortable environments), you can deliberately choose to create conditions that are more favorable to change. Exercising your human freedom may impel you to take risks in order to seek out the profound meaning of your life. This may involve:

- **Quitting denial:** Does your current life no longer satisfy you fully? Do you dream of something else? There is more to life than surviving. You must look at things head-on.
- **Daring to be yourself:** Accept that you are different and unique.
- **Going beyond simplistic solutions:** Take the time to research or invent responses adapted to your particular solution; avoid "copy-paste" solutions.

- **Staying positive, creative, and confident:** Do your best, and do it patiently. With time, and with opportunities that will inevitably arise if you remain determined, you will definitely succeed in your transition.
- **Celebrating life!** Each day provides a reason to rejoice, no matter how small it may seem. Remaining alive to these small (and large) joys will help you embrace unexpected occurrences and discover their latent meaning and potential.

 **PERMACULTURE PRINCIPLE 1:**
Observe and interact

### WHEN SHOULD I START?

The ideal time is now — both to commit to your personal journey and to join the great movement of global transformation! Once you have laid the groundwork, the design steps will be your guide as you build the only life that can fully satisfy you: your own!

## SEVEN BILLION UNIQUE INDIVIDUALS

Our need to feel recognized and loved often makes us try to conform to what we imagine others expect of us. Daring to be yourself means giving yourself permission to be different; it's about allowing yourself to express who you are, in your entirety, through the unique slant of your "niche," without fear of rejection. In our conditioned society, only a few "originals" dare to live in accordance with their deepest aspirations. They are the ones who feed the flame that lights the way to the new humanity.

## THE PERSONAL EXPERIENCE OF UNITY

Sooner or later in your search for meaning, you will stumble across an experience of unity, an awareness that every human is an element of the whole, inseparable from the flow of life that manifests the world. This experience will come with a feeling of fulfilllment and give you strength to overcome all obstacles along your path! This spiritual discovery may arise while you are immersed in nature or in the midst of an aesthetic emotion, meditation, or prayer.

The resulting change is commensurate with the intensity of the experience. Every person will find their own answers in the course of their evolution, depending on their values and the wisdom or spiritual tradition they feel closest to.

## Chapter 4

# Reconnecting with Our Deep Belonging to Nature

"THE HUMAN IS A DISTILLATE of the universe," said the researcher and philosopher Jean-Marie Pelt, in keeping with the teachings of ancient traditions *and* quantum physics. Belonging to nature is written deep inside every single one of our cells. "Nature" is our nature! If we mapped the history of life on Earth (3.8 billion years) onto the scale of a human lifespan, we could say that life appeared 38 years ago, the first humans four months ago (400,000 years), *Homo sapiens* two months ago (200,000 years), and consumer society one minute ago (60 years)! Seen in this light, we present-day humans are a tad young to presume to know how to safely reshape the world to suit our desires! It would undoubtedly be wiser to lean on the far more ancient wisdom of nature and of life itself.

For centuries, humanity has believed that it is sovereign, that it can (and must) dominate the world, and that our freedom consists of extricating ourselves from the laws of nature that shape us. We have lost sight of the fact that we form an integral part of the natural. To destroy nature is to destroy ourselves. To peel ourselves away from nature is to lose the profound meaning of our presence on Earth. The result is that human

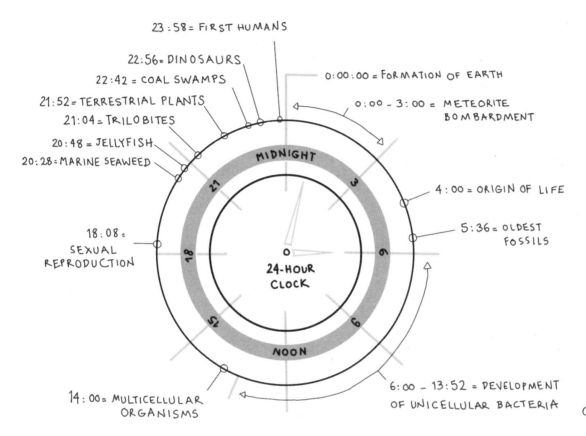

23:58 = FIRST HUMANS

22:56 = DINOSAURS

22:42 = COAL SWAMPS

21:52 = TERRESTRIAL PLANTS

21:04 = TRILOBITES

20:48 = JELLYFISH

20:28 = MARINE SEAWEED

0:00:00 = FORMATION OF EARTH

0:00 - 3:00 = METEORITE BOMBARDMENT

MIDNIGHT

4:00 = ORIGIN OF LIFE

5:36 = OLDEST FOSSILS

18:08 = SEXUAL REPRODUCTION

24-HOUR CLOCK

NOON

14:00 = MULTICELLULAR ORGANISMS

6:00 - 13:52 = DEVELOPMENT OF UNICELLULAR BACTERIA

*Clock of evolution.*

beings have seen themselves in exile and have searched with all manner of means — often illusory ones — to reconnect with the true meaning of life, one that is in harmony with the whole.

If we accept the idea that our planet is alive, we come to appreciate that each element of its "body," including each person, has a specific role to play. All that remains is to find out what our role is and put it into practice! The complexity of relationships among the natural elements keeps the system healthy and balanced. Elements that are not integrated or useful disappear. As the Anglo-French philosopher Edward (Teddy) Goldsmith, founder of the journal *The Ecologist*, reminds us: "In order for the ecosphere to conserve its stability, all living beings that compose it must obey a true hierarchy of laws, which themselves form the laws of nature." The problem is that modern humanity's way of life disturbs this order: "It is the inability of modern humans to respect the limits that protect the integrity and stability of the various social and ecological systems that trigger their destabilization and disaggregation." Of course, as Goldsmith recognizes, "We can transgress the laws of Gaia, but there will be a price to pay..."[1] Doing so may even result in the death of the system.

What if humanity learned to position itself in partnership with nature, taking part in the evolution and co-creation of the world? This permaculture book is here to help you be guided and inspired by the native, forgotten intelligence buried deep within you. Indeed, it's not learning we need so much as detoxifying: we need to break free from the conditioning that has stifled our true identity. The good news is that, in the right circumstances, our dormant potential cries out for reawakening. Living freely today means rediscovering the creative energy within us that powers all strata of life; it means rejoining the flow of evolution along with all other life forms, life forms which never stopped cooperating with creation — after all, they don't have the choice.

*What if humanity learned to position itself in partnership with nature, taking part in the evolution and co-creation of the world?*

**PERMACULTURE PRINCIPLE 4:**
Apply self-regulation and accept feedback

## RIPE FOR CHANGE?

Do you feel the confusion of meaninglessness in your life and the recurring dissatisfaction associated with this? Do you feel as though you're running without ever reaching your destination? If so, you are ripe for change. It's not about making the leap in response to some outside influence. The signal will come (if it comes at all!) from within, when you finally tire of your current situation. Little by little, you will learn how to deprogram your habits, your assumptions, and your dysfunctional behaviors in relation to nature. Gradually, you will want to simplify what can be simplified to make way for a vital and serene balance. "He who has grasped the immense simplicity of things, he who has heard the single note through the universal noise, owns the world," said paleontologist, theologian, and philosopher Pierre Teilhard de Chardin. That's wisdom!

# Chapter 5

# Nature's Blueprint

*Nature isn't like the economy: it works!*

— Jean-Marie Pelt

JEAN-MARIE PELT, the famous botanist, had a way with words. When we met with him in Metz, a city on the Moselle River in the Lorraine Region of Eastern France, he reminded us,

*In nature, no entity is isolated from the whole. Everything exists in relation to everything else. This is the principle of associativity: simple elements associate with each other to form complex entities with new properties. (Teilhard de Chardin is right when he says that the complexity of matter generates life, and that the complexity of life generates consciousness, and then mind.) But with their consciousness and capacity for freedom, humans — the most evolved beings in the universe — do not automatically apply the principle of associativity. Modern humans no longer want to be subject to universal laws. They see themselves as the owners, the exploiters of the world, rather than the gardeners. They idolize technology over ecology. Contemporary people, especially young people, experience the world through their computer screens. We are losing our intuition: the right brain is stressed by our binary computer systems. Modern thought, for example, has difficulty admitting that the whole is greater than the sum of the parts. The balance between micro and macro is being lost. The mission of the European Institute of Ecology (the institute Pelt founded in Metz) is to reincorporate humans into the vast system of nature. Nature can be useful in inspiring models of social and economic organization in our modern world.*

**PERMACULTURE PRINCIPLE 7:**

Design from patterns to details

Modern humans have forgotten their place in the great cycle of life. They invent systems that violate the laws of life and place our future in peril. The permaculture approach recommends looking to nature's models for the intelligence needed to revive, evolve, and adapt. We have everything to gain from this: our profound identity will flower, we will experience completeness by being reconnected to everything, and we will be free to be what and who we are. By imitating the *forms* of nature and emulating the *functioning* of ecosystems, human beings exercise their power to co-create the world.

Historically, the great Eastern and Western philosophers extended humans similar invitations. Lao Tzu said: "Understand unity and you will understand totality." Blaise Pascal, the 17 C French mathematician and philosopher writes in his *Pensées*: "I hold it equally impossible to know the parts without knowing the whole, and to know the whole without knowing the parts," and "the whole is greater than the sum of the parts." Brilliant artists such as Leonardo da Vinci and Antoni Gaudí also drew inspiration from nature. More recently, in his encyclical *Laudato si'*,[1] Pope Francis reminded humans that they belong to nature: "We have forgotten that we ourselves are dust of the earth, ... our very bodies are made up of her elements, we breathe her air, and we receive life and refreshment from her waters." He continues, in the chapter Integral Ecology:

*Everything is closely interrelated, and today's problems call for a vision capable of taking into account every aspect of the global crisis... We are part of nature, included in it and thus in constant interaction with it... It is essential to seek comprehensive solutions which consider their interactions with natural systems themselves and with social systems. We are faced not with two separate crises, one environmental and*

SOLAR SYSTEM

INFINITELY LARGE

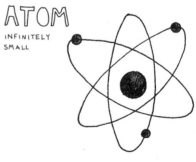

ATOM

INFINITELY SMALL

*the other social, but rather with one complex crisis which is both social and environmental. Strategies for a solution demand an integrated approach.*

## LEARNING HOW TO "LIVE WITH GRACE"

In the 20th century, scientists made the imitation of nature into a new discipline with very practical applications. The discipline is called biomimicry. The concept was defined by the American researcher Otto Schmitt and later developed by the American biologist Janine Benyus. Their essential point is as follows: "Do you have a project or problem? Observe nature; it will show you the solution." Benyus marvels at "the genius that lives, with grace, in nature." She is awestruck at the "yearly renewal of the miracle of the seasons… Who could coordinate so much complexity, so much beauty?" Continuing, in one of her online videos, she recommends, "Let's take advice from these organisms and ecosystems in our project designs!"

The premise of her approach is that no matter what challenge humans face, at least one other species on the planet has had to cope with an analogous situation. In the course of evolution, at least one species has developed effective and sustainable strategies that do not pollute, that do not consume more energy than is available, and that do not emit greenhouse gases. Human beings have every interest in drawing inspiration from these tried-and-true solutions to create effective and lasting organizations, products, and services. More generally, they also have an interest in learning to live "with grace," sustainably and intelligently interacting with other species. The Biomimicry Institute,[2] founded in the United States by Janine Benyus and her team, provides training for youth, students, and professionals in this approach. It also operates an online database to facilitate and share the process of nature-inspired invention: asknature.org. The site is an expanding storehouse of research from engineers, researchers, technicians, and architects who work in biomimicry and ecodesign.

## DISPELLING MISCONCEPTIONS ABOUT HIERARCHY AND COMPETITION…

In nature, there is no hierarchy among species: our anthropocentric perspective is what gives us such a hierarchical notion. We are the ones who crowned the lion as king of the jungle. It's true, of course, that each species has a defined and specific role. The role of a scavenger is different from that of an insectivore or a pollinator. And in a beehive, while the work of a drone may differ from that of a queen, it is no less valuable. A squirrel will find shelter in the hazel tree that supplies its food, then bury its surplus nuts here and there — but it will forget about a certain portion of them, thus unwittingly becoming a tree planter! Which is more important: the tree that provides habitat and food for the squirrel, or the squirrel that stewards future generations of the tree by planting its seeds? All players take part in a complex set of functions that allow life to continue. The same is true in the plant kingdom. The oak tree's role is in no way "superior" to that of the reed. The humble moss that carpets the forest floor, like many other life forms that are visible or invisible to the human eye, is just as useful as the towering trees overhead.

Effective cooperation can be seen both within and between the animal and plant kingdoms. Leguminous plants, for instance, fix nitrogen from the air, transform it into nodules in the soil, and use some of it for their own growth. When they die, they leave behind a large load of nitrogen, which other plants need in order to grow. Similarly, seed-eating birds are designed such that they can digest only a small fraction of the seeds they ingest. The undigested remainder, stimulated by the birds' gastric juices and encased in their droppings, is deposited here and there as the bird flies around, thus ensuring that new plants will grow. "Birds are the selfless actors in so many of our landscapes," as gardener, botanist, and author Gilles Clément so beautifully put it.

## ...AND ABOUT COMMUNICATION

Humans have the unique characteristic of using both verbal and nonverbal language. Words allow us to develop our thoughts, express our emotions, enrich discussions with our fellow humans — and to confront each other. Agree, disagree; I'm right, you're wrong… In our slow evolution to maturity, humans will ultimately discover that understanding a variety of viewpoints and honoring diversity of experience are practices that complement and enrich, with each person adding their own insights to the complexity of a situation.

**PERMACULTURE PRINCIPLE 8:**
Integrate rather than segregate

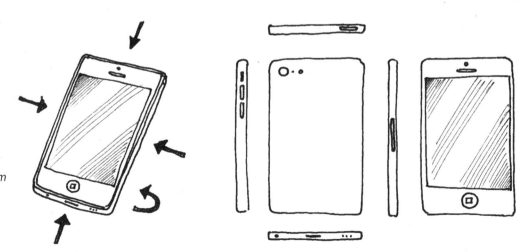

*One single reality from different points of view. All are true and complementary.*

## A CHANGE OF PERSPECTIVE IS NEEDED

Our society tends to neglect the notion of complementarity and instead overvalues some functions to the detriment of others: the work performed by the laborers who make our roads is often thought of as being beneath that of the engineers who design them. Yet the two roles are utterly dependent on and complementary to each other: what use would the engineers' studies and designs be with no one to create roads in the real world? Or, for that matter, with no motorists to use them?

The social ecosystems inspired by permaculture are meant to work to everyone's benefit, just as natural ecosystems do. In the same way that permaculture advocates restoration of the soil, which has been impoverished by decades of mistreatment, today human permaculture proposes that we restore the human realm by leaning on humanity's forgotten potential and the resilience of systems. Just as soil is spontaneously autofertile and bears a yield, humans are naturally creative if they find the right conditions to make their talents bloom.

Sometimes, human beings pass up wonderful opportunities. Imagine if the first Europeans to set foot in the Americas, rather than seeking to destroy the richness of Indigenous peoples, had instead welcomed their difference. They would have helped create a real New World, a product of the experiences of both cultures, a world much richer than the two merely added together: a civilization that was both respectful of nature and technologically advanced.

In France, as in America, some experiments in complementarity are working well: in community-supported agriculture (CSA) arrangements, the confluence of functions works to everyone's benefit. Consumers pay in advance for the weekly vegetable boxes they receive, and sometimes even lend the farmer a helping hand. The farmer receives financial security in addition to material and social support. Members get the satisfaction of consuming high-quality and locally produced organic food, supporting a business, and being part of a network. Everybody comes out ahead.

*Take the time to observe the models of nature, imitate them, and apply them in your designs.*

**KEY TO SUCCESS:** Take the time to observe the models of nature, imitate them, and apply them in your designs.

**Chapter 6**

# Applying the Ecological Niche Concept to Humans

A NATURAL ECOSYSTEM will be effective and lasting if each of its elements is in its place and performs a role in beneficial interrelationship with a maximum of other elements, thus generating life and energy. The same is true of human groups. The new humanity will be better off if each person arrives at their own "niche," their role, and functions in harmony and complementarity with others.

### THE ECOLOGICAL NICHE OF PLANTS AND ANIMALS

The notion of "ecological niche" was first defined by the Anglo-American zoologist G. E. Hutchinson in 1957. The niche determines both the position occupied by an organism, population, or species in an ecosystem and the conditions necessary to its existence. The niche encompasses the habitat in which the species evolves, its diet, the rhythms of its activities, its breeding grounds, its relationships with other species, its group survival strategies, and the balance of its ecosystem.

The American ecologist Eugene Odum clarified the distinction between niche and habitat in 1959 by stating that the niche of a species is its profession whereas its habitat is its address. For example, the ladybug's niche is to control the number of aphids in an environment by eating them. All ladybugs are programmed to carry out this task. All perceive aphids at great distances using their powerful antennas. Their jaws are in- geniously designed to ingest the aphids. Their vocation is unwavering. No ladybug has any other mission than this. If there are no aphids in a giv- en location, there is no reason for ladybugs to be found there. Their weakness is that they make easy prey for insectivorous birds that hunt in the same areas. To compensate for this weakness and keep ladybugs safe from predators — in other words, to ensure sustainable design — nature has devel- oped workarounds: ladybugs excrete a substance that repels birds. And their appearance — black spots on a red background — wards birds off too.

Among the social insects such as bees, ants, and termites, groups of individuals have comple- mentary functions that are useful to the whole species. Bees, for example, have their drones for mating, their queens for laying eggs, and their workers for successively occupying the roles of soldiers, fanners, nurses, etc. Members of social insect species exhibit morphologies and organs specially adapted to these functions in the bee- hive, ant colony, or termite mound.

In nature, all species work for the common good, each producing more energy than it con- sumes, each contributing to the longevity of the ecosystem. Even parasites make sure that they do not destroy the species they subsist on. There is just one exception: humans!

## HOMO SAPIENS, A SPECIES APART

Humanity as a whole does not deviate from the rule. Indeed, it has a collective role to play in the great Earth ecosystem, which we can summarize as follows: to contribute to the world's evolution by creating new ecosystems.

Of the many aspects that differentiate human- ity from the other animal species, one point is of particular interest in this chapter: in addition to occupying their species-level role, individual humans are endowed with their own particular identity, one that must be expressed and elabo- rated over time. This personal identity is not revealed at the outset of life. The human search leads each person (in principle) to chart their own path, to find their place, and to settle into their personal niche. This search is up to each in- dividual's initiative and tastes. It is the province of individual sovereignty, the exclusive attribute of *Homo sapiens*: the freedom to choose between the best option and the worst, or not to chose at all. Humanity's task, anomalous in the living world, is therefore uniquely thorny. "I have set before you life and death, blessing and cursing: therefore choose life, that both thou and thy seed may live," implores Moses in Deuteronomy 30:19. Thus, humanity has the power to choose to co-create the world — or to destroy it.

Another significant difference is that humans are probably the only beings that are conscious of their existence, their individuality, and their uniqueness relative to their fellows — the only beings capable of questioning their place in the world, the only creatures that delude themselves into identifying as separate from other humans and from the world, the only ones that must take a personal journey to re-access an awareness of belonging to the whole.

### AN INDIVIDUAL NICHE TO DISCOVER

Unlike animals and plants, whose role is written into their genetic program, humans must make a conscious effort to discover and develop the talents they carry with them into the world. From young childhood, certain children are hypersocial and attentive to others. Others build cathedrals out of Lego. Certain children always have tools on hand and use them to invent clever contraptions. Some are born with great intellectual facility and are above average at memorization or crafting baffling arguments. Others are endowed with scientific aptitude, artistic talent, or business acumen. It's possible to imagine educational systems designed to help children tune in to their natural inclinations and find their niche at an early age — but this is rarely the case. Rather, finding and growing into one's specific identity requires that we break free from the mold that education has fit us into.

The design process will help you pinpoint and assert your individual niche (design steps four and five). Making this discovery often comes with a sense of relief or even joy — the joy of homecoming. Deep down, many people feel that their true place is not where they presently are. But out of this introspection comes the beginnings of an answer to the nagging thought that haunts many modern-day people: "I don't know where I belong," "My life has no point," etc.

### THE UTILITY OF NICHES IN GROUP PROJECTS

Identifying individual niches is a must when one embarks on a group project: each person can fulfill the roles that mesh with their deepest longings, and the group is able to organize complementary skills and exchanges optimally. A word of caution: Don't box anyone into a role just to meet the needs of a group. It is up to each person to recognize and own their personal niche. It is hard to imagine asking a ladybug to do the work of a pollinator, even temporarily! Yet the equivalent of this remains a common practice in human affairs.

Permaculture has been so successful in recent years because it helps humans reclaim their place in the universe and in society: it offers them tools to fulfill their role of co-creator.

> **Language note: niche.** In this book, the word "niche" is used to define the role of people or elements within their physical, professional, and social situation (their habitat!), emphasizing the functions they may fulfill that enable them to be in harmony with their natural talents or traits.

 **KEY TO SUCCESS:** Take the time to discover your personal niche. Be patient and trust your intuition!

## The story of the sea anemone

"Daddy, what's on the other side of the reef?" asked the little sea anemone one day.

"Why would you ask such a question? Life is good here, on our big rock, safe from the ocean swell. You have all the food you could ever desire; and you are safe with your whole family around you! Who could ask for anything more?"

The little anemone learned that it was best not to ask this kind of question, which made her appear strange in the eyes of others. But her hunger for adventure was not satisfied. One day she noticed a detail in her surroundings: as tidal waves crashed against the reef, just where it hit, millions of tiny air bubbles formed, dancing as they rose to the surface. The little anemone imagined that if she caught enough bubbles, she too could rise to the surface and finally see what lay beyond the reef.

The time came for adventure. Soon enough, a nice big wave arrived, filling the little anemone's mantle with thousands of tiny air bubbles. Finally, she managed to detach herself from the rock! The little anemone allowed herself be swept up into the swirling water and bubbles. Being tossed in all directions was certainly not very comfortable, but she felt the most wonderful sense of freedom. What was not wonderful was hearing the worried cries from her family: "Be careful! It's dangerous up there! You're going to get yourself crushed! Come back! Have you lost your mind?"

But it would take more than that to hold back the little anemone. Even amid the swirling roar of the tidal wave,

she did not so much as shudder. She allowed herself to be pulled up and up, rising like a cork to the top of the swell, gently landing on the other side of the reef.

There, the water was calm and peaceful, warm and pristine. It was of a turquoise color that she had never seen before. There, on the bed of fine sand, white anemones straddled enormous shells as orange spotted clown fish joyfully cleaned the anemones' tentacles. Life had color and meaning at last.

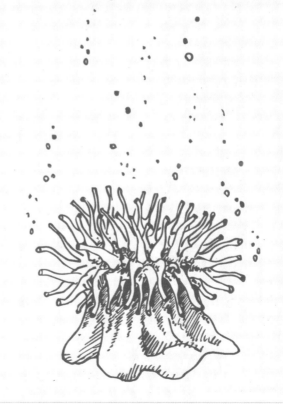

## Chapter 7

# Two Hemispheres Are Better Than One:
## Understanding Your Brain to Leverage Its Potential

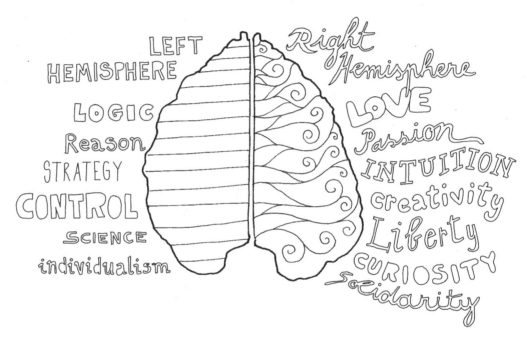

THE HUMAN BRAIN is made up of two hemispheres, among other components. Each hemisphere has a specific function that complements the other. Our modern lifestyle has led us to prize the qualities of efficiency and rationality associated with the left hemisphere — the part that classifies, reasons, argues, and excludes — over the intuitive qualities of the right hemisphere. The right hemisphere's oft-devalued qualities, considered "feminine," include the artistic, the emotional, the imaginary, the dreamlike, etc. Education in schools tends to emphasize left-brain development, leaving little room for the creative functions of the right brain.

### RIGHT BRAIN TO THE RESCUE

In permaculture, we work to restore complementarity between the two hemispheres, which are designed to function in concert and in perfect harmony. Thus, for anyone wishing to develop their full creative potential (and contribute to the evolution of humanity!) it is a good idea to stimulate the right hemisphere of the brain. The right hemisphere gives us access to the "memory of life," which is imprinted on each of our cells. Major figures such as Hildegard von Bingen, Leonardo da Vinci, Albert Einstein, Gandhi, and Janine Benyus exercised both their hemispheres, stretching their scientific, artistic, and spiritual capacities.

The left side of the brain is our "personal library"; it records our experiences (both positive and negative) as well as all the information we have gathered since birth. As we learn, our library expands. This enables us to find quick and comfortable solutions by referring to known benchmarks. It orients us toward the past. If we are presented with a leak, for example, experience is apt to tell us, "plug it." Using this approach by itself limits the creativity that the right hemisphere would bring us by expanding our field of possibility.

The left brain selects, sorts, and interprets the innumerable sensations captured by the right brain. It organizes them and verbalizes them. Language, reasoning, analytical ability, mathematical intelligence, the notion of time, and attention to detail reside in the left hemisphere. This is the voice that tells us it's time to pay our bills, to fill our gas tanks, to plant our radishes, etc. The left hemisphere is also the domain of thesis and antithesis, the seat of our interminable ruminations: "I shouldn't have… If I had

known… They'll never have me back… It's my fault… Yes, but still…"

The right side of the brain, always at the ready, apprehends and holistically presents (even without our knowledge) an array of images, information, and sensations, as well as the energy emanating from them. Through the emotions, it captures the "vibration of the world." It can put us in touch with bioinformation, i.e., the memory of the world, a knowledge that is inscribed in our cells from the time of conception. The right hemisphere is what allows us to converse with people who speak a different language from ours via nonverbal communication. It is what enables a Chinese child to understand a Spanish child. The right brain even allows us to make contact with the other kingdoms in the tree of life. To access bioinformation, we must first develop our attentiveness to the here and now. Walking in bare feet, breathing in the aroma of wet soil after a rain, feeling the wind on the skin, and taking in the silence of nature are sensory experiences that can make us more attentive. Such abilities are innate for some people, but anyone can develop them. The right hemisphere requires calm for its faculties to operate. Breathing slowly and moving gently help open up access to the right brain.

**The left hemisphere** brings consciousness of the *I*, of the *ego*, of details. If the left hemisphere operates without support from the right hemisphere, it produces a narrow, fragmented, and fixed view of reality.

**The right hemisphere** brings consciousness of the *we*, of the collective, a vision that is holistic, intuitive, and creative. If the right brain operates without the support of the left, it produces a confusing and dysfunctional view of situations.

## THE NECESSARY COOPERATION OF THE HEMISPHERES

Only by using both hemispheres of the brain in a coordinated fashion can we obtain a holistic and synthetic understanding of situations, just as we need both our eyes to capture information in three dimensions. Working like an antenna, the right hemisphere takes in information delivered through the senses and emotions and transmits them to the left hemisphere, which analyzes them and makes them available: "I have an idea!"

 **TRY THIS:** Stroke your arm paying full attention to it, while *simultaneously* thinking about your plans for tomorrow. You will see how difficult it is to feel and think at the same time! Either you feel the contact on your skin, or you think about tomorrow. To usefully occupy your left brain, you can ask it to perceive the pressure of your heel on the ground, the heat on your skin, sounds in your environment — without seeking to identify them. This voluntary act situates you in the present moment (right brain) and makes you permeable to your surroundings.

With experience, you can choose to orient your focus, shifting from one hemisphere to the other while learning to be still. Before making a decision, for example, you can deliberately pause for the duration of an in-breath and an out-breath to observe your sensations and inner images (right brain). Being attentive to the present in this way can make all the difference. The resulting decision (left brain) can only be a more enlightened one.

Let's consider the example of a bowhunter tracking an animal. All five senses are at play (right brain): with his eyes, he sees tracks on the ground; with his ears, he detects the slightest rustle; with his sense of touch (wind on his face), he positions himself downwind of his prey; his sense of smell and his intuition guide him in pursuit of the animal; and he can already taste the game he will eventually feast on. He is completely present and fully inhabits his right brain. Suddenly he spies his prey. He freezes, takes aim, and draws his bow. A subtle mix of experience and analysis (left brain) with holistic vision and intuition (right brain) cue the instant he sends his arrow flying. Both sides of his brain cooperate to enable him to reach his objective.

## YOUR BRAIN: A VERY NIMBLE ALLY

Here's some good news: your brain is a dynamic organ that is perpetually reconfiguring itself. This is how it can integrate new knowledge at any age. Networks and neuronal connections can strengthen, reorganize, expand... or disappear, depending on your need to adapt to new conditions (internal or external). Thanks to the brain's neuroplasticity and neurogenesis (the ability to create new neurons from its own stem cells), your future prospects are good: your brain can give you the power to transform your habits and reach your potential! All you have to do is call on it; this was demonstrated by the Italian neurobiologist Rita Levi-Montalcini, recipient of the Nobel Prize in Medicine in 1986 (who died in 2012 at the age of 103).[1]

**SOME TRICKS** for activating the right hemisphere of your brain

– Inhale, exhale. Focus your attention on your breathing. Breathe in, then visualize your out-breath. This will clear away anything cluttering the present moment. Imagine that everything you breathe out will "decompose" in the soil to serve other forms of life. Repeat as many times as you need to attain a calm and present state.

– Be quiet! The fact of speaking activates the left side of the brain and steals attention from the present moment.

– Avoid stress. Agitation is the enemy of the right brain. Breathe deeply, walk, and move as slowly as possible.

– Look at your surroundings using your peripheral vision, without paying attention to details.

– Avoid having a specific intention. Stay exclusively in the feeling of the moment.

– Don't ask yourself questions. Allow your thoughts to drift away like clouds in the sky without stopping to engage with them.

– If you feel an emotion, a contraction, or an expansion, simply notice it and then calmly continue the exercise, breathing out deeply. Stay in the feeling.

In your everyday life, get into the habit of connecting to what you find beautiful in nature: anything from soaking in the silence, the fresh air, or the warmth of sunshine on your skin (but be careful of ultraviolet rays!) to moonbathing, stargazing, walking barefoot in the rain, feeling the water running down your face, touching tree bark, gardening with your bare hands, listening to the wind in the trees, swimming in a lake or river with a minimum of clothing, and so on. If you live in the city, get out and see a painting exhibit, go for a stroll in the park, take in a concert, notice the beauty of people's faces, spend time with wise and serene people, or practice yoga or tai chi. Take the time to savor food.

It is up to each person to create the conditions that are right for them to re-enter into sensitive contact with the living world and to make their "natural" being resonate.

### EXPANSION AND CONTRACTION: MESSAGES FROM YOUR RIGHT HEMISPHERE

Once you are attuned to the present moment, you are poised to feel the sense of contraction or expansion that a given idea, place, person, or fact provokes within you. No doubt you are familiar with the subtle feeling of lightness in your chest that comes during moments of happiness and, on the contrary, the weightiness you feel in the

*The restaurant menu: between expansion and contraction.*

face of frustration or a harsh blow. The feeling instantly wells up, directly from the right brain, before it is understood and analyzed by the left brain. It's important to learn to detect this sensation to know what is best for you, and what your instinct and your inner intelligence are signalling to you. With practice, this feeling becomes more and more perceptible, and eventually automatic.

**KEY TO SUCCESS:** Exercise the agility of your right brain! Be attentive to your bodily sensations. Bit by bit, this will fine-tune your intuition.

For example, try this experiment at a restaurant: open the menu and read the descriptions of the dishes on offer. Pay attention to which ones prompt a positive signal (expansion). Once you have perceived the expansion, read the price column and note the difference! If you gravitated towards an expensive dish, you will feel the contraction right away. Conversely, if your choice is in a comfortable price range, you will remain in a state of expansion.

The first task for budding permaculturists is getting back in touch with this forgotten sense. It's about consciously feeling the life in yourself, and enriching designs with your intuition and experiences of life, both great and small. To develop this skill, you can consciously decide (until it becomes unconscious): "I am engaging my right brain; I am still; I am inhaling and exhaling slowly." You will be surprised at how willingly your brain cooperates and how quickly it understands what you are asking it to do.

Over time, you will make progress. Little by little, you will let images and sensations sink in for longer and longer before moving to the analysis stage. When working as part of a team, do the same thing before taking a position: listen to your feelings about your teammates or the project. Do you notice an expansion? A contraction? This will help you reflect on how to act next. This pause time is critical for fully grasping and comprehending all the elements and producing a viable design.

 **INDIVIDUAL EXERCISES**

### Japa walk

This exercise can be done anywhere, even in the city. It will help you find serenity and remain present to yourself and to others whenever you have a nagging thought or risk losing focus. Walk at a steady pace, look straight ahead while using your peripheral vision, breathe through your nose, and focus on your left heel. Every time it touches the ground, say in your head a one-syllable word of your choosing with a positive connotation — for example, "love," "vast," "good" — or imagine a musical note you like, such as "D." Or alternate the words "here" and "now." Change words if the effect diminishes.

### Stop and go, or Snail

Close your eyes and walk, barefoot if possible, indoors or outdoors, as slowly as you possibly can. For example, take ten minutes to travel one meter! Focus your full attention on the muscles in action, the weight being passed from one leg to another, the feelings you receive from the ground, your breath, and the images that appear in your head. Any time your mind wanders, simply pause, breathe out, and slowly begin walking.

 **PAIR EXERCISES**

### Trespasso

This exercise is great for learning how to stay present in your right brain despite any emotions you might feel. It is best performed with a partner but can be done alone with a mirror. You and your partner sit facing each other, close enough that you can look into each other's left eye. Start by closing your eyes, breathing deeply through your nose, and focus your attention on the air moving in and out of your lungs. When you are ready, both partners open their eyes and look into each other's left eye. (If you are practising alone with a mirror, look into your right eye in the mirror's reflection.) Try to find a sense of calm, free of tension and nagging thoughts. Simply observe what you feel, without leaving the present. Allow any attempts at distraction from your left hemisphere to pass away. If you experience mental chatter, embarrassment, or tension as a result of being close to the other person, get rid of the feeling with a deep breath. Perform this exercise for three to four minutes and repeat a few times. You will be surprised at how quickly it becomes easy to do. Later, at your leisure, you may choose to put yourself into this state of openness in any circumstance.

These exercises allow us to experience the shift from one hemisphere to the other. They develop your capacity to voluntarily make space for the right brain before the left brain gives any instructions.

## When the right brain boils everything down to basics

Dr. Jill Bolte Taylor is a neuroanatomist and alumna of Harvard University. In 1996, at age 37, she had a stroke after a blood vessel ruptured in the left hemisphere of her brain. She lost her speech, her ability to read and walk, and all her memories. Over an eight-year period, she painstakingly retrained her brain completely, eventually regaining all her faculties. In a book entitled *My Stroke of Insight*,[2] Dr. Taylor tells how, being both patient and doctor, she was able to observe the functioning of the right hemisphere of her own brain. While totally deprived of her ability to communicate and understand the words she heard, she intuitively absorbed everything that was going on around her. She felt good and peaceful despite the gravity of the situation.

This special experience (i.e., that of a researcher in the patient role) gave her wisdom that she has shared widely since then: meditation, artistic creation, and prayer stimulate the right hemisphere of the brain and make it possible to attain a feeling of peace, harmony, and oneness with the universe. Balancing the activity of the two hemispheres prevents us from being steered only by the left hemisphere, the seat of rationality and reasoning, which inclines us to doubt, fear, and anger.

**TO FIND OUT MORE:**
- François Joliat, *Henri Laborit: pour quoi vous dire* (Paris, L'Harmattan, 2000).
- Sally P. Springer and Georg Deutsch, *Cerveau gauche, cerveau droit à la lumière des neurosciences* (Brussels, De Boeck, 2000).
- Marie-Françoise Neveu, *Les Enfants "actuels": Le grand défi "cerveau droit" dans un univers "cerveau gauche"* (Paris, Exergue, 2006).

**Chapter 8**

# Teamwork or Collective Intelligence

*If you want to go fast, go alone;*
*if you want to go far, go together.*

— Popular saying

## CHOOSING BETWEEN INDIVIDUAL AND COLLECTIVE INTERESTS

HUMANS ARE RELATIONAL BEINGS. Each person is, by nature, bound to other people. A newborn baby is totally dependent on parents. Many long years pass before the child develops autonomy. In traditional societies, adult humans spontaneously work together to build shelter, meet their dietary needs, raise children, protect themselves from predators, etc. This is a form of solidarity that has almost disappeared in our "every man for himself" society, rendering the matter of personal survival much more precarious and agonizing.

Usually, when someone feels the need to get back in touch with their inner nature, they seek closeness with a group of people in which they feel able to express their individuality and receive support. Just as each individual must discover their niche to determine the right mix of parameters for personal balance and flourishing, each group must become conscious of its collective raison d'être (the group's niche) in order to reach its objectives effectively and sustainably.

If a group is to function well, it's important for each individual to have a clear idea of their role within the team as well as everyone else's. Each person's position must be accepted and recognized by all team members. This allows each member both to appreciate and respect their fellow members' strengths (and utilize them to benefit the project) and to accept and compensate for their own shortcomings. An air of trust and good communication within the group are key to striking this delicate balance.

In the living world, power is focused on a single objective: survival of the species. Only the strongest prevail and reproduce. The scuffles that play out among members of the same species serve to benefit genetic selection and assure the perpetuation of the species. Ants do not have any personal opinions or individual interests that they seek to defend against the rest of the colony, for instance.

In modern societies, humans pursue many objectives besides survival of the species — to the point where modern-day people sometimes seem to lose sight of this primary objective! While proverbial wisdom teaches us that there is "strength in numbers," we still tend to defend special interests (individuals, families, political parties, pressure groups, companies, countries, etc.). Today's collective emergency requires that we overcome our reflexive defensiveness and competitiveness and strengthen the sense of common good by creating networks, seeking complementarity, protecting the right to difference, and paying special attention to our most vulnerable.

**PERMACULTURE PRINCIPLE 11:** Use edges and value the marginal

### INDIGENOUS PEOPLES SET THE EXAMPLE

Certain Indigenous peoples developed communication mechanisms and decision-making systems that allowed them to live peacefully. They created the necessary space to allow each person's creativity to be expressed while expanding the number of zones

*Focus on your teammates' strengths, not their weaknesses! Accept that you will never appreciate every single facet of their personality.*

of exchange, which made for fertile relationships. Traditionally, the goal of all social, economic, cultural, and spiritual organization was the balance and continuation of the tribe.

In Inuit traditional populations, for example, the family unit comprised a couple, their unmarried children, and occasionally a widowed mother, sister, or foster child. The eldest active man was the family's spokesperson. The gathering of multiple families for hunting trips formed the second level of social organization. As the explorer Jean-Louis Étienne wrote,[1] one Inuk might come into contact with only a few hundred people in their whole lifetime, most of them connected in a web of solidarity. The more extensive this web was, the greater the chances of individual survival. Decisions were made jointly. Hunting group sizes depended on how plentiful the region was; if food was scarce, the group split into smaller units. Traditionally, Inuit had several means of strengthening group cohesion: marriages arranged in childhood (thus uniting parents of children promised to each other through a family tie), exchanging spouses, adoption, etc.

**KEY TO SUCCESS:** Focus on your teammates' strengths, not their weaknesses! Accept that you will never appreciate every single facet of their personality.

# TWELVE PATHWAYS
## TO BUILDING A UNIFIED AND FUNCTIONAL TEAM

Here are a few fun ways you can "permacultivate" your teams. These can be used in internships, in your family, at work, or in your neighborhood or village. They will help you build unified and enthusiastic teams. Within a few days or even hours, people from diverse backgrounds will form the bonds of trust. The *I* will be superseded by the *we*, and the group will develop amazing strength.

## 1  CLEARLY FORMULATE THE COMMON INTENTION OF THE GROUP

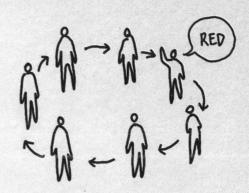

Who and what will be served by the group's proposed project? "If one does not know to which port one is sailing, no wind is favorable," said Seneca. This is true at both the personal and collective levels. Having a clear vision of the objective is key to channelling people's efforts towards the same goal and stimulating creativity. The objective also needs to light the group's fire and keep it going. When group enthusiasm is high, there is little room for unproductive conflicts between people.

### TRY THIS: Here and now

This is a lively activity to do in a circle before a work meeting. Taking turns, have each person express how they feel using a color, word, gesture, temperature, or sound. This activity expands consciousness, gets people attuned to the present, and facilitates group cohesion. This can be done three times a day if needed.

# 2   MOVE FROM "I" TO "WE"

In school, we are assigned individual marks for individual work. At work, we distinguish ourselves from our colleagues in hopes of garnering recognition and distinctions. Individual interest takes precedence over group interest, and this competitive atmosphere creates tension in human relationships: space is defended, power is imposed — and the *I* feels threatened by the *we*. Such competition no longer serves the continuity of the group. It becomes a rivalry, a pointless struggle to gain the most, own the most, and satisfy one's ego. What if, in our efforts toward personal and collective transition, we tried to focus on the good of the group, putting our personal baggage and opinions on hold temporarily, for the sake of achieving the best result?

**TRY THIS: I, us**

For the duration of a group meal, it is against the rules to say "I." This is an invitation to be present and take yourself out of the center. It is perfect for overcoming ego-related friction and building group awareness!

# 3   GET ACQUAINTED BY EVALUATING THE TEAM'S POTENTIAL

Flaunting one's best features is a very constructive exercise, though many find it difficult. When we know each person's strong points and determine the available human resources, we can recognize and appreciate areas of difference and complementarity. This establishes a positive outlook among members and facilitates fruitful interactions. At this stage, we avoid mentioning people's weak points!

**TRY THIS: Positives only!**

In breakout groups of five or six, have individuals take turns sharing what qualities they recognize within themselves: human qualities, technical skills, artistic talent, athletic ability, etc. Allot two minutes to each speaker, while the others listen and take notes. Then have each group report back to the larger group: taking turns, have each person present the assets of a fellow group member. Record all of these on a large sheet. The result is a wonderful chart of the group's human resources.

# 4   BE REAL AND AUTHENTIC

Opening up about ourselves is not easy; we fear judgement and rejection from others. Acting like someone else gives us a sense of protection. But trying to keep up an ideal image — or one that differs from reality — causes stress, which is the enemy of creativity and wellbeing. Cultivating an atmosphere of trust allows each person to regain a childlike innocence and reveal their true self. There is no harm in being who you are — or, rather, some risks are worth taking in the appropriate context.

**TRY THIS: Trust!**

Eight to ten people stand in a tight circle. One person stands in the middle with their arms crossed over their chest, their eyes closed, and their feet together. The people in the circle take turns gently pushing the middle person to each other and catching them. Once trust has been established, the next person takes a turn in the middle.

# 5   CONGRATULATE YOUR TEAM MEMBERS

A positive, encouraging, constructive word makes people feel valued and stimulates the group — provided the compliment is sincere, of course.

For he's a jolly good fellow

**TRY THIS: Congratulations!**

Choose a congratulatory song along the lines of "For He's a Jolly Good Fellow." Sing it in celebration of special occasions: birthdays, completed projects, good ideas, fruitful encounters, quitting smoking, arriving on time, etc.

#  6  LISTEN AND FEEL HEARD

Some people have a tendency to take up all the space in a group, while others take up none at all — both are extremes to be remedied. Here are a few tips for helping each person take up their fair share of the space:

- **Talking stick** (inspired by Indigenous traditions): The person holding the talking stick is the only one permitted to speak. Once they have finished, they pass the stick to the next person in line to speak.
- **Monitor:** Have one person in the group sit back and monitor the quality of the discussion and the speaking time, taking turns in this role. Monitoring requires listening and observation skills — a golden opportunity for those who feel they do not possess these qualities.

**TRY THIS: Posts, everyone!**

Find a useful task to be accomplished that requires strength and time, such as moving the contents of a shed, digging a ditch, or moving a piano. Have the group start by taking the time to organize itself — who does what, based on their strengths and skills. As soon as everyone is clear on his role, perform the task in silence and time how long it takes to finish. Amazing!

# 7 CREATE AN ATMOSPHERE OF DIALOGUE

Stay humble! We have to admit that there are a thousand possible visions besides our own. In an atmosphere of trust and respect, an exchange between differing viewpoints may enrich positions on all sides — or it may not. Making space for dialogue is a world away from compulsively arguing and imposing opinions, which is so common in group settings.

## TRY THIS: The blind and the lame

In this game scenario, two companions, one blind person (blindfolded) and one lame person (legs tied together), are travelling together when suddenly they are attacked by bandits. How will they survive? There's only one solution: cooperation! The blind person carries the lame person on their back while the lame person guides the blind person. Together, the two companions can escape the bandits. This game is best played in an open area outdoors!

# 8 MAKE DECISIONS BY CONSENT

Reaching a decision by "consent" means ensuring that no one is opposed. This differs from "consensus" decision making, in which everyone must be in favor and it only takes one opposing view to block the decision. Groups that function by consent aren't in search of a perfect solution (which could take a while!), but rather a common position that the whole group could "consent" to. This mode of decision-making avoids the drawbacks of a classic vote in which the majority is victorious and the frustrated minority awaits the opportunity to take their revenge.

## TRY THIS: Neither yes nor no

One person starts a conversation and engages the group in it. The object of the game is never to say yes or no. It can be good to come back to this exercise later to see the progress you have made!

## 9 ENCOURAGE SHORT AND FREQUENT MEETINGS

You are guaranteed better results. At the start of the session, set the agenda and determine when the meeting will be over. At the end of the meeting, review any decisions that have been reached and put any unfinished business on the next meeting's agenda.

### TRY THIS: The time bank

Take a pack of 52 playing cards. At the top of the meeting, deal each person a few cards. The value of the cards corresponds to the speaking time they are allowed. Make sure the participants receive a fair hand. Negotiating is allowed. This game invites people to focus their contributions.

 ## 10  PRACTICE DETACHMENT

How a project progresses can take a different turn from how you first imagined it. No big deal. Don't doubt yourself. If you have a concern, ask for clarification. Avoid making assumptions. Detach from the expected results.

### TRY THIS: A little silliness is a good thing

Have one group member show up with a disguise, a clown nose, a funny face, a funny hat, etc. You will see that people instantly let their guard down. This sets the stage for productive work and creativity. Make it someone else's turn for the next meeting.

## 11 CELEBRATE THE LIFE OF THE GROUP—KEEP IT JOYFUL!

With every day we live and every action we take, we have the opportunity for collective joy. Celebrating is a way to value each person's role, to become conscious of the group's effectiveness, and to maintain and strengthen the group's faith in the results of the project.

**TRY THIS:** Let's dance!

Surprise people by playing up-tempo music for a few minutes. Some will spring right up and dance. The shyer ones will follow!

## 12 DEVELOP NONVERBAL COMMUNICATION

Our attire, our tone of voice, our facial expression, our eye movements, our body language, our walking and sitting posture — all of these send messages to those around us. And they say more about who we truly are than any words could say. Are we aware of this? Long before they learn to speak, children are geniuses at expressing what they want. Adults who speak different languages, after some trial and error, manage to communicate just fine in spite of linguistic barriers. Politicians, communicators, and salespeople, all use body language to reinforce their messages.

**TRY THIS:** Mime

Have each person write a word, any word, on a slip of paper and put it in a basket. Taking turns, each person draws a slip and has to mime the word — no talking. The other people have one minute to guess the word.

**All teams have a certain amount of dysfunction.**
**This is normal; this is human. Certain errors are fairly easy to resolve.**

| Error to avoid | Potential solution |
| --- | --- |
| Ignoring your strengths and depriving the group of your skills. | Undertake the process of discovering your niche. |
| Jumping into action before establishing how the group will function and what steps are involved. | Clarify how people will take turns speaking and make decisions, and establish an action plan for successful project completion. |
| Giving *one* person the power (because of their credentials, skills, or enthusiasm). | Share decision-making power among all members. Have each person be responsible for their action items, autonomous in completing them, and accountable to the group. |
| Neglecting the silent minority. | Function by consent. |
| Allowing a growing number of members to become passive. | Ensure that everyone adheres to the common vision. Keep enthusiasm and participation levels high. |
| Letting meetings drag on forever. | Review your objectives. Refocus the debate. Enforce rules for discussion. |
| Forging ahead with the project and leaving slower people behind. | Verify that everyone is clear on the design before proceeding. Respect each person's pace. |
| Allowing yourself to be influenced by false experts. | Trust the group's intelligence. |
| Ignoring the advice of a professional. | Solicit multiple opinions. No one is infallible. |

INSPIRING EXAMPLE

# Dragon Dreaming: a method for successful group projects

Noting that 99 percent of innovative projects fail before they are completed, John Croft, an Australian permaculturist and co-founder of the Gaia Foundation, developed an approach to help groups make their dreams a reality. The goal is to give every person a chance at personal development by co-creating projects that serve life.

The approach, which is both fun and structured, invites participants to confront their personal dragons (fears), which underlie most conflicts. Inspired by Australian Aboriginal culture, it leaves a significant amount of room for intuition and celebration in order to keep the initial enthusiasm high.

John Croft proposes four steps:

**1 Dreaming and visualizing.** The project initiator's intuition must match the needs or expectations of a public in order for the project to take shape.

**2 Planning.** This is the time for those executing the project to ask the right questions and to confront the real world in order to come up with a solid action plan.

**3 Doing.** This is the concretization phase in which the action plan is implemented: contracts are signed, people are hired, seeds are planted, etc.

**4 Evaluating and celebrating.** This step is too often neglected. Here again, it's necessary to ask the right questions in order to draw lessons from the shared experience. This step helps you create better conditions in which to continue the collective creation process.

In the last 25 years, this method has been used to bring over 700 projects to life. Rob Hopkins used it successfully to launch the transition town movement and to write *The Transition Handbook*.[2]

# Part 2

## Design: A How-To Guide

## Chapter 9

# Definition of Design for Permaculture

THE WORD DESIGN refers to a set of practices for conceiving, planning, arranging, and structuring a space, project, group, relationship, or organization to make it fertile, abundant, and sustainable. The objective of a design is to organize beneficial and harmonious interactions among the greatest number of elements — including people, each of whom is a full-fledged component of the design. Each element has multiple functions that allow it to express its full potential, and every function can be performed by multiple elements, thus ensuring a dynamic and lasting system.

In permaculture, designs are inspired by the laws of nature in order to determine the best strategies and ensure the system is viable and resilient. The design will apply the structure best adapted to each situation. A successful design creates energy, produces diversity and abundance, and lessens the ecological impact of human activities, as the examples below will illustrate. The assembly of the constituent elements is what makes each design unique.

### HOW DOES A DESIGN WORK?

The great ecosystem that makes up our planet is designed such that it functions without human intervention. It evolved independently by adapting to varying situations. Similarly, once implemented, our designs will adapt to changes that arise. If a human-made ecosystem is totally dependent on outside intervention or unable to adapt to change, it is destined to vanish.

Take, for example, a person who depends exclusively on a salary, grant, retirement pension, or guaranteed income; or a home where one has to regularly repaint the walls, treat the wood, or empty the septic tank; or a company that has to replace its entire team every year and train new employees; or a garden that requires periodic inputs (even organic ones), repetitive tasks to activate fruit formation in trees, or soil tillage; all of these are signs that the system is not viable over the long term. Such systems demand significant time and energy. A permacultural design would achieve functionality in a less intensive way.

Certain interventions may prove necessary in the implementation of a design, of course. However, the ultimate objective remains the kind of self-sufficiency found in natural ecosystems. Our interventions should be limited to implementing and kickstarting the process. In nature, it takes a whole century to form two or three centimeters of soil. Through specially adapted actions, we can create fertile soil in a few years and then allow the soil to organize itself, as we will see in Part 3.

## AN EVOLVING PROCESS

Design is an evolving and creative process: we take stock of a situation at a given time and clarify the intentions and objectives of the person or group concerned. Design makes it possible to organize or reorganize a system to make it sustainable and versatile in adapting to change. If necessary, tweaks can be made to achieve the desired viability. As Bill Mollison often said, "design and redesign."

 **KEYS TO SUCCESS:** Take your time, and don't skip steps! It is easier to adjust a plan than it is to undo actions that have already been taken.

## THE INTENTION OF THE ACTORS: THE PROJECT'S UNIFYING THREAD

Before jumping in, it is important to understand the primary motivation, either yours or the group's, in carrying out the project. What lights your fire? What needs will the project meet? Who will it benefit? What is the objective? All participants are invited to answer these questions for themselves, either alone or in a group setting. The common intention that emerges from this reflection or sharing will be the unifying thread: the idea around which the project will be built and around which the team will be galvanized.

*Take your time, don't skip steps! It is easier to adjust a plan than it is to undo actions that have already been taken.*

## DEFINITION OF HUMAN PERMACULTURE:

Human permaculture is defined by the interaction of individuals in teams, all working towards a common project or goal. They do so in a manner in which each member has the opportunity to express their personal profile of niches, while applying the three ethics of permaculture: caring for the earth, caring for people, and sharing fairly.

## Chapter 10

# The Nine Steps of Design

steps: one to establish the niches of people and projects, the other to awaken creativity by stimulating the right brain through special exercises and games (the "dreaming and brainstorming" step). Here we present a nine-step approach to design. For clarity, we present these steps in order, from 1 to 9: OBRE-**NI-DREBRA**-DIM. In reality, the process is of course an interactive and non-linear one. Everything is connected to everything else! Each step leads us to adjust and refine what was imagined in previous steps. Start by simply following the steps and appreciating their effectiveness. With experience, you will be able to adapt this tool to suit any purpose.

1. **O**bservation
2. **B**orders
3. **R**esources
4. **E**valuation
   + 5. **Ni**che
   + 6. **Dre**aming and **Bra**instorming
7. **D**esign
8. **I**mplementation
9. **M**aintenance

PERMACULTURISTS originally developed a seven-step tool to guide beginners through the design process, a tool referred to by the acronym OBREDIM, which is made up of the initials of each of the steps described below.

Given that people in the West are generally conditioned to play roles for which they are not suited, we felt it was necessary to add two

# Methodology

### STEP 1) OBSERVE THE SITUATION WITHOUT ANALYZING IT

Whether designing a life, a location, or a project, beginner permaculturists should start by taking the time to be still and observe what they feel here and now, while taking care not to analyze, judge, or explain — and especially not to go off in search of immediate solutions! They need only become aware of the realities at play, in their full depth and uniqueness. They must apprehend these realities intuitively and allow themselves to be "spoken to" by the emotion that each generates within them, as a child would do. To re-access this open-minded view, "all" they need to do is call on their right brain, as we experimented with above.

*Contraction/expansion: a useful emotional indicator in any situation*

During this neutral observation phase, the permaculturist notes the intensity of their emotional reactions to whatever element is under observation, on a scale of 1 (weak) to 5 (strong). These emotions can be pleasant: as we have already seen, this is the feeling of "expansion," evoking a sense of lightness, joy, and confidence. By contrast, the "contraction" feeling expresses irritation, discomfort, and unease. There is no questionnaire or agenda for this first step. Allow yourself to be guided by the flavor of perception. Trust it! With a little training, this exercise becomes a useful emotional indicator in plenty of situations. It also teaches us to look for situations that bring us joy and to decode those that upset us. Expressing the expansion we feel relative to others creates an air of trust that calms the often-unconscious fear of not being accepted. This simple trick is indispensable for anyone wishing to be associated with human permaculture! It makes the group more comfortable, and practising it helps people reclaim the full creative potential of the right brain, putting it in service of the life within you and around you. That can be a challenging thing for humans today!

In this stage of observing without analyzing, the conditioning that compels us to find quick solutions to every situation can often be an obstacle, or even a handicap, to creating the right design. When we are in uncharted territory, we are often tempted to default to familiar responses or gravitate to what we imagine the group's position to be. But remember: diversity of perceptions is precious! Each member has a specific role to play. If even one person feels that they shouldn't express their opinion, the whole group is deprived of their unique contribution.

**KEY TO SUCCESS:** Focus on what you're feeling and share it with the group without worrying how others will see it.

**PERMACULTURE PRINCIPLE 1:** Observe and interact

### STEP 2) IDENTIFY THE BORDER EFFECT

All permaculture texts mention the "border effect." This term was used by David Holmgren and Bill Mollison to refer to the particularly fertile exchange zones that develop at the interface of two distinct environments. For example, a forest with 1,000 species (both plants and animals) located adjacent to an equally rich meadow with a further 1,000 species will have an edge (or exchange zone) with the combined 2,000 species *plus* an additional number of specific species that are attracted by the richness of this new environment that favors their fecundity. In warm regions, mangroves are the environment that forms between the sea and the shore, and certain animal or plant species are endemic to this exchange zone.

The border effect refers to a complex and subtle reality that is sometimes the product of millions of years of adaptation. The upper layer of soil (about 20 centimeters thick) represents an especially fertile exchange zone where the energies of the Earth and the sun converge, setting the stage for an exceptional proliferation of life, the most abundant in the terrestrial ecosystem. The same is true in the marine world, where the topmost layer of the ocean, i.e., the zone of exchange with sunlight, harbors an immense fertility. And human relationships are no exception: the diversity of talents assembled around a project creates an especially fertile zone of encounter — provided that the conditions are in place to make this diversity an asset and not a source of unproductive confrontations. In other words, all team members need to be on board with the venture at hand. Collaboration between a scientist and a poet might seem incongruous, for example, yet in human permaculture this is viewed as an opportunity: the scientist will contribute rigor while the poet brings flexibility, harmony, and beauty to the shared project.

The "exchange zone" is associated with the "border effect" observed in nature. It becomes richer by incorporating, superimposing, and amplifying the strengths and assets of each component. Happily, this exchange zone will emerge and be sustained in any human group that applies the "Twelve Pathways to Building a Unified and Functional Team" proposed in this book (see Chapter 8, "Teamwork or Collective Intelligence").

 **KEY TO SUCCESS:** Remember that the exchange zone is enriched to the extent that it integrates the strengths and advantages of the previously existing elements.

### STEP 3) DETERMINE THE AVAILABLE RESOURCES AND THE NEEDS TO SATISFY

In this third step, the person or group takes an inventory of the available resources, both internal and external to the system, identifying the limiting factors and determining their own needs and those of the other members. Note that this inventory is objective and fact based — so the left brain should feel completely at home — as opposed to the sense-based observation in step one. Viewpoint diversity being a source of richness, each member of the project will be able to make a contribution in this step.

**Internally available resources:** Human resources (each person's skills and tastes), natural resources (water, soil, land), material resources (housing, offices, vehicles, equipment), financial resources (income, credit), family resources (possible help on weekends), etc.

**Internal limiting factors:** Human factors such as conflicts or discrimination on the basis of age, race, sex, or ability.

**Resources external to the project:** For collective projects, see how similar projects have fared; study the tools used in those projects (charters, finances, legislation); contact specialized associations; find out about advisory services, resources available in the area, the natural environment (springs, lakes, rivers, forests, topography), local political authorities, economic and social activities (surrounding farms, businesses, and organizations), and access routes (bus or train stations, roads, river systems, airports); scope out alternative currencies; and don't forget to read *The Transition Handbook* by Rob Hopkins.

**External limiting factors:** Regulatory, economic, cultural, climatic, distance-related, and other constraints.

Next, the person or group identifies current and future needs:

**Material and immaterial needs:** Food, drinking water, facilities, income, transportation, support, training, client base, recognition, space, discussion time, rest, safety.

**A collective project** requires diverse and complementary skills (human resources, legal and tax advice), support (from the municipality, the bank), money, time, and a schedule. It also needs to meet individuals' safety, their need to feel useful to others, their need to lead a meaningful life, their need to be recognized as belonging to a group or ideology, etc.

**For an individual design,** list exactly what needs you have determined for your situation. This list will come in handy later. Next, figure out which one need is most important, the most urgent, the one that will open the door to the following steps.

## STEP 4) EVALUATE AND SORT THE DATA YOU HAVE GATHERED

Here, the data collected during step three are sorted. This is best done when the data are still fresh in your mind. The goal of this sorting step is to create a synthesis of all the parameters and to highlight the elements needed to determine your unifying thread — the roadmap that will guide you through the design process. This is where the raison d'être of your individual or collective project comes to light: how it is useful to society. Now is not the time to analyze or seek solutions — that comes later. Don't skip ahead!

Here is a trick to help facilitate this sorting operation:

**SORTING TRIANGLES**

- Draw a triangle on a large sheet of paper. At the topmost corner, write the needs of the people or system in question; at the lower left-hand corner, write the desired roles of the people

or system; at the lower right-hand corner, write the intentions, desires, and objectives of the people or system.

- Sort the data collected in step 3 under the corresponding headings. The three categories are closely related. If you can't decide which heading something belongs under, write it along the sides of the triangle, between the two points.

- Note the contents of the Zone 00 that emerges.

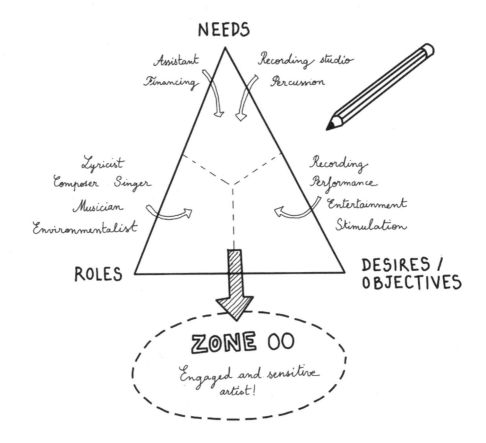

**KEY TO SUCCESS:** At this stage, don't come up with any solutions for the collective design. You risk blocking the creativity of your partners. Wait for the brainstorming step. There are always many possible solutions to a given situation.

## STEP 5) DISCOVER, CONNECT, AND ANALYZE THE NICHES

*Use T-charts for discovering and connecting niches*

Generally speaking, it is best to start by examining the human aspect of the project: what roles and functions would the people involved like to occupy spontaneously? What are their natural aptitudes? Even for elements of the system: what are their most obvious functions and roles?

Make a T-chart for each person and element of the system.

In the right-hand side of the T-chart, as applicable, record all the person or element's assets, skills, and ways of contributing to the group; their tastes, possible functions, and hobbies; and what sorts of things they do willingly, as established in step 4. Below this, make a section and record the strengths of the person or element, as perceived or expressed by the individual or by their teammates.

In the left-hand side of the T-chart, write the needs of the person or element, as formulated above. Below, make a section and record the weaknesses (as perceived by the right brain).

Through this synthesis of information, the niche becomes obvious and the unifying thread becomes more specific. This unifying thread is what links the niche *of the actors* to that of *the project*.

This process will yield fertile and creative combinations between people, functions, and systems. From this, groups, families, and clubs can form to help further the project.

The permaculturist who wants to play their part in the collective evolution can expand the design to include advancing the general interest: the common good can be included in one's personal objectives.

In a successful design, obvious convergences between the group members' niches and the raison d'être of the project will arise. The project niche can be adjusted to suit the talents of the group members, but the reverse would not be feasible! Indeed, each human being has an imperative to express their identity. The design must allow each person room for self-expression and self-actualization.

The role of permaculturists is to shape the design to match the needs and niches of the actors, not to make the actors adjust to the needs of the design at all costs, as is done in industrial society.

Once the niche and the unifying thread have been identified, it's time to identify, in just a few words, *the* main strength and *the* main challenge of the project. A successful design integrates the strength of people and projects and makes up

*Identify weaknesses of people or projects in order to compensate for them and strengthen the design.*

for their weaknesses in such a way that the system can be maintained over the long term. As in nature, humans will have to develop mechanisms and find solutions to compensate for their weaknesses.

*The participants' niches + the project niche provide the unifying thread of the project.*

Be sure not to rush through this step of discovering, connecting, and analyzing the niches. Hasty action could push you in the wrong direction. Identifying the unifying thread of the project is a critical step; there is no point in proceeding if this is not crystal clear. So, put down your pencil, take a step back, and recite the first

five design steps out loud, as in a movie screenplay. Look at your roadmap and confirm the raison d'être of your project with your teammates.

**KEY TO SUCCESS:** Identify weaknesses of people or projects in order to compensate for them and strengthen the design.

### STEP 6) DREAM AND BRAINSTORM

Call this step what you will: blue-sky thinking, brainstorming, spitballing, whatever. This is the dreaming step, where anything is possible. All you need to do is let your imagination run wild; daydream without limits, and watch as brilliant ideas from the right brains of your now-trained teammates spew forth. This is the most creative and stimulating part of the design. The previous steps allowed everyone to grasp the different components of the project and to gain an overview of needs and expectations. In this stage, each person allows their inspiration to follow the unifying thread identified in the previous step.

Here again, the right brain will be invited to go beyond the previously learned, often settled-upon forms — ramrod-straight rows of monocultures, houses with right angles, etc. The imagination should be free to wander toward shapes inspired by nature — curves, meanderings, fractal forms, etc. It is important to take your time and to think about the project often. Strolls, gardening, transportation time, meditation, and nighttime can all afford moments for the ideas to flow. Keep a notebook on your person to jot down images that spring to mind. You can go back to your notes during sharing periods with your teammates. Welcome all ideas, even off-the-wall ones, without limits. Don't hold back your own creativity or that of your teammates. There will always be time to eliminate the least pertinent ideas in the next step.

Be innovative! For example, have some fun sketching an idea tree or mind map. Graphical representations like these work like the brain does: through the association of ideas. Through potentially artful shapes, mind maps highlight connections between elements, related concepts, and complementary concepts. The most unexpected — or, who knows, brilliant — connections will appear at a glance, whether or not they are realistic. These connections will open the door to potential actions to take.

Don't hesitate to cook up multiple scenarios or explore all options. Some of them — perhaps ones that you suggested — will have to be jettisoned in the next step in favor of scenarios that seem more suitable to the situation at hand. What if that's not easy to accept? Well, that's human permaculture too: each person's ideas contribute to the collective advancement of the project.

**KEY TO SUCCESS:** Don't limit your creativity – or that of your teammates!

## STEP 7) CONCEIVE A FUNCTIONAL DESIGN

The design may take the form of a personal action plan, a landscaped plot of land, a scale model, a detailed workback schedule, etc.

After ensuring that you have followed the basic principles set out by the father of permaculture and validated the options selected from the brainstorming step, it's time for the team to verify that the proposed project will constitute a viable, lasting ecosystem:

- Does the project address an ecosystem-level need (within the group or society)? What is it?
- Will it generate a yield? For whom?
- Will it produce more energy than it consumes?
- Will the project benefit all elements or people in the system and beyond?
- Will each element exist in relation to the other elements in the system?
- Will each element or member occupy multiple functions?
- Have you fully taken into account the diversity of assets, strengths, and weaknesses of each person and of the project itself?
- Does the project have the means to realize its underlying ambitions? Is it viable?
- What will make it last?
- Have you evaluated its environmental, social, and economic impact?

If the proposed design proves solid and satisfying, the team continues by building a schedule

## Designing a space

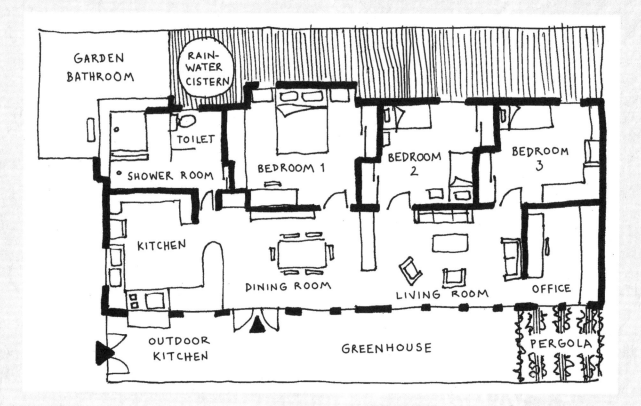

Given that this book is geared towards *human* permaculture, we have elected not to give examples of designing physical spaces as such. A number of books already deal with this topic in detail. In our view, the first zone that any spatial design is built around is Zone 00. The other zones (from 1 to 5) are structured around the people who live in the ecosystem you create.

with realistic steps (including the desired start and end of the project).

 **KEY TO SUCCESS:** Remember that the absolute top priority is for the system to be sustainable. All planned actions must be viable over the long term.

## STEP 8) INSTALL AND IMPLEMENT THE DESIGN

In previous steps (3, 4, 5, and 7), you identified the unifying thread of the project and the priority actions you can take to make the best use of the strengths and compensate for the main weaknesses of the people and the project. Now it is time to implement the design. Be flexible as you proceed, taking guidance from the right hemisphere of your brain. Embrace unexpected occurrences and adjust your plans if necessary. Don't be rigid about achieving a given objective at all costs. Remain humble and ready to listen to your partners and the surprises that occur in the course of events. To paraphrase Rob Hopkins in *The Transition Handbook*, let things go where they want to go.[1]

 **KEY TO SUCCESS:** Be very methodical, especially when it comes to budgeting and planning actions. Reflect, listen to your partners, consult experienced people, and take your time.

*Remember that the absolute top priority is for the system to be sustainable. All planned actions must be viable over the long term.*

## STEP 9) MAINTAIN THE SUSTAINABILITY OF THE DESIGN

Regardless of the project in question, maintaining and sustaining it into the future must always be in the back of the permaculturist's mind from step 4 (evaluate and sort the data) onwards. Step 9 is about verifying the project's capacity to self-regulate. Taking this precaution will ensure a smooth journey from coming up with your initial dreams to making them a concrete reality.

 **KEY TO SUCCESS:** Keep in mind that all projects need to be adjusted, rebuilt, or enhanced over time. As Bill Mollison says, "design and re-design."

## Three Examples of Design

# LIFE DESIGN
## PAUL

IN A PERMACULTURE DESIGN COURSE (PDC), PAUL JUST DISCOVERED HIS NICHE: HE IS AN ARTIST. PAUL CURRENTLY WORKS AS A FORESTER BASED IN MONTREAL. HE IS WELL PAID BUT NOT FLOURISHING. HE DECIDES TO TAKE TIME TO SEE HOW HE COULD START HIS TRANSITION. LET'S FOLLOW HIM THROUGH THE DIFFERENT STEPS OF HIS INQUIRY.

WHAT'S ON FOR TODAY -2

MY FUTURE PERSPECTIVES -2

MY MUSICIAN FRIENDS +5

MY BUDGET +4

SOLIDARITY OF MY WIFE +5

MONEY

SUPPORT

**1 OBSERVATION**

⇨ I TAKE STOCK OF MY SITUATION

**8 IMPLEMENTATION**

⇨ I BEGIN TO WORK ON MY PROJECT

**7 DESIGN**

⇨ I CONCEIVE MY LIFE DESIGN IN THE FORM OF AN ACTION PLAN

JANUARY

PLAN REHEARSALS AND CONCERTS IN JANUARY

CÉLINE   PAUL

END GOAL
RAISING PUBLIC AWARENESS ABOUT PERMACULTURE

**6 DREAMING & BRAINSTORMING**

⇨ I DREAM UP FUTURE PROJECTS

I dream of sharing the stage with Céline

Perform in nature

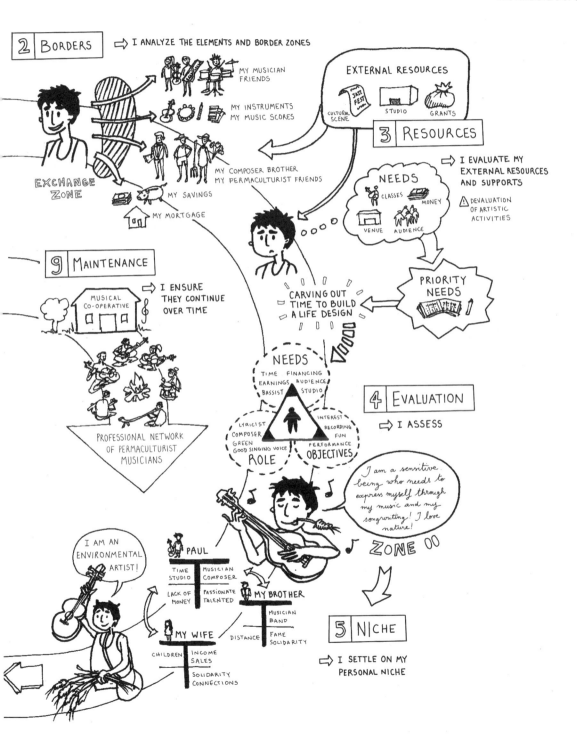

**2 BORDERS**  ⇨ I ANALYZE THE ELEMENTS AND BORDER ZONES

MY MUSICIAN FRIENDS

MY INSTRUMENTS
MY MUSIC SCORES

MY COMPOSER BROTHER
MY PERMACULTURIST FRIENDS

EXCHANGE ZONE

MY SAVINGS

MY MORTGAGE

EXTERNAL RESOURCES

CULTURAL SCENE    STUDIO    GRANTS

**3 RESOURCES**

I EVALUATE MY EXTERNAL RESOURCES AND SUPPORTS

⚠ DEVALUATION OF ARTISTIC ACTIVITIES

NEEDS

CLASSES    MONEY    VENUE    AUDIENCE

PRIORITY NEEDS

**9 MAINTENANCE**

I ENSURE THEY CONTINUE OVER TIME

MUSICAL CO-OPERATIVE

CARVING OUT TIME TO BUILD A LIFE DESIGN

PROFESSIONAL NETWORK OF PERMACULTURIST MUSICIANS

NEEDS
TIME  FINANCING
EARNINGS  AUDIENCE
BASSIST  STUDIO

LYRICIST
COMPOSER
GREEN
GOOD SINGING VOICE
ROLE

INTEREST
RECORDING
FUN
PERFORMANCE
OBJECTIVES

**4 EVALUATION**

⇨ I ASSESS

I am a sensitive being who needs to express myself through my music and my songwriting! I love nature!

ZONE 00

I AM AN ENVIRONMENTAL ARTIST!

PAUL
TIME    MUSICIAN
STUDIO   COMPOSER
LACK OF  PASSIONATE
MONEY    TALENTED

MY BROTHER
MUSICIAN
BAND
DISTANCE  FAME
SOLIDARITY

MY WIFE
CHILDREN  INCOME
SALES
SOLIDARITY
CONNECTIONS

**5 NICHE**

⇨ I SETTLE ON MY PERSONAL NICHE

# DESIGN IN AN URBAN SETTING FOR A BUYERS' CO-OPERATIVE

FOOD BUYERS' CO-OPERATIVE,
LAUNCHED BY A GROUP OF EMPLOYEES
AND LONG-TERM UNEMPLOYED PEOPLE
WHO WANT TO WORK TOGETHER TO FIND
ECONOMICAL SOLUTIONS. TWO OF THOSE
PEOPLE, A COUPLE TRAINED IN PERMACULTURE,
PROPOSE ESTABLISHING A BUYERS' CO-OP.

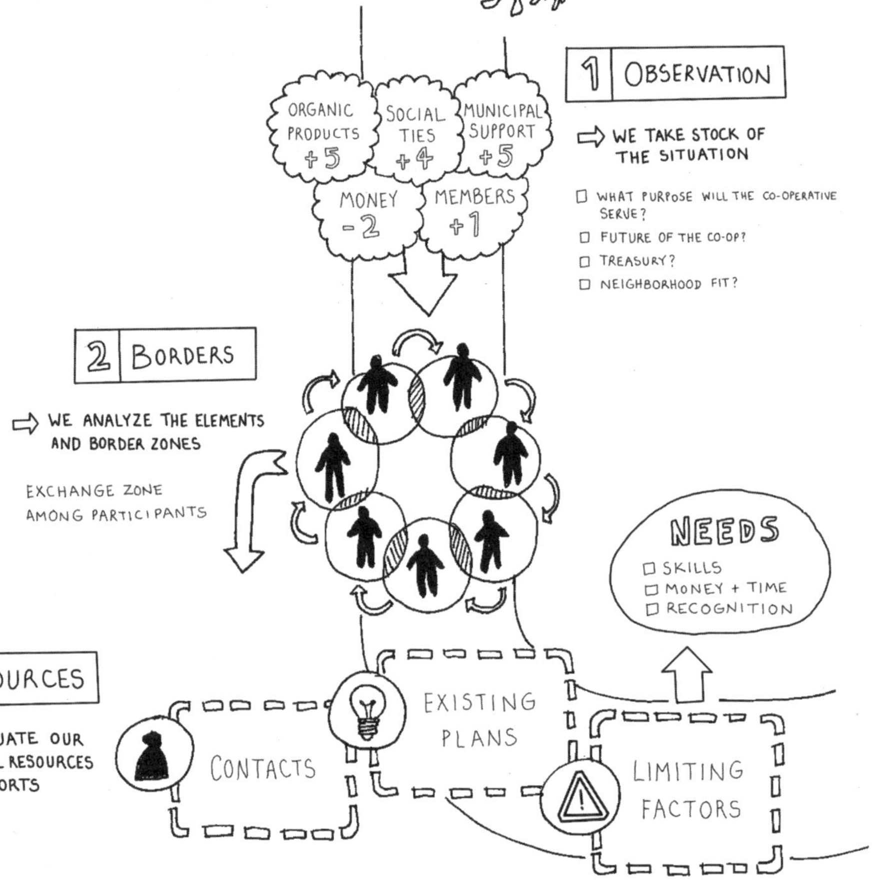

ORGANIC PRODUCTS +5

SOCIAL TIES +4

MUNICIPAL SUPPORT +5

MONEY -2

MEMBERS +1

## 1 OBSERVATION

⇨ WE TAKE STOCK OF THE SITUATION

☐ WHAT PURPOSE WILL THE CO-OPERATIVE SERVE?
☐ FUTURE OF THE CO-OP?
☐ TREASURY?
☐ NEIGHBORHOOD FIT?

## 2 BORDERS

⇨ WE ANALYZE THE ELEMENTS AND BORDER ZONES

EXCHANGE ZONE AMONG PARTICIPANTS

### NEEDS
☐ SKILLS
☐ MONEY + TIME
☐ RECOGNITION

## 3 RESOURCES

⇨ WE EVALUATE OUR EXTERNAL RESOURCES AND SUPPORTS

CONTACTS

EXISTING PLANS

LIMITING FACTORS

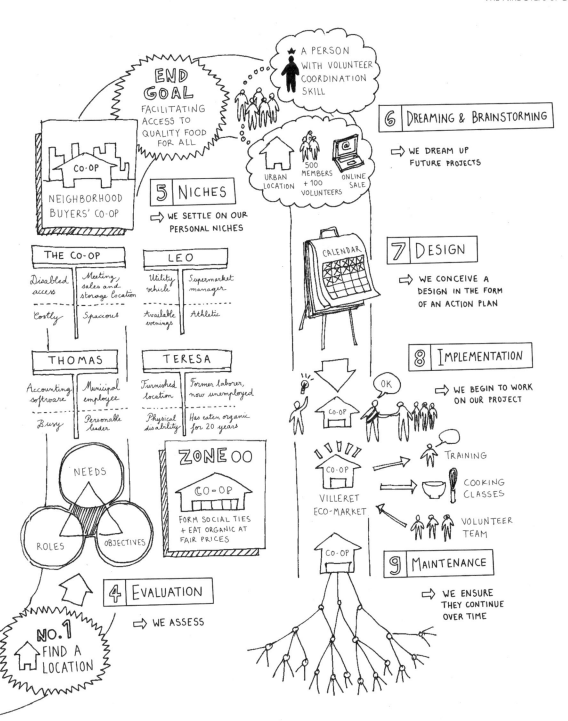

END GOAL
FACILITATING ACCESS TO QUALITY FOOD FOR ALL

CO-OP
NEIGHBORHOOD BUYERS' CO-OP

A PERSON WITH VOLUNTEER COORDINATION SKILL

URBAN LOCATION — 500 MEMBERS + 100 VOLUNTEERS — ONLINE SALE

6 DREAMING & BRAINSTORMING
⇒ WE DREAM UP FUTURE PROJECTS

5 NICHES
⇒ WE SETTLE ON OUR PERSONAL NICHES

THE CO-OP
Disabled access | Meeting, sales and storage location
Costly | Spacious

LEO
Utility vehicle | Supermarket manager
Available evenings | Athletic

CALENDAR

7 DESIGN
⇒ WE CONCEIVE A DESIGN IN THE FORM OF AN ACTION PLAN

THOMAS
Accounting software | Municipal employee
Busy | Personable leader

TERESA
Furnished location | Former laborer, now unemployed
Physical disability | Has eaten organic for 20 years

8 IMPLEMENTATION
⇒ WE BEGIN TO WORK ON OUR PROJECT

OK

NEEDS
ROLES   OBJECTIVES

ZONE 00
CO-OP
FORM SOCIAL TIES + EAT ORGANIC AT FAIR PRICES

CO-OP
VILLERET ECO-MARKET

TRAINING

COOKING CLASSES

VOLUNTEER TEAM

CO-OP

9 MAINTENANCE
⇒ WE ENSURE THEY CONTINUE OVER TIME

4 EVALUATION
⇒ WE ASSESS

NO.1 FIND A LOCATION

# RURAL EXAMPLE DESIGN
## FOR GROUP HOUSING

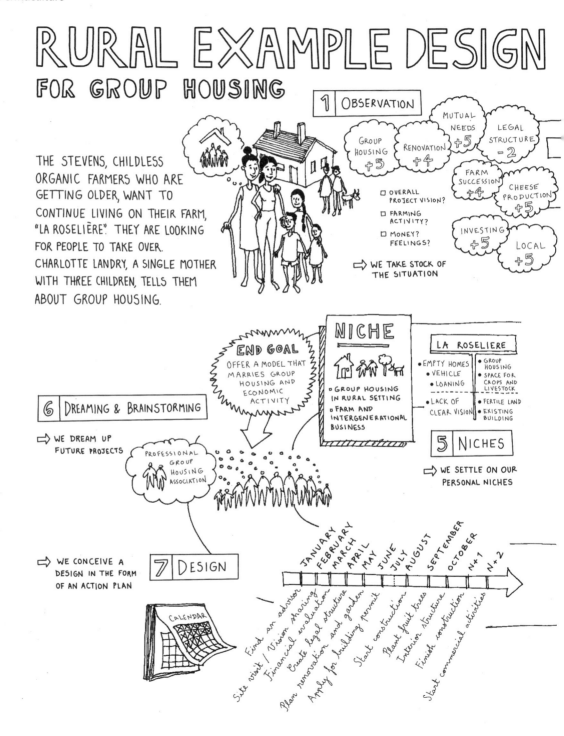

THE STEVENS, CHILDLESS ORGANIC FARMERS WHO ARE GETTING OLDER, WANT TO CONTINUE LIVING ON THEIR FARM, "LA ROSELIÈRE". THEY ARE LOOKING FOR PEOPLE TO TAKE OVER. CHARLOTTE LANDRY, A SINGLE MOTHER WITH THREE CHILDREN, TELLS THEM ABOUT GROUP HOUSING.

### 1 OBSERVATION

GROUP HOUSING +5
RENOVATION +4
MUTUAL NEEDS +5
LEGAL STRUCTURE -2
FARM SUCCESSION +4
CHEESE PRODUCTION +5
INVESTING +5
LOCAL +5

☐ OVERALL PROJECT VISION?
☐ FARMING ACTIVITY?
☐ MONEY? FEELINGS?

⇨ WE TAKE STOCK OF THE SITUATION

### NICHE

☐ GROUP HOUSING IN RURAL SETTING
☐ FARM AND INTERGENERATIONAL BUSINESS

**END GOAL**
OFFER A MODEL THAT MARRIES GROUP HOUSING AND ECONOMIC ACTIVITY

**LA ROSELIERE**
• EMPTY HOMES
• VEHICLE
• LOANING
• LACK OF CLEAR VISION
• GROUP HOUSING
• SPACE FOR CROPS AND LIVESTOCK
• FERTILE LAND
• EXISTING BUILDING

### 6 DREAMING & BRAINSTORMING

⇨ WE DREAM UP FUTURE PROJECTS

PROFESSIONAL GROUP HOUSING ASSOCIATION

### 5 NICHES

⇨ WE SETTLE ON OUR PERSONAL NICHES

⇨ WE CONCEIVE A DESIGN IN THE FORM OF AN ACTION PLAN

### 7 DESIGN

CALENDAR

JANUARY  FEBRUARY  MARCH  APRIL  MAY  JUNE  JULY  AUGUST  SEPTEMBER  OCTOBER  N+1  N+2

Find an advisor
Site visit / Vision sharing
Financial evaluation
Create legal structure
Plan renovation and garden
Apply for building permit
Start construction
Plant fruit trees
Interior structure
Finish construction
Start commercial activities

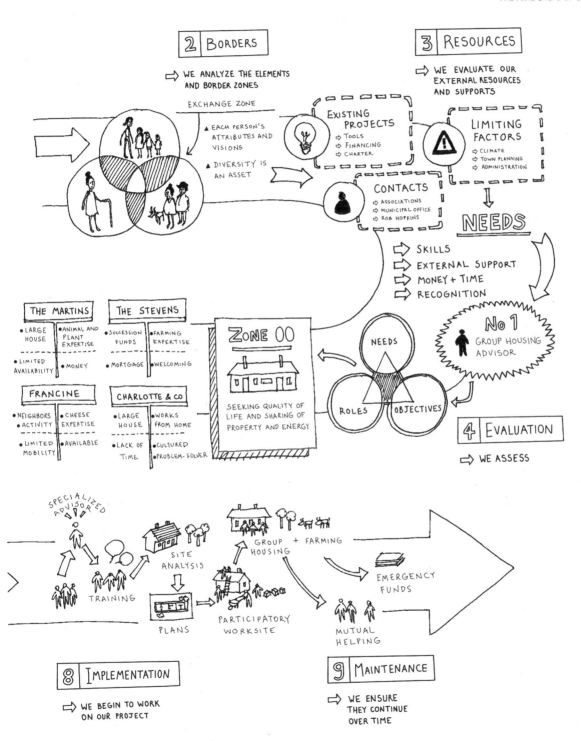

**2 BORDERS**

➡ WE ANALYZE THE ELEMENTS AND BORDER ZONES

**3 RESOURCES**

➡ WE EVALUATE OUR EXTERNAL RESOURCES AND SUPPORTS

EXCHANGE ZONE

▲ EACH PERSON'S ATTRIBUTES AND VISIONS

▲ DIVERSITY IS AN ASSET

EXISTING PROJECTS
⇨ TOOLS
⇨ FINANCING
⇨ CHARTER

LIMITING FACTORS
⇨ CLIMATE
⇨ TOWN PLANNING
⇨ ADMINISTRATION

CONTACTS
⇨ ASSOCIATIONS
⇨ MUNICIPAL OFFICE
⇨ ROB HOPKINS

**NEEDS**

➡ SKILLS
➡ EXTERNAL SUPPORT
➡ MONEY + TIME
➡ RECOGNITION

No 1
GROUP HOUSING ADVISOR

**THE MARTINS**
- LARGE HOUSE
- ANIMAL AND PLANT EXPERTISE
- LIMITED AVAILABILITY
- MONEY

**THE STEVENS**
- SUCCESSION FUNDS
- FARMING EXPERTISE
- MORTGAGE
- WELCOMING

**FRANCINE**
- NEIGHBORS
- CHEESE EXPERTISE
- ACTIVITY
- LIMITED MOBILITY
- AVAILABLE

**CHARLOTTE & CO**
- LARGE HOUSE
- WORKS FROM HOME
- LACK OF TIME
- CULTURED
- PROBLEM-SOLVER

**ZONE 00**

SEEKING QUALITY OF LIFE AND SHARING OF PROPERTY AND ENERGY

NEEDS

ROLES          OBJECTIVES

**4 EVALUATION**

➡ WE ASSESS

SPECIALIZED ADVISOR

TRAINING

SITE ANALYSIS

PLANS

PARTICIPATORY WORKSITE

GROUP + FARMING HOUSING

MUTUAL HELPING

EMERGENCY FUNDS

**8 IMPLEMENTATION**

➡ WE BEGIN TO WORK ON OUR PROJECT

**9 MAINTENANCE**

➡ WE ENSURE THEY CONTINUE OVER TIME

# DISCOVERING MY PERSONAL NICHE

## APPLYING THE 9 STEPS

BEFORE LAUCHING INTO A LIFE DESIGN OR COLLECTIVE PROJECT, IT IS INDISPENSABLE TO DISCOVER ONE'S PERSONAL NICHE.
WE ARE CLOSEST TO OUR INNERMOST NATURE BETWEEN THE AGES OF 9 AND 11, BEFORE WE ARE INFLUENCED BY OTHERS.

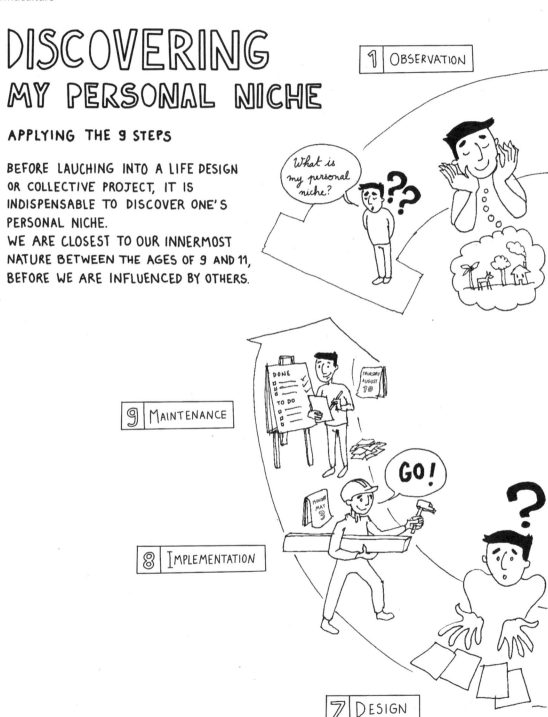

2 | BORDERS

3 | RESOURCES

NEEDS | MEMORIES

WEAKNESSES | STRENGTHS

4 | EVALUATION

5 | NICHE

6 | DREAMING & BRAINSTORMING

# Part 3

## Caring for the Earth

# Chapter 11

# Biodiversity, the Key to Balance

HUMAN BEINGS, like all living, breathing creatures, rely on a complex set of natural elements. Humans exert no influence over some of these elements, such as the Earth's revolution around the sun, gravity, the cycle of the seasons, etc. Our activities have a neutral or negative effect on other elements — but we can also have a positive impact if we choose to restore environments we have destroyed or thrown off balance through reckless actions.

In Part 3 of this book we highlight the vital ties that bind human beings to water, the soil, and the forest. For the last century, human activity has exerted a major impact on these three elements with unpredictable domino effects, especially on the climate and biodiversity. Most resources, despite the damage they sustain, will be able to regenerate eventually. But what about humanity? How long will we be able to continue in the face of the problems we are causing? How long will we be able to survive in an environment that has become hostile? When will our species realize that neglecting or destroying our environment means destroying ourselves? Let's not give in to pessimism or discouragement: humanity has some latitude to set things right and to consciously adopt more virtuous behaviors in harmony with the laws of nature. This is the role of a permaculture design.

## UNDERSTANDING IN ORDER TO PLAN AND ADAPT

Realizing how fragile and complex the mechanisms of nature are, and understanding the cause-and-effect relationships between our behavior and the disturbances we may be causing, is the key to finding the motivation to alter our habits. This is especially pertinent at a time when scientists are announcing average projected temperature increases of 1 to 5°C, which guarantees that severe turbulence is in store for us. An increase of 1°C increases water evaporation by seven percent. Given that evaporation is a key driver of atmospheric circulation, weather events will become more intense: more heavy rains, sudden flooding, drought, more extreme heat, etc.

Before we examine the three ecosystems in turn (water, soil, and forest), here are a few basics to keep in mind:

– An ecosystem is a living whole that brings together different species in interrelationship with each other and with their environment within a given area. It is composed of producers (notably plants), consumers (including animals), and decomposers (notably microorganisms), which are aided by solar energy. The association of all these elements creates life. If nothing prevents it from doing so, a natural ecosystem will theoretically evolve towards a stable state ("climax"). It adapts constantly thanks to a complex set of actions and feedback mechanisms.

– Every natural ecosystem has multiple and complex ecological functions, which are essential to the proper operation and balance of the ecosystem of Earth. The innumerable interactions and exchanges of energy and matter among ecosystems allow them to stay in dynamic equilibrium and to evolve. All of the natural ecosystems serve to keep alive gigantic reserves of biodiversity, which are themselves the key to the ecosystems' resilience and ability to balance and adapt.

**PERMACULTURE
PRINCIPLE 4:** Apply self-regulation and accept feedback

– Biodiversity performs ecological or ecosystem "services" free of charge to all living species, including humans, which benefit in multiple ways with no action required on their part:

*Supply services:* Ecosystems provide water, food, energy, and resources such as wood, textile fibers, metals, etc.

*Regulation services:* Oceans, rivers, the soil, and forests store, transport, filter, purify, and restore huge reserves of biodiversity and fresh water, which carry large amounts of nutrients and microorganisms — all with no need for human intervention! Their resilience allows them to regulate diseases and serve as climate buffers.

*Support services:* Ecosystems provide habitats to plants and animals, primary materials for human dwellings, and all the conditions

## AMAZING DATA

In less than two human generations, the population size among wildlife species has shrunk by half worldwide. This information comes from the World Wildlife Fund (WWF), an international NGO, in its 2014 *Living Planet Report* (figure based on a representative sample of over 10,000 populations of mammals, birds, reptiles, amphibians, and fish since 1970). As the report reminds us, "These are the living forms that constitute the fabric of the ecosystems which sustain life on Earth — and the barometer of what we are doing to our own planet, our only home. We ignore their decline at our peril."

## Biodiversi... what?

The word *biodiversity* encompasses all forms of life on Earth, from the very smallest to the very largest — the sum total of the complex interactions they perform, their functions, and their life strategies. This biological diversity is the product of billions of years of evolution. The whole community of life, of which humanity forms an integral part and on which it is totally dependent, has a common origin: the same DNA, which differentiates over time. This means all species spring from the same family tree. In this chapter we learn about our kinship with the plant and animal world!

to produce the nutrition needed for plants, animals, and humans.

*"Cultural" services or "amenities":* Natural ecosystems also offer humans immaterial services such as the beauty of landscapes, which inspire art and invite contemplation, the thrill of scaling mountains or surfing on ocean waves, and the chance to learn by observing nature and sharing discoveries.

**PERMACULTURE PRINCIPLE 10:**
Use and value diversity

# Chapter 12

# Water Is Life

*Nothing is lost, nothing is created,*
*everything is transformed.*

— Antoine-Laurent de Lavoisier (1743–94)

## WATER, AN INDISPENSABLE ELEMENT TO ALL LIFE FORMS

WHEN LIFE FIRST AROSE on planet Earth, it did so in water. And it is in the salty water of the amniotic fluid that human life gets its start. The human body, largely made of water (70 percent by weight on average), carries in its cells the traces of the marine origins of life.

Fresh water is vital to all terrestrial animal and plant species, allowing them to hydrate and breathe. If deprived of water, most animals will die within a few days, well before they die of hunger; many plants won't last long without it either. All our organs need water, including our skin and lungs, which depend on moisture in the air. Even species adapted to desert life or species that hibernate still depend on water.

Water's role in the Earth ecosystem is to keep all species alive — nothing less! The oceans play a fundamental role as thermal buffers to regulate the climate; water stores heat from the sun, and it takes much longer to change temperature than land. The oceans also function as carbon sinks, with their upper layers recycling about 100 billion tonnes of carbon per year, or 60 times more than is contained in the atmosphere.

The vital character of water is woven into most human cultures and spiritual traditions. How many stories and rituals associated with fertility, birth, purification, or even death have water at their center?

## WATER FROM THE SKY

Where does water come from? "Water comes from the stars!" cheerfully answers biologist Pierre Mollo. "In the beginning (15 billion years ago), there was the Big Bang. The universe was concentrated into a minuscule point at an unimaginable temperature (billions of billions of degrees). Later, five billion years ago, this planet was mineral and bathed in $CO_2$. Life came from the sky when icy comets and meteorites melted as they grazed the Earth, carrying fresh water and anaerobic bacteria (which can live without oxygen). One fine day, thanks to volcanic eruptions that released mineral salts from the bowels of the Earth, a bacterium (cyanobacterium) started producing oxygen through photosynthesis.

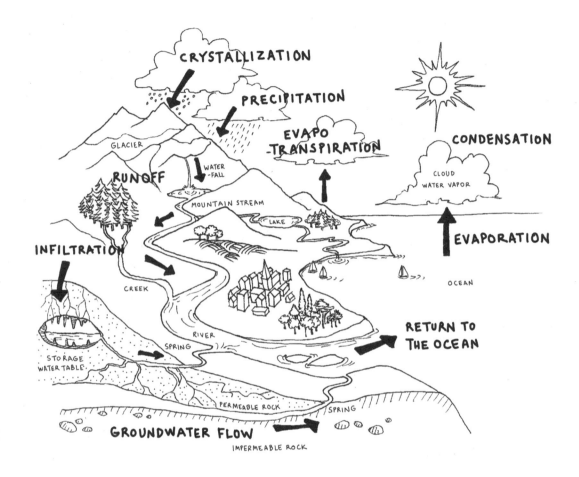

The bacteria multiplied as they absorbed $CO_2$ and all sorts of toxic particles. Little by little, they settled, forming contours and continents. Since then, wind loaded with sand from the deserts (silica) has fed the oceans and enabled the development of diatoms (phytoplankton) in the water. This plant plankton produces oxygen, which in turn feeds animal plankton." This is how water gave rise to life, first as the marine chain of life, which subsequently gave rise to the terrestrial chain of life.

**PERMACULTURE PRINCIPLE 5:**
Use and value renewable resources and services

Scientists have advanced a number of complementary hypotheses regarding the origin of water, which are regularly called into question when new discoveries are made. It is now acknowledged that "water is present throughout the cosmos in the form of ice or vapor. But there is no liquid water outside the solar system, in which our dear planet is the only one to be graced with liquid water," the French National Centre for Scientific Research (CNRS) states. Scientists continue to study the "cosmic water cycle" in the interstellar environment, gradually finding bits of information that overturn the conceptions accepted thus far.

### WATER HAS YET TO REVEAL ALL ITS SECRETS

Contemporary science defines water by the *chemical* composition of its molecule: $H_2O$ (one oxygen atom bonded to two hydrogen atoms through electrostatic forces). However, some of water's *physical* properties defy fluid mechanics and remain mysterious to this day. Many researchers are trying to unlock these mysteries, sometimes at the risk of losing their careers.

**TO FIND OUT MORE:** Dossier scientifique: l'eau, French National Centre for Scientific Research (CNRS), sagascience.cnrs.fr/doseau/decouv/proprie/MenuProprie.html

### AN EVER-CONSTANT VOLUME OF FRESH WATER

The amount of fresh water available on Earth has been limited and constant since its origins. "The water we drink has already been drunk many times," the landscape architect Gilles Clément likes to remind people in his talks. "Maybe even by a dinosaur!" chimes in an online commenter.

## Water, soil, forest, and humanity: a family history (1 of 3)

### Marine plankton, the world's greatest oxygen producer

The first form of life appeared on Earth (more specifically, in the ocean) some 3.8 billion years ago. Thanks to the presence of minerals discharged by volcanic eruptions, bacteria evolved into the plant form of plankton, known as phytoplankton. From this initial unicellular form came blue-green algae, the oldest algae of all, later followed by all varieties of algae and aquatic plants. This marine biomass, which today outweighs that of all the forests combined, produces over half the oxygen needed for life on Earth via photosynthesis. What's more, phytoplankton absorb over 50 percent of the $CO_2$ from the atmosphere. This makes these marine photosynthesizers one of the lungs of the planet, allowing the soil and all plant and animal species to breathe. (Part 2 continues on page 97.)

The same water is always circulating, endlessly feeding rivers, glaciers, water tables, and soil — not to mention our taps. It is estimated that the sun's rays evaporate 1,000 cubic kilometers of water from the oceans every day. This water becomes gaseous and forms clouds, which eventually descend back to the Earth's surface in the form of rain or snow. Of this precipitation, 31 percent evaporates again, 16 percent flows overland and joins various watercourses, 23 percent filters down and feeds water tables, and underground rivers and caves. A portion of the water that falls on the soil enters plants via their roots. A fraction of this water is returned to

## Humans have access to less than one percent of the Earth's fresh water

### WATER ON EARTH

 **97%** SALT WATER

**3%** FRESH WATER

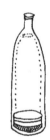 **2/3** FROZEN WATER

**1/3** LIQUID WATER

 **3/4** GROUNDWATER (partly inaccessible)

**1/4** SURFACE WATER (accessible)

**97%** salt water

**3%** fresh water, two-thirds of which is frozen (ice and glaciers) and the rest of which is liquid. Of the liquid third, three quarters is underground water that is partly inaccessible to humans (for the time being). Humans have easy access to just one quarter of the liquid third. Using more complex analysis many scientific organizations have concluded that, in practice, humans have access to only about one percent of the fresh water on Earth.

SOURCES: WORLD WATER COUNCIL, INTERNATIONAL OFFICE FOR WATER, FRENCH NATIONAL CENTRE FOR SCIENTIFIC RESEARCH (CNRS).

the atmosphere in its gaseous form (water vapor) via transpiration from the leaves. The water in circulation on the planet remains constant in total volume — though it spends variable periods of time in the different "reservoirs" (from eight days in the atmosphere to several million years in glaciers). On its return voyage to the ocean, fresh water carries terrestrial organic material, which perpetuates the development of plankton and therefore of oxygen and the entire marine chain of life.

Water is a rare and precious resource. Moreover, its unchanging volume must be shared among a growing number of humans and activities. Given that the world's most water-rich people have 10,000 times more water than the most water-poor, fresh water reserves are very unevenly shared around the world — and unequally utilized. The Northern Hemisphere has more volume in its reserves and consumes an enormous amount. The Southern Hemisphere has less volume and consumes much less, despite its higher demographic pressure. Thus, water stress varies greatly in different regions of the world.

## VAST RESERVES OF (NEARLY) FRESH WATER UNDER THE OCEAN?

An international scientific study published in December 2013 in the journal *Nature*[1] states that enormous volumes of water have been trapped under oceans for millions of years. The volumes are estimated at three times the surface water volume, or 100 times the amount of water removed by humans in one century of excessive consumption (the 20th). The water in these reserves is in fact brackish (i.e., salty, but less so than seawater) and therefore easier to desalinate. The prospect of exploiting this resource is tempting for countries running short on fresh water, and especially for supporters of limitless consumption! But it does not bode well for the preservation of our still undiscovered natural resources.

## THE HUMAN PROPENSITY TO BE NEAR WATER

Human communities most often settle in proximity to water, such as by riverbanks, along estuaries and coasts, and around inland lakes. Not only is water a resource necessary to life, but it also holds high energetic potential and offers populations easy access to inland regions. The great civilizations were born beside rivers. In Mesopotamia, in the fertile land watered by the Tigris and Euphrates rivers, humans developed highly innovative irrigation techniques 60 centuries before the common era. These techniques enabled the development of agriculture. And once the basic need of food could be satisfied, cultural fertility was free to blossom: it was also on the fertile banks of the Tigris and Euphrates that writing was born some time afterward.

Nine countries share 60 percent of the world's fresh water reserves: Brazil, Russia, the United States, Canada, China, Indonesia, India, Colombia, and Peru.

*Urban water cycle.*

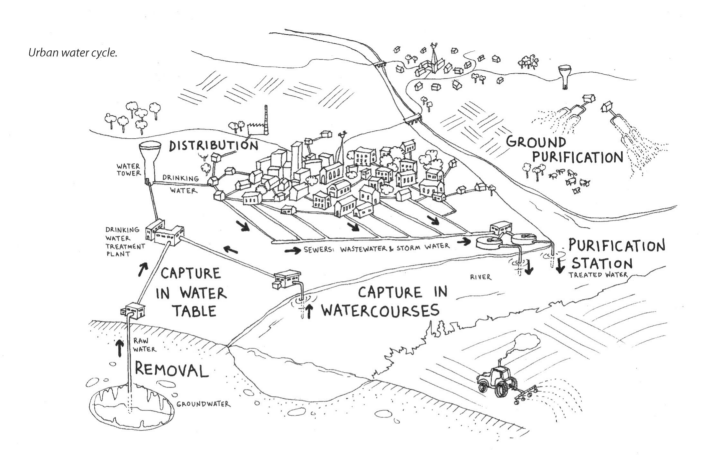

**PERMACULTURE PRINCIPLE 5:**
Use and value renewable resources and services

### A DESTABILIZING CHAIN OF POLLUTION

Given the proximity of populations to water, we find that rivers, lakes, and oceans serve as both resource and receptacle for human activities. Ancient civilizations knew how to use water without polluting or wasting it. Today, our lack of awareness of our belonging to nature, together with the density of populations situated along rivers, has rendered the situation critical. While fresh water is of course a renewable resource (by virtue of the cycle of evapotranspiration and precipitation), it is still under threat. Indeed, domestic and especially agricultural and industrial activities in rich countries generate pollution that starts off terrestrial and ends up aquatic (via runoff). This degradation destabilizes natural terrestrial and oceanic environments, imperilling the health and life of many species, including humans. This chain of water pollution is now fairly well understood by authorities and the general public. It is a situation that requires widespread mobilization.

**WATER TABLES IN DANGER**

Another serious risk is much less well known: in many parts of the world, the water that our modern societies use so lavishly is essentially permanently removed from water tables. Once it goes down our kitchen and bathroom sinks, our showers, and our toilets, this water is most often fed into the collective wastewater system (sewers) and subsequently into water treatment plants. There, the wastewater is "cleaned" and fed into a river, which flows into the ocean. This means that almost none of the water removed from our water tables cycles back, making it unavailable to feed the underground reserves. This situation is compounded by reckless deforestation, which dries out soil (and unbalances the climate). For years, water specialists have been sounding the alarm about the risk of draining the underground reserves, but the authorities don't seem to be listening. For this reason, we strongly urge citizens to divert their rainwater and their wastewater to the ground, the latter following treatment by pedo- or phytodepuration (soil or plant purification). With a view to preserving terrestrial and marine life (and therefore oxygen production), permaculture proposes measures for taking care of water.

**PERMACULTURE PRINCIPLE 6:**
Produce no waste

**HUMAN FRESH WATER NEEDS**

According to the World Health Organization (WHO):

- 100 liters of fresh water per person per day (LPD) is needed to live "comfortably."
- 50 LPD is needed to live "decently."
- 20 LPD is needed to survive. Of this volume, 2 to 3 LPD must absolutely be potable for the water that humans drink and use to prepare food.

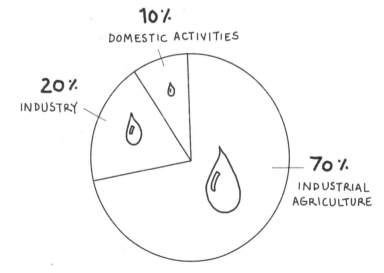

*World water usage.*

SOURCE: SUSTAINABLE DEVELOPMENT DEPARTMENT, "AGRICULTURE'S USE OF WATER," *CROPS AND DROPS: MAKING THE BEST USE OF WATER FOR AGRICULTURE*, ROME, FOOD AND AGRICULTURE ORGANIZATION OF THE UNITED NATIONS, 2002, FAO.ORG/3/Y3918E/Y3918E03.HTM.

## AMAZING DATA
## World access to potable water (UN)

- One in three humans has no access to potable water and lives in a situation of "water stress" (where needs exceed resources).
- Half of humanity drinks water that is "suspect," or even hazardous, and must travel kilometers to reach a water source. This is an infringement of human rights as defined by the international community.

## Water consumption varies greatly among regions of the world

|  | liters per person per day |
|---|---|
| United States* | 600 |
| Canada* | 300 to 400 |
| Europe | 130 to 250 |
| France | 130 to 160 |
| Asia, South America | 50 to 100 |
| Sub-Saharan Africa | 10 to 20 |

*Many urban North Americans pay a flat fee for their water. For many others, the price of water is built into public taxes. These methods are not an incentive to saving water!*

*A true revolution in potable water usage is needed, both individually and collectively.*

39%

20%

12%

10%

6% 6%

6%

1%

DRINKING

COOKING

CAR WASHING & GARDENING

DISH WASHING

LAUNDRY

FLUSHING

BATHS

VARIOUS

**Domestic use of potable water in rich countries**
*Yes, only one percent of tap water is consumed as drinking water (seven percent if you include food preparation)! Ultimately, 93 percent of potable water is used for hygiene and cleaning. This is waste that we need to recognize and reduce.*
Source: "Les usages de l'eau: les usages domestiques," Centre d'information sur l'eau, cieau.com/les-ressources-en-eau/en-france/les-usages-domestiques.

## GIVING PRIORITY TO WATER IN ALL DESIGNS

The mobilization of national and international authorities to reduce consumption of fresh water (especially potable water) and preserve water quality grows stronger with each passing year. That's a good thing. These top-down actions are necessary, but they are far from sufficient. If we are to quickly reverse our tendency to waste and pollute, we need every individual on board. A true revolution in potable water usage is needed, both individually and collectively. The availability and quality of fresh water dictate the economic, social, and cultural development potential of a site or region, which is why all permacultural designs place priority on this element.

Including water in the designs that you undertake is key — and it doesn't have to be complicated. The hardest part is grasping how urgent it is to alter our habits and perspective.

Here are a few simple and effective measures that all concerned citizens, especially permaculturists, can implement to preserve, recover, and enhance water resources in their homes, in their gardens, and on their land:

- Stop using products that pollute
- Calculate, limit, and control consumption of potable water
- Ensure that water is used multiple times before returning it to the land
- Install dry composting toilets

- Identify leaks in the drinking water network (15 to 20 percent of distributed water)
- Harvest rainwater
- Facilitate the slowing of rainwater, its dispersion, and its infiltration into the water table using swales and infiltration trenches (the three Ss: *slow it, spread it, sink it*)
- Purify and energize water
- Store water at high points (to facilitate distribution) and set up basins and/or other reservoirs

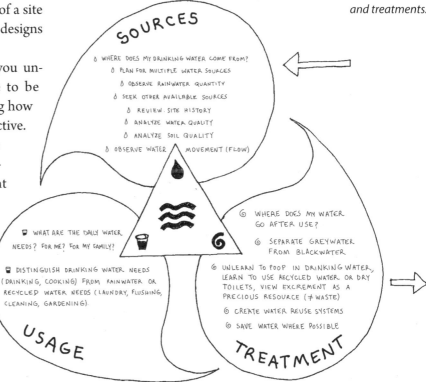

*Observing water sources, uses, and treatments.*

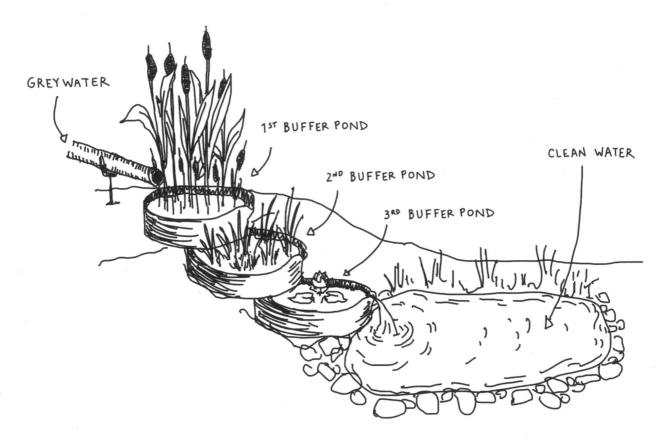

GREY WATER

1ST BUFFER POND

2ND BUFFER POND

3RD BUFFER POND

CLEAN WATER

– Limit watering (and select plant varieties accordingly) and curb evaporation from soil using straw or mulch
– Water deeply and infrequently rather than sparsely and frequently
– Process greywater (shower, dish, and laundry water) through pedo- or phyto-depuration (soil or plant purification)

– Stay informed about water resources in one's area (source, quality, treatment).

**PERMACULTURE PRINCIPLE 9:**
Use small and slow solutions

# Water pioneers

**René Quinton** (1866–1925): "We are truly a living marine aquarium in which some billion cells are swimming."

According to this French biologist and doctor, the plasma that surrounds mammalian cells (including ours) is identical to the original sea liquid (apart from the dilution factor). Diseases arise when the balance among certain elements is off. According to Quinton, all that's needed is to absorb sea water that is purified and isotonic to physiological concentrations in order to re-establish equilibrium and help the organism bounce back from illness or fatigue. The "Quinton Plasma" process, widely practiced when the researcher was alive, including in hospitals, was subsequently abandoned in favor of more "modern" remedies. Today it is used in naturopathy.

**TO FIND OUT MORE:**
René Quinton, *L'eau de mer, milieu organique: Constance du milieu marin originel, comme milieu vital des cellules, à travers la série animale* (Paris, Masson, 1912).

**Louis-Claude Vincent** (1906–88): "Water captures the vibratory forces of the universe and relays them into all living environments."

An associate of Dr. Jeanne Rousseau, this founder of bioelectronics highlighted the resonant quality of water and its capacity to relay the cosmo-electromagnetic information it receives into living environments. He developed a physicochemical technique for measuring the potential of hydrogen (pH), electrical potential ($rH_2$), and electrical resistivity ($\rho$) of aqueous solutions and thus for assessing the vitality of water or food, and the state of a person's biological "terrain," as he terms it. Under this approach it is also possible to correct a terrain to keep it in good health. Through bioelectronics, it is possible to obtain quality potable water by associating the filtration and revitalization processes. "The fundamental notions of purity and vitality are ignored by the official services, which are more concerned with the quantity of water to sell than with the quality of water to drink," volunteers from the bioelectronics association say regretfully.

**TO FIND OUT MORE:**
Votre santé naturelle, votre-sante-naturelle.fr.

**Jacques Benveniste** (1935–2004) and **Luc Montagnier** (1932–): "Water conserves the electromagnetic imprint of the molecules that have been in contact with it."

The French physician and immunologist Jacques Benveniste became known to the public through his work on "water memory" in the late 1980s. He showed that water conserves the electromagnetic imprint of molecules that come into contact with it, even after these molecules have disappeared after very strong dilutions. A portion of the scientific community disagrees with this vision. The French biologist Luc Montagnier, who won the 2008 Nobel Prize in Medicine for discovering the human immunodeficiency virus (HIV), which causes AIDS, bases his current research (detecting chronic bacterial infections) on the discoveries of Dr. Benveniste.

**TO FIND OUT MORE:**

Documentary film, On a retrouvé la mémoire de l'eau! by Christian Manil and Laurent Lichtenstein, 2013, france5.fr/et-vous/France-5-et-vous/ Les-programmes/LE-MAG-N-28-2014/articles/ p-20549-On-a-retrouve-la-memoire-de-l-eau. htm

**Chapter 13**

# Soil, Too, Is Life

*A dead leaf on the ground is not dirt; it's food.*

— Gilles Clément, planetary gardener

## SOIL, SUPPORTER OF LIFE

WE ARE BORN ON LAND, we walk on the land, we get our food from the land, we build our homes and roads on it, we carry out all our activities on it, and yet we are barely aware of the life that teems beneath our feet: seven million invertebrates live under the footprint of a single hiker! Most Indigenous peoples venerate the soil as the source of all fertility. Even to this day, Andean peoples make offerings to Pachamama, the nourishing Earth mother.

The nature of soil and the life that thrives in its layers doesn't count for much in the collective consciousness of modern society. We forget that subtle balances play out under our feet, unseen by the naked eye yet vital to all the cycles of terrestrial and marine life, and therefore to our survival. Indeed, most of terrestrial biodiversity dwells *in* the soil, not on the soil. In one square meter of healthy soil exists a fragile balance of up to 260 million animal species and twice as many plant species, each with specific functions in the wider ecosystem. Every gram of soil contains up to 100,000 bacterial species that are necessary to the life-sustaining equilibriums of terrestrial organisms!

The soil represents the meeting place between Earth energies, which come from the depths of the planet, and the cosmic energies from the stars and planets that influence life on Earth. This makes soil an especially rich zone of exchange, a living treasure for the planet and the organisms that call it home.

## VITAL FUNCTIONS FOR THE WHOLE ECOSYSTEM

Soil fulfills numerous complex functions within the ecosystem that are structural, physical, chemical, and biological in nature. They produce and maintain the biomass (forests, meadows, crops) from which we derive our food (production function). The greater this diversity is, the more that soil microorganisms are able to process, digest, and convert organic material (dead plants and animals — and, to some extent, our garbage) into food for plants (processing function). The end result is fertile humus, with its capacity to keep the innumerable plant and animal populations that live there in good health (habitat function).

Soil plays an important regulatory role: it stores, transports, filters, purifies, recycles, and restores gigantic reserves of fresh water. In other words, it plays a buffering role, both in terms of massive water circulation and in terms of climate, thanks to the thermal mass of the water it contains (resilience function).

Soil is an excellent substance for removing pollution from water (filtration function) thanks to the biogeochemical cycles of carbon and nitrogen associated with plants. It also plays a major role in water quality and carbon sequestration.

In summary, soil is a priceless asset to life on Earth — and a fragile one too, given that even

small amounts of damaging action can quickly render it sterile.

## ECOLOGICAL SERVICES FOR HUMANITY, FREE OF CHARGE

The soil beneath us provides multiple services — for free — including materials for our homes, fiber for our clothes, minerals, and petroleum. It is a storehouse of nutrients (especially minerals) critical to the health of plants, microorganisms, animals, and humans. And it provides a genetic reservoir as a source for scientific innovations (therapeutic and otherwise).

Finally, soil provides beautiful landscapes that we can use for physical, psychological, cultural, and spiritual fulfillment.

## SOIL: A NONRENEWABLE AND FINITE RESOURCE

Soil is made up of both a mineral portion and an organic portion that contains a lot of water and air. The mineral portion (clay, silt, sand) results from the breakdown of the parent material from weather (precipitation, wind, temperature changes), with the support of the multitudes of organisms living in the organic part of the soil (bacteria, fungi, earthworms, insects and other invertebrates, plants, living and dead animals) and complex biochemical processes (involving nitrogen, phosphorus, potassium, trace elements). Based on how

*Cycles of matter.*

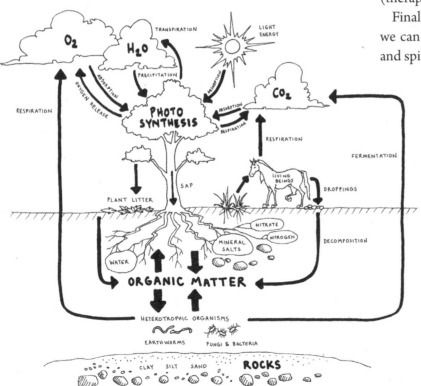

these different elements are combined, the soil is structured into clayey, silty, or sandy aggregates of varying homogeneity, which determine its properties, especially water retention. Based on the topography of the location (exposure to erosion, water flow, slope), the soil forms successive layers: these are termed the soil "horizons."

In any case, a significant amount of time is needed for soil formation to occur: centuries or millennia depending on the circumstances (an average of 100 years is needed for one centimeter of soil to form) — so much time, in fact, that soil is considered a nonrenewable resource. In temperate environments, soil thickness (i.e., the amount of soil sitting above the parent material) varies from 0 to 2 meters. This can reach 10 meters in tropical zones. Soil is considered good for agriculture if it contains 45% mineral matter, 25% water, 25% air, and 5% organic matter.

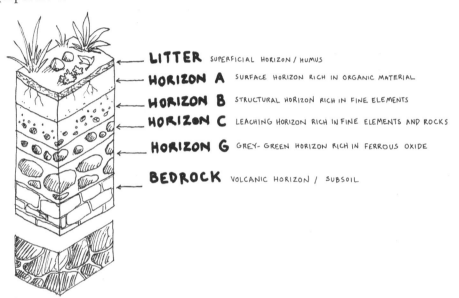

**LITTER** SUPERFICIAL HORIZON / HUMUS

**HORIZON A** SURFACE HORIZON RICH IN ORGANIC MATERIAL

**HORIZON B** STRUCTURAL HORIZON RICH IN FINE ELEMENTS

**HORIZON C** LEACHING HORIZON RICH IN FINE ELEMENTS AND ROCKS

**HORIZON G** GREY-GREEN HORIZON RICH IN FERROUS OXIDE

**BEDROCK** VOLCANIC HORIZON / SUBSOIL

## Water, soil, forest, and humanity: a family history (2 of 3)

### Soil's debt to aquatic life

For the last 3.5 billion years, marine plankton has been reproducing and dying. Enormous quantities of micro-algae have settled to the bottom of the sea, forming contours. As the ocean gradually retreated, continents and landscapes appeared. This is how the calcium-rich skeletons of coccolithophores (tiny algae) forged the famous chalk cliffs of Étretat, in France and the similar white cliffs of Dover, England, over millions of years! Similarly, the silicate rocks of Auvergne and Ardèche formed through the sedimentation and fossilization of diatom skeletons, diatoms being the most widespread species of phytoplankton. It is partly from the degradation of this parent material that soil was born, which, in turn, enabled terrestrial life to develop. (Continued on p. 112.)

## WHERE IS THE ARABLE LAND TODAY?

The arable layer of soil — i.e., the part that can be farmed and used to produce food — is 15 to 30 centimeters (6 to 12 in.) thick.

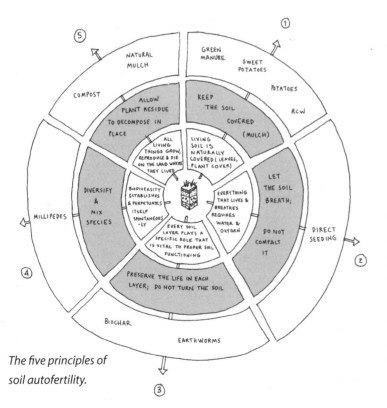

*The five principles of soil autofertility.*

Arable land is a limited resource by virtue of the planet's limits, which you can visualize by cutting up an apple:

- Three-quarters of the Earth's surface is covered by ocean.
- Of the remaining quarter of the apple, two-thirds is covered with desert, mountains, or ice.
- This leaves only one-third of this quarter of an apple to feed all of humanity. Now peel this slice: the peel represents eroded land, weakened by our practices and which humans can restore.

## THE FIVE PRINCIPLES OF SOIL AUTOFERTILITY

For millennia, plants have been propagating with no human intervention whatsoever! Let's learn about the conditions that allow the soil to generate its own abundance. This will allow us to replicate these conditions, to restore the vitality of our soil and minimize the work needed to cultivate our gardens.

Everything that lives — plants, animals, humans — inevitably dies. The microbial life in the soil digests and transforms all plant, animal, and mineral remnants into materials that can be assimilated, and can in turn feed plant life. Soil can be regarded as the digestive tract of the biosphere. The quality and fertility of the soil directly depend on the presence of organic material in the soil and the microorganisms' capacity to process it — and so does the health of the plants that grow there (just as the health of the human body depends largely on the vitality of the gut flora).

## SOIL IS NATURALLY AUTOFERTILE

Soil autofertility relies on five complementary and interdependent principles which, of course, apply all at the same time. If humans take inspiration from these principles and employ them for long enough on degraded land, the soil will regenerate and regain its autofertility.

### 1st principle of autofertility:
### Keep the soil covered

In its natural state, soil never remains bare (except in deserts). Left to its own devices, wild soil cleared accidentally (by fire, flooding, volcanic eruption, etc.) never remains unoccupied for long. Several elements conspire to cover it again: through the action of the wind and birds, pioneer plants — which we ungratefully call weeds — establish. Seeds buried in the ground come out of dormancy and germinate. Thus, plant cover regenerates and forests regrow, producing biomass, which creates new humus as it decomposes. And plant and animal life resume their course.

For this reason, permaculturists take care to cover the soil with mulch. Any organic material

| Principles of soil functioning in nature | Five measures for restoring soil autofertility |
|---|---|
| Living soil is naturally covered (leaves, plant cover) | 1. Keep the soil covered (mulch) |
| Everything that lives and breathes requires water and oxygen | 2. Let the soil breathe; do not compact it |
| Every soil layer plays a specific role that is vital to proper soil functioning | 3. Preserve the life in each layer; do not turn the soil |
| Biodiversity establishes and perpetuates itself spontaneously | 4. Diversify and mix species (polyculture) |
| All living things grow, reproduce, and die on the land where they lived | 5. Allow plant residue to decompose in place |

makes good mulch: dead leaves, ramial chipped wood (RCW), cut branches, wood chips, lawn clippings, newspaper, cardboard, carpeting or cloth made of natural fiber, sheep wool, etc. The presence of these materials activates life underground, which in turn activates the decomposition of the materials, which creates humus

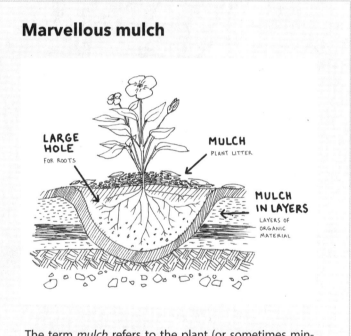

## Marvellous mulch

The term *mulch* refers to the plant (or sometimes mineral) covering that is spread on the ground at the base of plants in order to limit evaporation, mitigate runoff, and retain soil moisture. Applying mulch, or *mulching*, keeps the soil soft, facilitating humus formation through the decomposition of organic material. Moreover, mulching limits the growth of pioneer plants.

and restarts the cycles of life. Even a plastic tarp can protect the soil from weather and erosion and stimulate the activity of soil microorganisms.

### 2nd principle of autofertility: Let the soil breathe; do not compact it

Water and oxygen are vital elements for the plants, microorganisms, and animals that make their home in the soil. Therefore, water and oxygen must be allowed to circulate deeply in the soil to feed all strata of life. Through the tunnel-digging action of earthworms, moles, and foxes, and the soil-mixing work of ants, woodlice, spiders, and millipedes, animals keep the soil aerated, allowing water to penetrate. After ensuring that the soil is covered (first principle), permaculturists ensure that this respiration can take place: they designate walking paths on the land to avoid packing the soil everywhere with their steps. They especially avoid walking or trampling on cultivated areas so that the spaces created by wild animals are left intact. In this way, the land stays soft, fertile, and penetrable to water and air, which are crucial to the life of its inhabitants.

### 3rd principle of autofertility: Do not turn the soil

Each layer of soil has a special role that is vital to the proper functioning of the whole. The life in each layer is adapted to the availability of oxygen: certain microorganisms, insects, and fungi live on the surface and fulfill the role of processing fallen plant and animal material. They live in symbiosis with a number of elements which, like them, are found on the surface and require air and light. Other species live deeper down and do the work of making soil nutrients assimilable by plants. These species dwell in the darkness in anaerobic (oxygen-free) environments. All it takes is for a gardener to turn the soil, and all this organization goes topsy-turvy. A large fraction of the soil life declines: anaerobic organisms die from exposure to the air and sun while the surface species, now deprived of oxygen, asphyxiate to death.

Why exactly have humans become accustomed to turning the soil? The goal, of course, is to oxygenate it. Ploughing by humans compacts the soil. But we should ask: why is the soil compacted in the first place? Because humans ploughed it before that. When exposed to runoff from rain, and the assault from the sun and wind, the turned-over soil dries out and becomes depleted. Ploughing compacts a few centimeters of the soil, creating what is termed a plough pan: a hard layer that is difficult for air, water, and plant roots to penetrate. This compaction lowers yield by 10 to 30 percent. So, ploughing creates a vicious circle: destroying all these species lowers soil fertility and the vitality of plants, which can no longer play their symbiotic roles. In turn, they become vulnerable to disease and exhibit signs of weakness, which attracts pests. The wastefulness is twofold: the work performed is counterproductive, and the soil fertility declines. No miracle product can make up for this lost vitality in a sustainable fashion.

Permaculturists prefer to use the natural action of microorganisms in the soil. It's the soil animals, especially earthworms, and microfauna that do the work!

Contrary to popular belief, it is the act of working the soil — not the growth of the crops — that saps the soil. Only 5 percent of the components that make up plant biomass is removed from the soil itself (about 2.5 percent nitrogen and 2.5 percent various minerals). The rest comes from water (about 75 percent) while the remainder of the biomass is created through photosynthesis (20 percent, thanks to light).

### 4th principle of autofertility: Diversify and mix species

Plants are living, social beings, capable of "emotions," and "prefer" to live in the company of other species rather than in monoculture. In nature, biodiversity arises and self-perpetuates spontaneously; different plants mingle with each other in interactive diversity. This mixing benefits the plant balance and, by extension, the soil life. In our immense crop fields planted in straight rows and dominated by monoculture (a product of the left hemisphere of our brains), there are few exchange zones, those areas where the rich features of multiple environments are mutually reinforcing. Monoculture leads to mineral depletion (all the plants use up the same nutrients) as well as genetic depletion (no crossing occurs). In their weakened state, the plants attract the same viruses, diseases, and predators, which recognize the same signs of weakness in the plants at great distances and come to feast. Like larger predators, they pick off the weak individuals, which are easiest to attack. The more weakened plants the pests find to eat, the more the pests reproduce and propagate (slugs, for example).

To summarize, the more we grow in monoculture, the more sapped the soil becomes, the more fragile the crops that grow there become, and the more liable they are to attract viruses, pests, and diseases. To break this vicious circle, permaculturists foster interactions among plants by mixing crops in the same location. They also rely on allelopathy, a set of biochemical interactions by which plants emit substances that protect them from predators or diseases. In addition they utilize symbiosis between plants and soil fungi: the latter are able to transfer directly to plant roots substances that plants need but cannot absorb alone. In exchange, the plants provide the fungi with plant matter manufactured through photosynthesis. This arrangement increases productivity considerably.

### 5th principle of autofertility: Allow plant residue to decompose in place

When they die in nature, plants and animals stay where they die and transform into humus, with no human intervention. We should imitate this process and allow the unused parts of our plants to break down where they are. This could be leaves, stems, roots, straw, or even whole garden "weeds" provided they have not yet gone to seed.

This biomass serves as natural mulch, which feeds microorganisms and protects them from temperature variations. It helps create humus and improves the natural fertility of the land.

### SIGNS THAT AUTOFERTILITY HAS BEEN ACHIEVED

When autofertility is present, signs gradually start to appear:

- Plant health is the first indicator; plants are productive and reproduce in abundance.
- Many earthworms are present.
- A variety of insects and birds are present.
- The soil is soft and the undergrowth has a pleasant odor.
- Finally, mycorrhizae are present in plant roots: these are long white filaments that establish in plant roots and smell a lot like mushrooms. They are the result of the association among fungi, roots, and bacteria. Their role is to break down the large lignin molecules found in woody tissue, thus giving bacteria access to the inside of the wood. If mycorrhizae are found all over the land (not just in compost residue), the soil has attained autofertility.

If you spot all these signs on your land, it is time to stop adding inputs, even compost. Overnutrition is harmful to plants, just as it is for humans! Once the biological activity in the soil has been restored, all you need to do is maintain

# SOIL AUTOFERTILITY

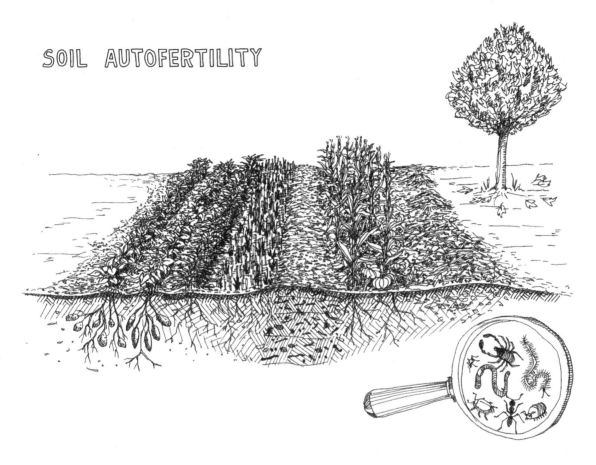

your mulch and allow the soil to self-regulate. Cultivate a patient mindset. Take the time to observe. Give nature the time to do its work!

## SOIL – TOO OFTEN MISTREATED AND IN DANGER

Humans use land to grow food, build homes and roads, harvest plant fibers, provide forage for their animals, store and extract water and energy, entertain themselves, and wage war. All these activities require larger and larger areas of land and cause deforestation, drying, the erosion and pollution of farmland, and loss of biodiversity — too often going so far as to destroy this irreplaceable resource and the life it contains.

Compacted, polluted, acidified, ploughed — the mistreatment of soil by industrial agriculture, mainly in the last 60 years or so, has destroyed microorganisms and the biodiversity of plants and animals. Soil lost to erosion is carried to rivers

## The earthworm: the gardener's greatest ally

Did you know that healthy soil contains a metric ton (2200 lb.) of earthworms — or 3 million individuals — per hectare (2.5 acres)? (That's 300 individuals per cubic meter.) Each hectare of good soil contains 15 kilometers of tunnels and an incalculable amount of castings. Castings are twisted bits of worm waste found on the ground; they are rich in humus and mineral salts. Earthworms are laborers that only enrich the soil and never disturb it! They work every day, for free, without burning any oil. Give them the right habitat and food (organic material), and their generosity will surprise you. There is never a risk of being overrun by a profusion of earthworms: when they reach the upper limit of population size, they simply stop reproducing.

The surface worm *Eisenia foetida,* commonly referred to as the red wiggler, has an average life expectancy of seven years. It lays about 65 eggs per year, which produce up to 260 babies (incubation period: 28 days). Nightcrawlers, which live deeper down in the soil, have a life expectancy of 15 years. Their presence helps plants fight parasites, especially nematodes.

Source: French National Research Institute for Development, ird. fr.

and oceans, and with it travel synthetic chemicals that destabilize other fragile environments. Given that all natural ecosystems are indissociably linked together, wherever the soil ecosystem begins to lose its balance, the domino effect will spread disequilibrium to other ecosystems too.

Collectively, humans lack awareness about the gravity of the impact their actions have on soil resources. They bury their heads in the sand when it comes to the long-term consequences these reckless practices could have, especially when it comes to water, food production, and global warming.

The international community is just starting to measure the situation. *The Status of World's Soil Resources Report,* the outcome of the work of 200 scientists in 60 countries, was published in December 2015 under the auspices of the Food and Agriculture Organization of the United Nations (FAO). Global plans for action to halt the escalating degradation of soils call for promoting sustainable management practices. Without this, the FAO cautions, the carbon contained in the soil "could be released to the atmosphere, aggravating global warming linked to the burning of fossil fuels."

Among other things, permaculturists aim to quell the negative impact of their activities on the soil in order to maintain its precious balances. Whether you live in the country or the city, the designs that we invite you to implement in your own life will help you make step-by-step

## AMAZING DATA
## Soil under pressure

- Around the world, one-third of soil is moderately or highly degraded by erosion, nutrient depletion, acidification, salinization, compaction, or chemical pollution.
- 40 percent of land is affected by desertification.
- The increase in world population will translate into a 60 percent greater demand for food, forage, and fiber by 2050.
- Since the 19th century, 60 percent of the carbon stored in soil and vegetation has disappeared through the effect of land clearing for intensive agriculture and urbanization, according to the FAO and the UN.
- France is the world's third-largest consumer of pesticides (after the United States and Japan) and by far the largest within Europe, according to the French Senate.
- In Quebec, the agriculture sector consumed over 90 percent of pesticides sold in the province in 2014, which represents over 4 million kilograms. Quebec's environment department reports that these were the highest sales since 1992.

progress and ask useful questions towards creating a space suited both to the site and to your needs. The answers you come up with will of course be specific to your situation.

### A FEW ENVIRONMENTAL METHODS TO IMPROVE YOUR SOIL

Whether in a garden or on a balcony, anyone can take simple actions wherever they live to help the soil recover its vitality and autofertility — the ultimate objective being not to take any action at all!

- **Ramial chipped wood (RCW):** This method replicates what occurs naturally in all forests: the ground is covered with fine branches — young branches, freshly chopped with a lawn mower. They are high in minerals, amino acids, enzymes, proteins, cellulose, sugars, starch, and bacteria, making them especially useful when it comes to enriching, irrigating, structuring, and regulating the soil life.
- **Biochar** (charcoal for agricultural use) or **terra preta** (black earth): This is useful for creating particularly fertile soils, like those observed in pre-Columbian sites in Amazonia. The method consists of permanently burying in the soil certain quantities of charcoal produced at low temperatures through pyrolysis, which makes it richer in

carbon. The highly porous material filters water, stores soil moisture, improves nitrogen and carbon cycles, and provides habitat for many microorganisms. It also produces exceptionally high yields.

- **Green manures:** These include phacelia (purple tansy), clover, vetch, and buckwheat. These nitrogen-fixing plants are temporary crops that retain nutrients in the soil and protect it in the period between crops and seasons. They produce organic material and leave behind a large quantity of nitrogen nodules for the next crops to use. They are later used as mulch or compost. Additionally, their flowers attract pollinators and other auxiliary insects.

- **Direct seeding under plant cover:** This consists of seeding the future crop (for example, different varieties of wheat) into an existing crop of green manure covered with straw. A specially adapted seeder deposits the seed in the soil and closes up the soil in its wake, without disturbing the underground microfauna and microflora. This practice enriches the organic matter of the soil and protects it from weather. It is highly economical in terms of time, inputs (none), water, and petroleum. It is a low-cost way to increase yield.

- **Composting:** While waiting for your soil to regain its autofertility, you can help it along by adding compost. Mix your green material (fruit and vegetable scraps, yard trimmings)

with brown material (straw, dead leaves, cardboard) and aerate it by turning it periodically. Maintaining the proper moisture level will help with decomposition. *Never bury compost: it will produce methane, which kills microorganisms.* Compost restores soil and allows communities to save on household waste treatment.

**Variations:**

**Surface composting:** Same principle. Simply spread your vegetable and fruit scraps on the beds you wish to enrich and cover them with dry material. Be careful of pests!

**Homeopathic composting:** Spread decomposing (semi-mature) compost on the surface and cover it with dry matter. The influx of bacteria will stimulate the soil vitality.

- **Surface manure spreading:** High-quality manure (check on the animals' diet and veterinary treatments), preferably already enriched with dry material (bedding) and, of course, mulched, will also feed your soil as it regains autofertility.

- **Preparing soil by growing potatoes:** This is an effective method in temperate climates for turning a lawn or vacant land into a productive garden! First designate beds that you would like to become autofertile. Flatten the grass — don't bother pulling it out — and plant seed potatoes of a robust variety every 40 cm (16 in.). Cover the seed potatoes with 50 cm (20 in.) of straw to keep them dark. Once the potato plant has pierced through the covering (don't worry; it will come!) you can plant leeks or dry beans. After you harvest the vegetables, leave the residue in place. Your land will be ready for the following spring!

– **Preparing the soil by growing sweet potatoes:** In hot climates, this crop prepares the soil the same way regular potatoes do in temperate climates. Germinate the sweet potatoes and start them in potting soil. Once they have a root system developing, transplant them into the ground, even grassy ground, with a little manure, at a

spacing of 30 cm (12 in.). For the first few weeks, water frequently after the heat of the day. After one year, the soil will be covered with vegetation and the sweet potatoes will be ready. After harvesting, leave the biomass in place and add mulch. The soil will now be ready to accept whatever crop you choose.

In Part 4, Caring for People, you will find some examples of forest gardens, agroecology, agroforestry, and biodynamics that apply the principles of soil autofertility to produce food in ideal conditions.

## Soil pioneers

**Masanobu Fukuoka,** Japanese microbiologist (1913–2008): "Cultivate the art of doing nothing. Let nature do the work!"

Mulch! Just mulch! No tillage, no fertilizers — not even compost — no chemicals, no weeding, no pruning, no machines, no petroleum. The "wild agriculture" promoted by this hands-on grower steeped in Buddhist philosophy inspired Bill Mollison and David Holmgren in their definition of "permanent agriculture." Thanks to the yields he achieved in rice and other grains, citrus and other fruits, and vegetables,

he was able to persuade the FAO to adopt his idea; the organization now recommends reduced tillage to preserve soil.

**TO FIND OUT MORE:** Masanobu Fukuoka, *The One-Straw Revolution: An Introduction to Natural Farming* (Emmaus, Pennsylvania, Rodale, 1978).

**Percival Alfred Yeomans,** Australian mining engineer (1905–84): "Clean water and healthy soil: these are the foundations of human and social health."

Beginning in the 1950s, Yeomans advised farmers in arid regions to collect and store rainwater and runoff water in their soil using the contours of the land. With his "keylines" system, "in a matter of two or three years, soils which take a century to evolve under forest can be recreated by man." He invented a plough, which bears his name and is used today in many countries. The device, designed for field crops, aerates the soil without turning or compacting it. "If nations would set a goal for soil health, the other situations which plague us would resolve themselves," stated the visionary.

**TO FIND OUT MORE:** *Percival Alfred Yeomans, Water for Every Farm: A Practical Irrigation Plan for Every Australian Property* (Sydney, K.G. Murray, 1973).

**Lydia Bourguignon** (1949–) and **Claude Bourguignon**, French agronomic engineer (1951–): "RCW is a fast and effective way to revive dead soil."

In the 1980s, Lydia and Claude Bourguignon stated that "90 percent of the micobiological activity in European soil has been destroyed by intensive agriculture." In 1989, they founded the Soil Microbiological Analysis Laboratory (LAMS) and helped disseminate the idea of soil as a complex and fragile ecosystem. They advocate a return to using hedgerows and agro-silvo-pastoralism to restore soil.

**TO FIND OUT MORE:** Claude and Lydia Bourguignon, *Le sol, la terre et les champs: Pour retrouver une agriculture saine* (Paris, Sang de la Terre, 2015).

**Chapter 14**

# Forest: Bridge between Land and Sky

*Forests precede civilizations. Deserts follow them.*

— François-René de Chateaubriand (1768–1848)

## THE FOREST:
## A BASTION AGAINST CLIMATE CHANGE

FORESTS PRODUCE almost half the oxygen the living world requires to survive, while their vegetation and soil absorb 40 percent of the carbon dioxide. By forming plant cover with their leaf litter, trees create humus, which stores and filters large quantities of water and moisture.

Billions of cubic meters of water pass through the roots of trees and into the air via transpiration and evaporation. Without forests, a portion of the world's rain would not form. The significant foliage of trees allows them to play a role in the water cycle. For every square meter of ground surface, trees provide 3 to 10 square meters of foliage. When rain occurs in a forest, 20 to 50 percent of the rainfall is retained by the foliage.[1] Tree roots function as a special hydraulic network, diverting water to water tables. Tree roots prevent soil erosion and leaching. When trees die, their roots decompose in the soil and maintain its natural fertility.

Forests serve as windbreaks and mitigate extreme weather events. Like the oceans, they too act as climate buffers. They are special and immense reserves of biodiversity, a provider of food

and shelter for animals, and a source of fuels, clothing, medicinal plants, etc.

The forest also plays an important social role in that it provides humans a point of contact with nature. We use them for walks, games, relaxation, sports, creativity, learning, travelling, and contemplation that awakens our consciousness — all activities necessary for the physical, mental, and spiritual balance of humans. "Forest bathing" is becoming a popular activity among city dwellers. Forests also serve the vital role of sanctuaries to the rare human populations that have forever lived harmoniously in them, taking all they need without destroying the forest. These Indigenous populations are without a doubt the only true guarantors of forest preservation.

## HOW ARE FORESTS BORN?

In nature, different types of plants arise in succession to create a forest. The English horticulturist Robert Hart (1913–2000) classified them into seven stories (levels). The plants in each story leave behind biomass that prepares the land for the next story's arrival. Each story gives creative energy for the next.

## ROBERT HART'S SEVEN FOREST STORIES

1 **Pioneer plants.** The first to arrive on bare soil are herbaceous perennial plants, also known as "weeds," whose role is to quickly cover the soil and feed it. Members of the grass family are part of this (often unwanted) group. They spontaneously reseed, form roots, and die, leaving behind carbonaceous biomass, which feeds the microorganisms. They require a lot of light and disappear where too much shade is thrown by trees.

2 **The shrub story.** Birds and some mammals are attracted by these rich environments and

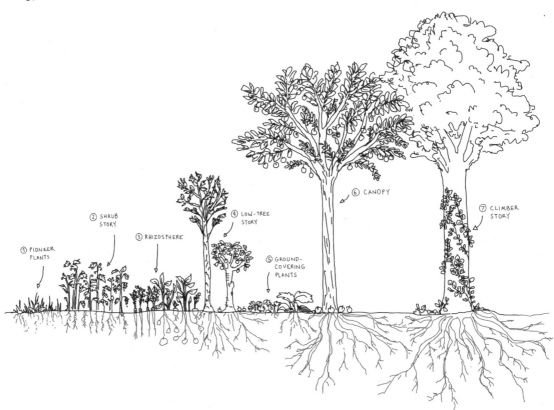

*The seven stories of the forest.*

① PIONEER PLANTS
② SHRUB STORY
③ RHIZOSPHERE
④ LOW-TREE STORY
⑤ GROUND-COVERING PLANTS
⑥ CANOPY
⑦ CLIMBER STORY

leave behind their droppings, which contain seeds from the fruits of thorny plants they have eaten elsewhere. Once processed in the animals' digestive tracts, these seeds are now in the prime conditions to germinate. Other seeds arrive freely on the wind or hitch a ride on hikers' boots. Raspberry, blackberry, blackcurrant, and wild currant bushes develop in this fashion. The thorns of these shrubs protect young tree sprouts from herbivores, allowing them to grow up through the shrubs.

3 **The rhizosphere** (root development area). Rhizomes break up and soften the soil. They leave dead root structures behind them, creating tunnels that allow air, water, and nutrients to circulate in the soil. This story includes carrots, turnips, potatoes, dandelions, ferns, quackgrass, asparagus, etc.

4 **The low-tree story** (under 5 meters) is made of young woody plants, some of them fast growing. These pioneers generally have brittle wood and short lives. They leave behind on the soil an abundant biomass of leaves, branches, and trunks, which form the forest cover. This story includes dwarf fruit trees, birch, and staghorn sumac.

5 **Ground-covering plants** develop on the surface, including certain cucurbit species (zucchinis for example) and, via their aerial roots or runners, strawberries.

6 **The canopy** is the upper part of the forest (5 meters and greater). It cuts through the other plant stories and grows in the middle of this diversity. This story includes hardwoods such as oak, beech, and large fruit trees. They provide shade, live for many years, and leave large quantities of biomass on the soil.

7 **The climber story** (ivy, kiwi, wisteria, Virginia and other creepers). Their role is to (eventually) suffocate and bring down the largest trees to regenerate the forest. They climb up trunks to the treetops to receive the light they need in order to fruit. Little by little, climbers create environments around the trunks they colonize that are prime territory for bark diseases. After several years, the tree eventually falls, creating a clearing. And the cycle of the stories begins again.

Over time, soil that is accidentally cleared (by a naturally occurring fire or other natural disaster) gradually becomes covered over again with these seven stories, eventually re-creating a forest. This mechanism of regeneration occurs everywhere on Earth, though of course with different species depending on the region. If you organize these stories into interrelations with each other on the same land, with "a little" patience you can create a forest! It takes seven centuries, cautions the French botanist and biologist Francis Hallé,[2] for a human-planted forest to accumulate the characteristics of a real primary forest.

By choosing plants that provide fruits and vegetables, we create an edible and

## Water, soil, forest, and humanity: a family history (3 of 3)

### Our ancestors the trees

Whereas phytoplankton began populating the oceans over 3 billion years ago, part of the plant world exited the sea to begin colonizing dry land "only" 450 million years ago. Thereafter, all types of terrestrial plants developed. Later still (230 million years ago), dinosaurs (the first large land animals) came on the scene, and "only yesterday," humans arrived. These life forms are all links in the same chain of evolution; all are members of the same living family. Humanity, the baby of the family, has a lot to learn from the wisdom of its "ancestors," the trees, which embody resilience. All you have to do is notice the sense of wellbeing that most people feel in the presence of large trees. This feeling has been formally developed in Japan as the practice of Shinrin Yoku, which means Forest Bathing or Forest Therapy. For more on this visit shinrin-yoku.org.

self-sufficient "forest garden"! The greater the plant diversity in these stories, the more varied the animal habitats and the greater the soil vitality. The presence of trees creates a moist microclimate that encourages the formation of rain.

### PRIMARY FORESTS ARE BECOMING INCREASINGLY RARE

Forests currently cover one-third of the Earth's land area and contain more than half the carbon accumulated within terrestrial ecosystems. The three great tropical forests are found in the following locations:

– The Amazon (primarily Brazil, Peru, and Colombia)
– Democratic Republic of the Congo
– Indonesia

These three zones contain two-thirds of the planet's primary forests.

Forests untouched by humans represent only 5 to 10 percent of all forests on the globe. They are becoming both rarer and more fragmented, especially in the northern hemisphere, where such forests often cover areas of only 20 to 300 hectares (50 to 750 acres), often in poor and acidic soil.

### HOW DOES A FOREST WORK?

The amount of carbon on Earth is constant, but carbon goes through transformations that make it a powerful force in the recycling of plant matter. The availability of carbon is critical to the development of living beings, as the element is the basis of organic cells. All foods produced by agriculture and consumed by humans (carbohydrates, fats, proteins) are made of carbon chains. Through photosynthesis, plants capture some of the atmospheric $CO_2$ and use it to create biomass. This biomass stores and conserves $CO_2$, even after its return to the soil. Its role is considered that of a "carbon sink."

The world's largest carbon reserves are located in sediments accumulated on the ocean floor (over 50 million gigatonnes of carbon, or GtC) and in animal and plant life in ocean waters (39,000 GtC). Carbon reserves in the atmosphere and biosphere (soil, plants, forests, animals) are much more modest (less than 2,000 GtC) but still vital to life on Earth. The main forms of carbon present in the atmosphere are carbon dioxide ($CO_2$) and methane ($CH_4$).

The disequilibrium in carbon flux (exchange) among these various reservoirs is having consequences for all life cycles.

Carbon is soluble in water. This is why the carbon sequestration capacity of the oceans greatly exceeds that of the atmosphere — by a factor of 63, in fact. Through their respiration and decomposition, both plants and animals release $CO_2$. Through photosynthesis, plants also fix carbon into biomass and produce oxygen. Peatlands alone store twice as much carbon as living biomass.

In a situation unprecedented in the history of humanity, the concentration of atmospheric $CO_2$ is now 35 percent higher than it was for the last 420,000 years: about 400 parts per million by volume (ppmv) in 2015. This concentration is increasing between 10 and 100 times faster than before.[3] The reason is the burning of huge amounts of fossil energy, which releases $CO_2$ much more rapidly than carbon sinks can absorb. Deforestation exacerbates this disequilibrium, as felled forests can no longer play their role.

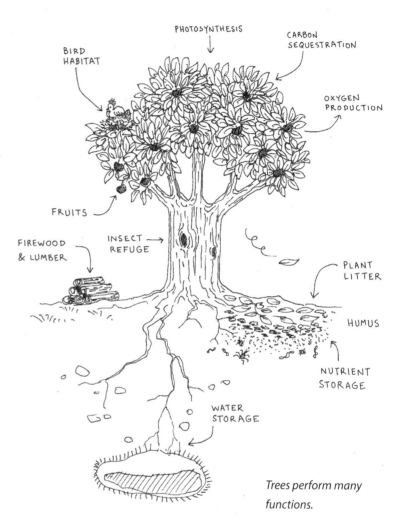

*Trees perform many functions.*

The processes of photosynthesis, plant respiration and transpiration, decomposition, and biomass combustion maintain the natural circulation of oxygen and carbon between the forest and the atmosphere. Clearing land without giving forests enough time to regrow has significant consequences for the carbon cycle. As a result, there is less forest vegetation to perform photosynthesis, and major stocks of carbon accumulated over long periods in forest ecosystems are exported far from where the trees grew. Thus, the carbon cycle is broken.

## AMAZING DATA

Three-quarters of the disturbances in the world's carbon cycle are directly attributable to the burning of fossil energy.

## SMART OR UNCONTROLLED LOGGING?

Wood is an environmentally friendly and renewable resource as long as it is not overexploited. Hardwood regenerates in 100 years in temperate zones and sustainably stores $CO_2$. In certain cases (to make paper pulp or lightweight housing materials, for example), wood can be replaced by hemp, which has a life cycle of one season.

Traditionally, logging occupied a hallowed position in development policies. Primary forests were logged only along roadsides. After the Second World War, as military machines were being repurposed as farm machines, logging activities scaled up and began reaching deep into primary forests, with no consideration for their

## What do we do with the forests we log?

Out of all the wood logged on the planet, 15 to 30 percent is cut illegally, often to make room for lucrative grain crops for livestock consumption. The black market for wood generates sales of $100 billion per year. Crime associated with wood smuggling is becoming more organized and is frequently connected with other crimes including murder, corruption, fraud, and theft — especially to the detriment of Indigenous peoples.

**Of the 70 to 85 percent of wood sold legally:**

53% becomes firewood
27% becomes lumber, veneer, and plywood (buildings, furniture)

16% becomes paper pulp, packaging, particleboard, and fiber
4% goes to various other uses

Sources:

– Interpol and United Nations Environment Programme, *Green Carbon, Black Trade: Illegal Logging, Tax Fraud and Laundering in the World's Tropical Forests*, 2012.[4]

– Food and Agriculture Organization of the United Nations, *State of the World's Forests: Enhancing the socioeconomic benefits from forests*, 2014.[5]

renewal. Since the 1980s, an awareness of this pillage has been (too) slowly growing among wood industry players, from producers to processors, from sellers to politicians and, further down the line, the public and consumers. There has also been, of course, significant resistance from lobbies representing industries that derive great profits from uncontrolled exploitation. In this commercial jungle, there is one card ordinary citizens can play: their ability to make wise consumer choices, which requires that they become aware of how their daily behaviors impact forests. To this end, one first needs to distinguish between smart logging and uncontrolled logging.

Felling large primary forests to replace them with fast-growing, lucrative farm crops is the main cause of deforestation of the world's largest wooded areas. This destruction is the work of powerful industrial groups that place their short-term profits over sustainable forest management practices and sometimes flout international regulations. This logging makes it possible to produce soybeans for livestock feed, to manufacture biofuels (palm oil, sugarcane), or to profit from the precious woods. Demographic pressure and economic development in the most heavily wooded countries, coupled with increased demand for wood products, aggravates the situation further.

The illegal wood trade also weighs heavily on the resource. In Madagascar, overlogging and illegal trading in rosewood and ebony have destroyed four-fifths of the island's forest heritage in the space of a century.

Cutting down primary forests with no consideration for the time they take to regrow constitutes a crime against life: forests require centuries to regenerate, not to mention the fact that the human, animal, and plant biodiversity they harbor are most often permanently destroyed.

The international community is moving towards sustainable forest management, which seeks to reconcile biodiversity with the fulfillment of human needs. This is of course a step in the right direction. Nonetheless, the resulting industrial forests, most often planted in monoculture, bear no relationship — ecologically speaking — to primary forests. They are engineered to grow quickly and produce profits cheaply, such as the use of eucalyptus for pulp and paper and oil palms for biofuels. Like all monocultures, these plantations have negative effects on the environment, such as invasions of spruce budworms (an insect pest), which are fought with aerial pesticide treatments. Cutting down forests and replacing them with soybeans for the agri-food industry, urban sprawl, road construction, and poor land-use planning also contribute to the destruction of large areas of forest.

**TO FIND OUT MORE:**
See *Forest Alert* (1999), a Canadian National Film Board documentary by Quebec artist and activist Richard Desjardins and filmmaker Robert Monderie, which speaks out against the clearcutting of Quebec's boreal forest for the pulp and paper industry.

## WHAT IS THE RELATIONSHIP BETWEEN OUR CONSUMPTION AND FORESTS?

**A lifesaver:** The Forest Stewardship Council (FSC) eco-social label guarantees that the wood or wood-based product was produced in accordance with the principles of sustainable forest management.

Besides our consumption of meat and leather (used in footwear, accessories, and furniture), which involves ever more intensive cutting of trees, we consume a lot of toilet paper, facial tissues, paper towels, coffee filters, diapers, wipes, and packaging (that often serves little purpose). It's a good idea to take the time to list the products made of trees around us and see which of them we could remove or replace with forest-friendly alternatives.

## ENTERING "SYLVILIZATION"! CONCRETE ACTIONS TO SUSTAIN THE FOREST

Diversity spontaneously arises in nature. If we want to help to re-create territories that are as

## AMAZING DATA
## Forest treasures

- Forests are home to 80 percent of terrestrial biodiversity.
- They cover a third of the Earth's land surface.
- Tropical forests untouched by humans cover six percent of the Earth's land surface. They are home to three-quarters of terrestrial biodiversity and contain a precious resource for possible medicinal compounds.
- Forests are the last refuge for a large number of animal and plant species.
- Half of tropical forests have disappeared since 1945.
- A cubic meter of wood can store the carbon from a metric ton (a tonne) of $CO_2$.
- Worldwide, about 13 million hectares of forests disappear every year (an area the size of England).

- Over 1.6 billion people depend to varying degrees on forests for their livelihood.
- 300 million people live in or around forests.
- 60 million people depend virtually entirely on forests (especially Indigenous populations).
- In highly deforested areas, the risk of contracting malaria is 300 times greater than in intact forested zones.

SOURCES:
- WORLD WILDLIFE FUND, *SAVING FORESTS AT RISK*, LIVING FORESTS REPORT 2015.[6]
- FOOD AND AGRICULTURE ORGANIZATION OF THE UNITED NATIONS, *STATE OF THE WORLD'S FORESTS*.

harmonious as the complex ecosystems that make up forests, we need to forget about monoculture solutions! They are not sustainable and do not fulfill the multiple roles of natural forests.

We need to enter a paradigm of "sylvilization," valuing interdependence, co-management, co-responsibility, and solidarity. Wherever we are, we need to learn how to make room for the forest, to coexist with it, to protect it, and to revive it. Permaculture proposes a number of concrete actions to this end.

*What you can do to protect the forest as an individual citizen:*

- Evaluate the impact of your food habits on natural resources and rethink the products you consume, especially your meat purchases. Anyone can do this, including city dwellers.
- Learn to read product packaging, become familiar with labels, and boycott products made from exotic

**Sylvilization** is a term invented in the 1950s by a Métis person from Quebec and used by the Mi'kmaq Magamigo. See sylvilisation.com.

*Forest preservation actions.*

woods. Ensure that your flooring, furniture, and lumber bear the Forest Stewardship Council (FSC) label.

– Limit your consumption of paper and paper-based products (wipes, toilet paper, diapers, facial tissues, paper towels, coffee filters).

– Develop Zone 5 areas on any land you own, areas where the seven stories of spontaneous vegetation can establish and ultimately foster the full dynamic of plant and animal biodiversity.

– Plant edible forests!

*What associations, networks, and municipalities can do to protect the forest:*

– Raise public awareness about forest-related issues: films, testimonials, visits, and meetings with subject-matter experts to help change people's awareness and collective behavior.

– Plant trees (fruit trees if possible) or encourage them to be planted on land under their jurisdiction.

– Lobby political officers so that all projects maintain or restore an untouched Zone 5 where construction is prohibited. Citizens can only make changes in this area through a democratic voting process.

 **KEY TO SUCCESS:** Increase the number of ecological corridors (forested, if possible) and Zone 5 areas. Let biodiversity flourish!

## EDIBLE FORESTS TO "LIBERATE SOIL FERTILITY"

Following in the footsteps of Robert Hart, we should plant food forests where we live. Hart's original aim was to provide his disabled brother with delicious organic food. He was also sensitive to the issue of world hunger and wanted to find a simple way to address it that would be replicable in any country. His personal experience left him convinced that small plots could be used to cultivate productive gardens that would provide pleasure, beauty, and quality nourishment for humans and animals, as well as a way to help others, fight soil erosion, and even contribute to a flourishing of spirituality. He drew his inspiration from the small self-sufficient and democratic communities promoted by Gandhi (1869–1948) and the alternative "brotherhood economics" of the Japanese activist Toyohiko Kagawa (1888–1960). Starting in the 1930s, Kagawa promoted the planting of fruit and nut trees to protect soil and provide food for humans and animals.

For 30 years, on his small plot of 500 square meters in Wales, Robert Hart showed that humans' role in gardening was limited to maintaining the conditions to "liberate the fertility" naturally present in the soil by allowing roots and earthworms to build their energy circulation networks. When maintained in this fashion, soil does not suffer from weather variations (excess heat or humidity). To grow heliophilous (sun-loving) plants, all that's required is to create a clearing by occasionally cutting down one or

FOREST GARDEN

two large trees. Robert Hart's personal experimentation demonstrated that such a miniature forest (with its seven stories) can reach maturity within four years in temperate zones.

*Robert Hart's tips for starting a forest garden:*

– Choose common plant species (or exotic ones if preferred).
– Start by planting large fruit trees 6 meters apart in all directions.
– Plant dwarf fruit trees halfway in between.
– Plant small fruits and currant bushes between the trees or along the borders.
– Put in herbaceous plants and perennial vegetables.[7]
– Contain plants that encroach on other plants. This will be a daily chore in peak season for the first few years!
– Keep the soil mulched. Covering it with chopped branches (RCW) will increase the soil's natural defences against insect pests and diseases without destroying the micro-fauna. The mulch will limit undesirable

effects and maintain soil fertility and moisture.
– Apply nettle, seaweed, or comfrey tea as needed.

Generations of permaculturists have followed these tips (adapting them to diverse situations, of course) to obtain maximum production with minimal work!

**TO FIND OUT MORE:**
– American design teacher Dave Jacke has written a two-volume book on edible forest gardens with his

# Forest pioneers

**Akira Miyawaki** (1928–): "Native trees have the power to heal the Earth."

A Japanese botanist and specialist in forest restoration on severely degraded soil, Miyawaki planted 40 million trees in Japan and elsewhere using the ecological engineering method now named after him. From among native pioneer and secondary species, he selects trees that are complementary in their functions and work with mycorrhizae, planting them close together to re-create forest cover. He brings together a wide diversity of companion species (40 to 60 plant types, and even more in tropical zones) as "support." Competition among plants strengthens those that survive. Miyawaki often has children plant the trees to encourage randomness in the layout, as occurs in nature.

**Francis Hallé** (1938–): "Being around trees puts humans in their rightful place."

This French botanist, biologist, and admirer of equatorial forests, reminds us that forests got along just fine before humans arrived, i.e., for at least 350 million years! In his view, trees, the largest and longest-lived living things, are the model of autonomy, slowness, depth, and resilience that our society so greatly needs. Humans, by contrast, are utterly dependent on the plant kingdom (often unknowingly), live with a sense of urgency, tend to be superficial, etc. This specialist considers agroforestry, with its high yields, to be a response that intelligently reconciles the needs of humans, animals, and plants. "Ultimately the tree is given the role of protector that it always had in traditional cultures. Hundreds of years of research will be needed to truly understand the promise of these giants," the researcher says.

associate Eric Toensmeier: *Edible Forest Garden* (White River Junction, Vermont, Chelsea Green, 2005). It tells you everything you need to know to start a fruit forest and understand the evolutionary mechanisms at work in forests.
– British author Patrick Whitefield: *How to Make a Forest Garden* (East Meon, UK, Permanent, 2002).

 **KEY TO SUCCESS:** Consider that your immediate influence over the quality of the water, soil, and forest, comes from your consumer choices. As Quebec ecosociologist Laure Waridel reminds us, we vote with our dollars.[8]

 **TO FIND OUT MORE:** Francis Hallé created the documentary film *Once Upon a Forest*, produced by Luc Jacquet (2013).

**Sebastião Salgado** (1944–) and **Lélia Salgado** (1947–): "By replanting trees, we replant springs."

After covering all kinds of human-caused disasters as a photographer (genocides, outmigration, famines), Sebastião Salgado, together with his wife Lélia, set out to replant the Atlantic forest that once existed in the Northeast Region of Brazil, where Sebastião was born. The area had experienced desertification in the wake of unchecked forest logging. After several attempts, the couple — aided by schoolchildren — succeeded in planting 2.5 million trees of 300 different species on the 750-acre family farm. Within 15 years, the water, life, and even wild animals had returned. The land has been designated a private natural heritage reserve. Outreach efforts include a number of complementary activities including environmental education, integration programs for people in need, seed production, and research. The forest is an inspiring example for those who wish to keep (or restore) hope, and a model for all damaged areas of the planet.

 **TO FIND OUT MORE:** Sebastião Salgado has created many books and photo expositions. *Le Sel de la Terre*, a documentary film produced by Wim Wenders in 2014, charts Salgado's journey. For information on the Instituto Terra, visit institutoterra.org.

INSPIRING EXAMPLE

# Planting forests to save oysters!

**Shigeatsu Hatakeyama** is a Japanese oyster farmer. In 1989, his oysters became unfit for consumption following a red algae infestation. In response, he observed, investigated, and found an original solution to the problem.

The man now known as "Grandpa Oyster" noticed that the toxic red algae were feeding on pollution from the neighboring river. This reminded him of a trip he had taken in the French department of Loire-Atlantique a few years earlier. He observed that the broadleaf forests on the banks of the Loire River naturally filtered terrestrial rainwater while the river carried the nutrients that oysters fed on out to sea. He realized then that the ecosystem could only be understood in a holistic sense. "The solution consists of rebuilding the ecosystem, from the land to the sea," he decided. "Humus is needed to feed oysters!" (Humus contains iron and fulvic acid, which allow for photosynthesis and the fixing of chlorophyll on the plankton that the oysters feed on.) He brought the local mayors and residents together — knowing it was impossible to accomplish his aim unless everyone living along the river shared the same vision and values. And he proposed that a broadleaf forest be planted upstream of the estuary. Farmers joined in, a local poet created a movement under the banner "The forest is longing for the sea; the sea is longing for the forest," and the miracle was performed: gradually, the water quality improved and oyster farming was able to begin again. Now, over 25 years later, 30,000 trees have been planted along the river, and programs to reduce pesticide usage in crops and to regulate runoff are being run. The story is famous all across the country and on other continents as well. Today it is included in school programs in Japan. Every year, 10,000 children are invited to the site to plant trees and learn about the relationships between human activities, the river water, the soil, the forest, and the ocean. Kyoto University has created a department that straddles the disciplines of forestry and ocean studies. And the ingenious oyster farmer received the United Nations Forest Hero Award.

After the tsunami devastated the region in 2011, Shigeatsu Hatakeyama observed that the ocean was devoid of life. A few months later, he and his team were surprised at how quickly the underwater world bounced back to life. Such resilience was possible because there was a complete, complex, and balanced ecosystem. This is an encouraging example for oyster farmers and foresters who are prepared to cooperate.

**TO FIND OUT MORE:**
– Mori-Umi organization (in English): mori-umi.org/english/history.html.
– Forest Hero Award: youtube.com/embed/vhaVXrUhkHU.

# Part 4
## Caring for People

## Chapter 15

# Permacultivating Our Food

OF ALL HUMAN NEEDS, our need to eat and to drink are the most immediate, the most urgent, and the most "emotional." Our food habits, which we inherit from childhood, shape our individual identities and mark our cultural belonging. For this reason, it is especially upsetting for us to see them called into question. However, whether we like it or not, people's current eating habits in industrialized countries will need to change: they are neither generalizable nor sustainable.

*Food is necessary for life and living beings are in competition to get their share.*

They create social and economic vulnerability that is untenable over the long term; they are predicated on a dangerous dependence on oil and produce stark inequalities among different regions of the world, which are incompatible with the principles of food sovereignty and social justice. Our food habits cause many kinds of pollution and threaten biodiversity; they deplete natural resources, generate enormous waste, and cause major health problems. In short, the time has come to change our models!

Many nutritious, economical, environmentally friendly, and delicious food sources are overlooked, underutilized, and underestimated. Some of them suffer from negative perceptions. To give permaculturists and concerned citizens like you a leg up, we present here a number of ideas to fuel your consciousness and creativity. We also recommend a few menu items that — we hope — will make you want to expand your palate and seek out new types of food. You are sure to discover unexpected sources of enjoyment and health!

In 1948, the United Nations included the right to food in the Universal Declaration of Human Rights. Half a century later, international law specified that to feed oneself in dignity, to grow one's own food, or to buy it is a "human right." Growing food assumes that one has the right to land, seed, and water. Buying food assumes that it is "available, accessible, and appropriate," that is to say "culturally acceptable," as stipulated in international law. But how does this basic right fare in the 21st century, when nearly a billion people survive in an undernourished state while another billion suffer from obesity and other pathologies associated with an unbalanced diet? In rich countries, a growing number of citizens depend on food assistance. What will the right to food mean in 2050, when humans number nine billion — more than two-thirds of them living in cities? What will it mean given the fact that several indicators are already in the red: farmland constantly shrinking as a result of sprawling cities and endless paving, crops being developed for livestock and biofuels, soil worn out from 60 years of intensive chemical treatment, and fish stocks crashing from overfishing?

The member states of various international organizations agree that the problem rests not so much with lack of food availability on the planet, but rather the growing number of people who lack food access because they cannot afford it. Thus, it is the commercial system that causes humans' needs to go unmet.

**PERMACULTURE PRINCIPLE 3:**
Obtain a yield

## LOCAL, SUSTAINABLE FAMILY AGRICULTURE: A RECOGNIZED SOLUTION

How do we make "proper" nutrition available to all? Today, a choir of experts has a solution to recommend: develop family farming! In the last ten years or so, international organizations have been coming around to the idea that the key to worldwide agricultural disorder lies at the local, sustainable, family level. The question is no longer how many tons to produce, but how to produce them. The merits of agroecology are supported in both scientific and political circles today. This global revolution in the vision of agriculture has been made possible by farmers, researchers, and NGOs, which for the last two decades have been coming up with innovations in food production all around the world. They have proven that sustainable practices can achieve high yields, maintain farmers' autonomy and quality of life, and protect the environment — all while remaining economically viable.

Alternative food sources remain largely underexploited to date. The ocean offers inestimable resources: outside of fishing (which is in crisis), there is great potential in plankton and algae farming and in sustainable aquaculture. The same is true of insect farming; the tiny creatures are a traditional protein source in certain cultures already. Though unfamiliar to most in the West, this resource has the advantage of being accessible to artisans operating on small plots of land. Insect farming requires little water or fossil energy input.

**PERMACULTURE PRINCIPLE 10:**
Use and value diversity

It is high time we diversified our food sources and found alternatives to the prevailing dietary trends in rich countries. It is also high time we shortened the distance between where food is produced and where it is eaten (mostly the city).

Agreeing to alter our behaviors presupposes that we have a solid grasp of the globally detrimental consequences our current lifestyles have on the wellbeing and future of humanity. Permaculture offers pathways to easing this transition: new practices that have social, economic, and health benefits for individuals and society.

Part 4 of this book, with its emphasis on food, presents compelling alternatives in plant farming, animal husbandry, and aquatic and entomological resources (insects). There are so many avenues to explore, so many solutions to emulate and adapt to our surroundings, and so many ways in which we can inspire others. These examples serve as arguments in favor of new eating patterns that hold potential to balance the needs of humans with those of the planet.

**PERMACULTURE PRINCIPLE 12:**
Creatively use and respond to change

### THE SEARCH FOR A JUST DIET

How should we choose our food? How do we find the most "just" diet for ourselves (i.e., in harmony with the laws of nature and with the environment)? Should we eat vegetarian, macrobiotic, raw food, fruitarian, locavore, insectivore, dietary vegan, or full-on vegan (abstaining from all animal products in our lives, including honey and wool, for ethical reasons)? Should we follow an Okinawa, paleo, Mediterranean, instinct, gluten-free, Viking, DASH, or alkaline diet? The choices are endless. It's hard to develop our own ideas about the best diet for our needs when debates on the subject are so passionate and visceral. Followers of certain diets are often convinced that their way is best and that it is the one and only path to proper health. The strength of their convictions has a way of overshadowing the valid points associated with other options.

Rather than letting yourself to be seduced or pushed into this or that trend, you are invited instead to reflect on the material we present here, ask the relevant questions, and reach your own conclusions. Any option you choose will skew in favor of certain criteria. It is up to you as an individual to design the diet that suits you best; the final equation you settle upon will take into account your geographical situation, activities, personal beliefs and, of course, potential health risks. But whatever you settle on, your answer will need to cover your energy and nutritional costs, which are multiple, nuanced, and complex. You can use your family design as inspiration for your dietary design. The following chapters offer avenues for transitioning toward a diet tailored to the needs of modern human life and the environment — in short, ways to "permaculti-vate" your diet.

Depending on the cultures, geographic location, and resources at play, most govern-ments — and most dietitians — issue dietary recommendations for staying healthy. These recommendations are sometimes summarized in the form of "food pyramids": according to chosen criteria, the foods at the base of the pyramid should form the foundation of the diet, while those at the top should be exceptions. Accordingly, there is no single diet we can say is universally good. Each culture develops its own vision of the ideal diet. Health-conscious peo-ple can even design their own pyramids. The Swiss Nutrition Society (among other sourc-es) has an online test to help you calculate your personal pyramid in minutes and assess how balanced it is: sge-ssn.ch/fr/toi-et-moi/tests/test-pyramide-alimentaire. Recommendations are also offered on how to bring your diet more in line with what the organization considers the ideal balance.

## A UNIVERSAL LAW:
## EAT TO LIVE – AND TO BE EATEN!

Human beings, like all living beings, must ab-solutely eat to live. Subsistence occupies a significant portion of our daily activities (as is the case for other animals). This dietary prima-cy undergirds the other imperative of all species: reproduction. Without sufficient health-giving food, there is no fertility or continuation of the species. Feeding ourselves with quality food is an absolute priority.

Everything that lives eats what is (or was) alive in order to survive. This is how the food chain works, from the smallest to the largest organisms. A bird swallows insects and profits from the plant material eaten by the insects. A lion hunts a gazelle and benefits from the grass grazed upon by the gazelle. A vulture, like the soil microorganisms, consumes dead bodies. In this way, life energy is passed on, through death, to perpetuate life. This is an iron-clad law; there are no exceptions. It is up to us to refine our obser-vational abilities and develop our consciousness: like all organisms, our vital energy comes from our diet and the forces we receive from nature. Wheat, apples, and fish are all conveyors of life. Their vitality deeply nourishes the body and mind of the person who absorbs them, extend-ing far beyond the nutrients themselves. We need these subtle signals of life just as much as we need the calories that nourish our bodies.

When we die, humans become food for bac-teria and other soil microorganisms. These organisms convert the corpse into matter that can be assimilated by other forms of life, such as trees and other plants. The great cycle of life and death engenders more life. We must hum-bly accept our place within it. And bear in mind that nature, marvellously designed though it is, has not yet revealed to us all it has to reveal. Our consciousness of life remains limited. We must remain attentive, curious, open minded, and open to surprise! Our right brains are there to help us in this endeavor.

## HOW WILD ANIMALS EAT

As permaculturists, we have an interest in observing how nature works, especially wild animals, to understand how we as omnivores function. We can draw inspiration from these observations to fashion a lifestyle that is sustainable and in tune with our needs and environment.

*Animals' anatomies are adapted to the available food where they live*

- Using the hair-like structures of their baleen, baleen whales filter huge quantities of seawater, from which they retain only the tiny plankton, the basis of their diet.
- The hummingbird's beak is perfectly formed to collect nectar from the calyx of flowers. The beating of their wings in turn pollinates the flowers on which they feed.
- Parrots' massive beaks allow them to crack the large seeds that make up their food source.
- Chicken feet have large claws to scratch the soil, while ducks have webbed feet for swimming and diving.

*Animals' physiology is adapted to the available food*

- Bears and groundhogs accumulate large quantities of fat before winter, then hibernate until spring arrives. Their heartrates are

low during hibernation, and they moult in the warm season.
- During winter, geese, whales, and monarch butterflies migrate toward milder climates, where food is available.

*Animals' diets are adapted to the available food in their territory*

- Bats are adapted to a variety of environments around the planet depending on what food is present where they live. Certain species eat only fruit, while others consume insects. Still others suck the blood of vertebrates and have developed saliva with anaesthetic properties. Some obtain nourishment from flowers, which they pollinate in their travels.
- Whale sharks prefer to eat plankton, which is abundantly available, rather than attacking prey.

*Feeding rates directly depend on needs and circumstances*

- A lioness expends an enormous number of calories to catch and kill her prey. Once she has achieved satiety, she can go for a week without eating: her meaty, energy-rich diet enables her to eat irregularly and take time to digest.
- The herbivores hunted by the lioness also expend a lot of energy. But unlike carnivores, their physiology demands that they spent most of their time eating small

amounts of plants and digesting them in multiple stages inside a digestive tract with multiple chambers.

*Group strategies*

– Certain fish, such as tuna, live in tight schools to protect themselves from predators. Certain birds, such as sparrows, live in flocks for the same reason.
– Lactating lionesses stay with the cubs while the other mothers hunt prey, which they share upon their return.
– Coyotes and wolves hunt in packs.

## NATURAL SELECTION ENSURES CONTINUATION OF THE SPECIES

– Only the most vigorous salmon make it through all stages of the difficult run from the ocean to their river spawning sites, where they lay their eggs and reproduce.
– The female praying mantis devours her male mate after they copulate, thereby avoiding any risk of inbreeding with her future progeny.

Jane Goodall studied chimpanzees extensively. In her book *Harvest for Hope: A Guide to Mindful Eating*,[1] the British primatologist wrote about the similarities between these primates and humans. Like chimpanzees, humans are omnivorous. The anatomies of both species make them adept at many tasks: picking fruit in trees, cracking nuts, pulling roots out of the ground, making tools to catch insects, hunting, and fishing. Their metabolism does not require that they store significant fat reserves. Because chimpanzees are nomadic, they have access to fresh and varied food all year long. They can have their food needs met with just four hours of effort per day. The rest of the time is spent engaging in social relationships. Now there's some food for thought when it comes to social organization in humans![2]

## THE HUMAN SPECIES: AN EXCEPTION TO THE LAWS OF NATURE?

Observing nature shows that:

1. Given their metabolism and life strategies, all nonhuman species are adapted to their environment. Only humans attempt to adapt the environment to their needs.

2. All species eat foods that are available where they are. Only modern humans consume foods imported from the other side of the world.

3. Following on the previous point, the foods required for a species' development are found in its immediate environment. This was the case for humans before the era of urban concentration. Humans' economic choices increasingly allow them to flout this rule.

4. The diversity and quantity of food ingested by animals are proportional to their energy needs. Humans can eat more than they need, to the point of making themselves ill.

**5** A species' reproductive ability depends on the availability of food. Here too humans are exceptional; the birthrate in certain countries is inversely proportional to food availability.

Today, a large proportion of naturally food-rich spaces have disappeared. For most modern-day people, the quest for food becomes the quest for employment, which (if all goes well) provides enough money to buy groceries at the supermarket. But at what price? What is the ecological footprint? And what are the health impacts? Populations in the Northern Hemisphere get 80 percent of their food resources from countries in the Southern Hemisphere, and most food travels an average of 5,000 km before arriving on Western tables.[3] Think of the tea, coffee, chocolate, sugar, rice, citrus fruits, and exotic fruits that regularly grace our palates. Even the seeds of the potatoes, tomatoes, and beans that grow in European gardens were originally imported from the other side of the world during the Age of Exploration.

Can our species be the only one that deliberately organizes its food to be dependent on environments external to its own? The only one that reproduces without adjusting its population to fit the available food supply? Is "*Homo industrialis*" losing touch with the information inscribed in its genes to the point that its body no longer intuitively recognizes what is good or bad for it? Under normal circumstances, signs would alert it to the danger of toxic substances in its diet. This is no longer the case. For decades, many studies have converged in suggesting that human remains, rife with pesticides and preservatives, are taking longer to decompose. Will humans one day escape the cycle of life altogether — never to return to Earth to feed another life? Will human's dreams of omnipotence and immortality be pathetically reduced to clogging up cemeteries?

## HUMANS: OMNIVORES BY CONSTITUTION

Let's go back to where it all began. Unlike animals that migrate, hibernate, or store fat for winter, and unlike plants that go dormant, *Homo sapiens* has no physiological mechanism to contend with seasonal variations or store significant amounts of energy. Humans must eat a varied diet every day. By constitution, we are omnivorous. Our lower limbs allow us to move towards available food depending on the season. In fact, early in our history, humans were nomadic. Our "group intelligence" allowed us to develop complex strategies to find, gather, scavenge, hunt, or fish our food. In time, humans invented tools and learned how to domesticate animals to accomplish this aim more easily. With the invention of pottery, humans began to store and cook food in containers. The invention of the wheel around 3500 BCE in Mesopotamia (present-day Iraq), revolutionized daily life: working the soil became much easier. Agriculture developed, producing grains that could be stored. Humans no longer had to travel to find food. We became sedentary.

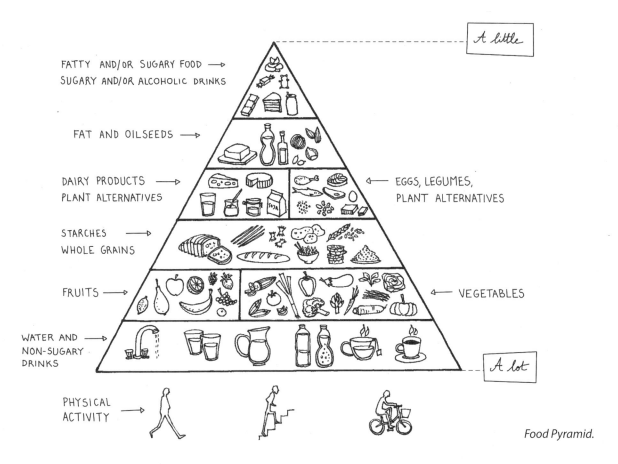

FATTY AND/OR SUGARY FOOD →
SUGARY AND/OR ALCOHOLIC DRINKS

A little

FAT AND OILSEEDS →

DAIRY PRODUCTS →
PLANT ALTERNATIVES

← EGGS, LEGUMES,
PLANT ALTERNATIVES

STARCHES →
WHOLE GRAINS

FRUITS →

← VEGETABLES

WATER AND →
NON-SUGARY
DRINKS

A lot

PHYSICAL →
ACTIVITY

*Food Pyramid.*

Then, with the nearly simultaneous invention of writing, humans exited prehistory and entered history!

The dentition of *Homo sapiens* allows us to feed on a wide variety of foods. With our incisors we can pierce the skin of fruits, and with our molars (used properly) we can crack nuts and grind plant roots. With our canines we can tear up meat. While many herbivores have a multi-chamber rumen enabling them to digest plants completely, humans have a single stomach that can digest many kinds of foods.

## MODERN HUMANS IN SEARCH OF ANOTHER WAY TO FEED OURSELVES

Growing numbers of citizens are acknowledging the environmental and health issues associated with industrial food; they envision a mode of food production that is family-centered, local, flavorful, and healthful. Individual and community

## AMAZING DATA

In 2015, 1 billion people were obese, while another 1 billion people were malnourished.

### Food for whom?

- Three-quarters of the world's farmland is used to raise livestock and produce livestock feed.
- Nearly half of the world's grain production is used for livestock feed.[4]

### Empty plates in rich countries too

- In France, charities serve about 180 million meals per year to the country's poorest people.
- Across Europe, 18 million people are dependent on food aid. In Canada, this figure is 841,000 people and has increased by 25 percent since the economic crisis of 2008.

### Loss and waste

- 57 percent of calories produced in the world never reach a plate.[5]
- Along with this waste, we must factor in the land, water, fertilizer, energy, labor, and time needed to produce these calories.

### The ecological footprint of meat and wheat

- Producing 1 kilogram of beef requires 15 cubic meters of water, 6 kilograms of grain, and 8 square meters of land.
- Producing 1 kilogram of wheat requires 1.3 cubic meters of water and 1.5 square meters of land.[6]

gardens are flourishing in cities and rural areas. Wild edible plants are being appreciated and foraged. Alternative diets abound. Like permaculturists, plenty of people are using all tools at their disposal to find a mode of eating that is in harmony with nature.

### WHAT ARE OUR TRUE NEEDS?

Our physical, intellectual, creative, and mental activities all require a certain number of calories. It is food's job to supply these. The more active we are, the more calories we need; the inverse is also true. Accordingly, the energy content and amount of food consumed should be proportionate to our activity level. An office worker who spends all day sitting will have different needs from those of, say, a stonemason. Excess calories accumulate in the form of body fat and cause problems. More often than not, the modern diet is dictated by an economic model (i.e., fuelling the food industry) rather than by our actual energy needs. Starting in the 1940s, Dr. Catherine Kousmine[7] demonstrated the link between an unbalanced diet and cancer and devised a diet adapted for her patients.

The rate at which we ingest food is, in principle, regulated by our biological clock: our caloric needs create the sensation of hunger. But Pavlov's famous experiments showed that social customs prevail over this biological aspect. The ritual of sitting down to a table at specific times has separated us from our physiological needs.

## THE ANTI-LIFE MESSAGE OF INDUSTRIAL FOOD

The hybrid grains and genetically modified products that increasingly crowd our supermarket shelves have been altered to prevent the plants from reproducing naturally. The message encoded into their cells is this: block continuation of species. When these plants are eaten, animals and humans incorporate this message: block the continuation of the species. What if this deadly injunction were to be inscribed in the genetic code of our own cells? Consider that a significant drop in men's fertility has already been observed clinically; sperm counts have been in decline for decades. Some explain this by pointing to excessive stress levels. But stress has always been with us! What about the stress experienced by prehistoric humans as they hunted mammoths? Or the stress of soldiers on the front lines of battle? Stress sometimes plays a positive role by making humans more effective

in perilous situations; it helps us protect our families and pass our exams. The cause of the drop in human fertility is to be found elsewhere. Scientific studies have highlighted the causal link between the consumption of commonly used chemicals included in the official list of "carcinogenic, mutagenic, and reprotoxic" substances and dropping fertility. Furthermore, consuming meat from large industrial operations sends our cells a different message than eating the meat of wild animals or those raised on small farms.

Today, even the fruits of the soil are cut off from their roots. In its natural state, only a mature seed can germinate, i.e., perpetuate life. This message of life from the mature fruits we eat in turn fuels our human vitality. In the industrial economy, fruits and vegetables are typically harvested prior to maturity to facilitate their transportation and to gain a few weeks (and a few dollars) from their maturation cycle. They ripen in containers while in transit, far from soil, sun, and precipitation. Obviously, the message they carry is not the same. The spring or mineral water we drink from plastic bottles has been similarly sapped of its original vitality.

## MAINTAINING OR RESTORING BALANCE IN THE TERRAIN

At the start of this book, we established a parallel between the soil and "human terrain." Both are living, both can be cultivated, and both produce a yield — if all goes well. The microscopic underground life, not unlike the gut flora of animals, assimilates everything that lives and dies on the ground and directly influences plant health, partly by balancing the pH. In the soil and in their own bodies, permaculturists seek to rebalance the terrain in keeping with a holistic vision, rather than treating individual symptoms that may arise from an imbalance. A terrain (soil or human) with balanced pH will allow the individual (human or plant) to mobilize its own immune defences to respond to outside attacks (disease, parasites, extreme weather conditions, etc.).

## GREEN, CHLOROPHYLL-RICH MATERIAL BALANCES PH IN THE SOIL – AND IN THE HUMAN TERRAIN

Modern food, like phytosanitary chemicals (an ambiguous and misleading term) tends to acidify terrains (both agricultural and human), thereby making them vulnerable to disease. How do we balance pH? For humans, balance can be restored by maintaining a diet made up of about 80 percent alkaline foods (essentially fresh fruits and vegetables) and about 20 percent acidifying foods (certain grains and legumes as well as animal products). In other words, eating plants that are green, fresh, living, and raw (or only slightly cooked) balances pH. There is no such thing as eating too much: in practice, the human body cannot be too basic.

# Chapter 16

# Water, a Vital Element

## DRINKING TO LIVE

A HUMAN BEING CAN LIVE for quite some time without eating but can survive only a few days without ingesting water. Drinking hydrates the body and maintains the organism's constitutional water level: an average of 45 liters for an adult weighing 70 kilograms, or 65 percent of their weight! The vital organs — brain, heart, kidneys, lungs, liver, and pancreas — as well as the blood, muscles, and skin are 70 to 80 percent water. Some of the body's water is eliminated through excretion — in the urine, sweat, and stool — and

DESIGN FOR WATER

through the breath. It's a good idea to compensate for these losses as regularly as possible. This is why it is advisable to ingest about two and a half liters of water per day (a volume that of course varies based on age, activity level, the temperature, etc.). Eating can provide the equivalent of a liter of water, and drinking can provide the remaining liter and a half.[1] Caution: diuretic drinks (tea, coffee, and alcoholic drinks) accelerate elimination and cause dehydration. The feeling of thirst is a sign that the organism lacks water. So, the trick is to drink before you become thirsty! This is easily forgotten in our fast-paced lives. It helps to keep some water handy. Our cells most readily assimilate water when it is closest to body temperature, i.e., between 30 and 40°C.

Drinking water also helps the body meet its requirements for mineral salts and trace elements. These substances are picked up by naturally flowing water that comes into contact with underground rocks and are also a key part of regulating the human body's vital functions: fluoride, chloride, phosphate, calcium, magnesium, potassium, sodium, iron, copper, manganese, zinc, selenium, and silicon. Mineral salts account for four to five percent of our body weight, while trace elements will suffice in tiny quantities — though they are just as essential.[2] As the professor Louis-Claude Vincent demonstrated, human beings are magnificently and vitally dependent on the water that gushes out of the Earth's innards to regulate their most subtle internal functions. Yes, we are indeed *one* with the Earth, and one with the universe!

## WATER, A COMMON GOOD – YET POORLY SHARED AND THREATENED BY POLLUTION

The ideal drinking water is spring water that is vitalized by contact with the land and air, rich in minerals and available near where you live. Unfortunately, such "raw water," as specialists call it, is often rendered unfit for consumption by exposure to numerous pollutants. Today, people are strongly encouraged *not to drink* water from streams and rivers. In France, "50 percent of surface water and 40 percent of underground water is in poor chemical condition," France's Water Information Centre tells us. Excesses of nitrates and pesticides used in industrial agriculture run off when it rains, eventually reaching rivers (and later the ocean) and infiltrating water tables, wells, and catchment areas. And let's not forget the toxic particles suspended in the air that fall with precipitation, either.

As mentioned earlier, one in two humans alive today must travel several kilometers to access water. Yet permanent access to potable water is a human right defined by the United Nations in 2002: "The right to water entitles everyone to sufficient, safe, acceptable, physically accessible and affordable water for personal and domestic use." The text goes on to specify that water "must be free from micro-organisms, chemical substances and radiological hazards that constitute a threat to a person's health."[3] A third of the world's population lacks toilets or even latrines. This creates the major risk that natural water reserves will be polluted, which of course affects drinking water quality.

In rich countries, drinking water reaches people either in taps or in bottles. Running water is a recent luxury (it was only in the late 1980s that the last of the houses in France were hooked up to running water). Could our ancestors have ever imagined a day when water would be sold in plastic bottles? In recent years, pioneering citizens have been working to make rainwater drinkable in homes, a movement that stands to gain momentum (see p. 144–145).

In France, the most controlled food product is tap water. The authorities assure us that it is "some of the safest water in the world." However, users complain that too often it contains large amounts of chlorine. A total of 62 percent of France's potable water comes from underground resources — collected from a spring or drilled from a deep water table — while 38 percent comes from surface water, including rivers and lakes.

## TAP OR BOTTLED?

Thanks to significant publicity, the bottled water industry has succeeded in convincing a large portion of the public that bottled water is superior to tap water. With rare exceptions, it is nothing of the kind.

Analyses are conducted regularly by a number of organizations. For two years, the World Wildlife Fund (WWF) conducted comparative analyses in France with a laboratory accredited by the Ministry of Health. The NGO tested tap water in people's homes in 50 cities as well as bottled water taken from 15 different sites. The tap water was tested for 180 molecules, including endocrine disruptors (polyaromatic hydrocarbons, polychlorinated biphenyls, bisphenol A, organochlorines, and pesticides) whose effects, even in small doses, may be highly deleterious, especially if mixed together in a "cocktail." Nineteen molecules were detected: mainly nitrates, chlorine and bromine residues, and aluminum, all in proportions that fell within the applicable standards. Traces of hydrocarbons were also detected in over 20 percent of the water samples. "To obtain drinking water, communities have to use increasingly sophisticated and costly treatment methods as pollution levels gradually increase," the NGO notes in its report.[4] "We are seeing more closures of polluted catchments, as well as more interconnections among networks in order to dilute the pollution. This headlong rush cannot continue," alerts the WWF, which regularly engages in environmental protection actions.

The bottled water tested by the WWF from 15 sources was found to contain four micropollutants (nitrate, aluminum, antimony, and lead) in concentrations that fell within the regulatory standards. The conclusion: both tap and bottled water contain a variety of molecules that, though present in small doses, present long-term (and poorly understood) health risks. Rather than coming out against tap water and bottled water, the WWF investigation demonstrates that "it is urgent to protect water resources upstream and raw water resources more generally."

## France's water market

**Bottled water**

- About 6 billion liters are sold every year.
- An average of 154 liters of flat (non-bubbly) bottled water per person are consumed per year.
- This generates 240,000 tonnes of plastic waste.
- Sales figures: about €2 billion in 2012. Top sellers: Nestlé (the world leader) and Danone.

**Tap water**

- No waste or transportation once infrastructure is in place.
- Sales figures from the leader, Veolia: €4.5 billion in 2011.

There are big differences between tap water and bottled water, but these play out economically and environmentally. For starters, bottled water is 100 to 300 times more expensive than tap water! The energetic cost of manufacturing plastic bottles out of petroleum is also high. Once filled, the bottles often travel great distances, generating $CO_2$ emissions along the way. Finally, they generate thousands of tonnes of waste that is expensive to recycle, some of which makes its way into the environment. Furthermore, like any natural substance cut off from its environment, water that sits around in bottles loses its original vitality. Energetically speaking, it carries a message of inertia — an effect that many modern-day people are starting to discover as they learn more and become attuned to their right brains.

People in rich countries who are lucky enough to have access to quality tap water should use it! Why purchase bottled water if tap water supplies their mineral salt needs? Drinking one liter of tap water per day provides 15 to 25 percent of a person's daily calcium needs.

### WHAT CAN WE PERMACULTURISTS DO CONCRETELY?

Recall that in permaculture we try to ensure that every function is supported by three elements if possible. This precaution is especially important in the case of water.

Thus, aside from the tap, which makes us forget about the potential fragility of the supply, we should also help maintain wells, streams, or rivers located near us — if we are fortunate enough to have these in our environment. If we analyze the quality of these natural waters, we can use the results to help us see what actions could be taken upstream, perhaps by mobilizing municipal officials and/or citizens who live near the river to reduce pollution and restore the water's health. Obviously, pesticide-free agriculture will help. So will storing rainwater, even in areas that receive plenty of rain. By filtering, energizing, and revitalizing water, we can make it safe to drink. We can also ensure it returns to the ground to feed the water tables and the water cycle.

Let us not to squander this precious resource. As permaculturist citizens, let's stop using drinking water to irrigate our gardens (which do better with rainwater anyway), flush our toilets (opting for dry toilets instead[5]), or wash our cars (rainwater or greywater does the job just fine). It is each individual's responsibility to care for water, to recycle greywater, to work to ban any products that are toxic to the soil or water, and to allow nothing into the sewage system that is likely to harm the water. Let's open up our cleaning closets and have a good, hard look at the toxic (and often useless) products we have in there. Let's round up anything that could pollute the soil or water and take it to the landfill (more and more landfills are processing hazardous waste in a separate stream). Let's stop buying products that pose a threat to humans and the environment. Plenty of natural alternatives exist for personal hygiene and home and garden maintenance.

## REVITALIZING THE WATER WE DRINK!

How can we access drinking water that contains as much life as possible where we live? Natural water is not sold in bottles in stores, nor generally is it found under our feet — and the effectiveness of miracle solutions proposed by the often expensive dynamizers or revitalizers remains unproven. If we change our perspective, we can see water as a resilient element capable of regenerating itself, like all living things. A number of processes may be used in combination:

- Tap water treated with chlorine or ozone may be enhanced prior to drinking by running it through an active carbon or reverse osmosis filter.
- It can also be whisked before being left to decant for a few hours. The motion oxygenates the water and facilitates the evaporation of some of the chlorine.
- Tap water can be perked up with a sprig of fresh mint or any other aromatic plant, a few petals of edible flowers (rose, calendula, nasturtium, dahlia), a drop or two of fresh lemon juice or essential oil (peppermint, for example). Plants impart some of their properties to the water. The pitcher also adds a decorative element to the table, which is always pleasing.
- Expose the water to the sun for a few minutes. It will capture the life force of the star and pass it on to you when you drink it; the chlorine will evaporate more quickly too.

# What does it mean to energize water?

By observing nature, **Viktor Schauberger** (1885–1958), an Austrian forest ranger, noticed that water flowed in a vortex without consuming energy. This spiral motion allowed water to capture more oxygen and energy. "When water swirls in a vortex, it becomes energized, purified, and vivified," he stated. This observation set the stage for obtaining better water. Schauberger noted that water is extremely sensitive to vibrations. His research led him to describe water not only as the support of all life, but also as "the support of terrestrial consciousness." The inventor was a biomimicry enthusiast before his time and drew inspiration from the motion of fish in vortexes to create prototypes for implosion motors that do not consume fuel.

**TO FIND OUT MORE:** Alick Bartholomew, *Hidden Nature: The Startling Insights of Viktor Schauberger* (Edinburgh, Floris, 2004).

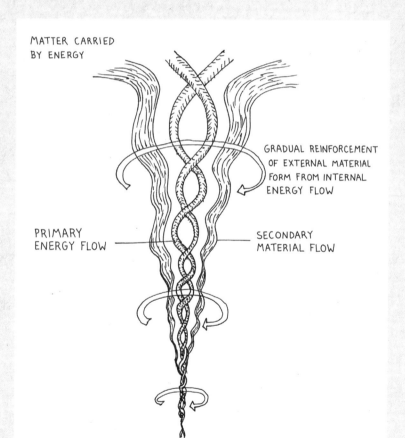

MATTER CARRIED BY ENERGY

GRADUAL REINFORCEMENT OF EXTERNAL MATERIAL FORM FROM INTERNAL ENERGY FLOW

PRIMARY ENERGY FLOW

SECONDARY MATERIAL FLOW

*Water vortex.*

– You can create your own vortex by pouring water back and forth from one container to another. This will increase its bioavailability, thus facilitating cell hydration and the elimination of toxins. Water energized in this way must be drunk right away rather than stored for later. The same vortex principle can be used on a larger scale on a terrain that collects rainwater.

– Glass containers are preferable: glass is made of sand, a material present in riverbeds. Water is at home in glass, whereas plastic can pass on certain particles and alter its quality.

## MINDFUL DRINKING

According to studies conducted by Masaru Emoto, the fact of actively caring for the water we drink imprints a message of life into the water's "memory," a message passed on to our cells, one that strengthens the body and mind. This is also true if we formulate a positive intention before drinking water, the researcher reports. It's easy to imagine that drinking mindfully — just like eating, talking, or working mindfully — fosters physiological and psychological balance.

**TO FIND OUT MORE:** Masaru Emoto, Hidden Messages in Water (New York, Atria, 2005).

DRINKING MINDFULLY

**INSPIRING EXAMPLE**

# Drinking water from the sky

Imagine you could become "water self-sufficient" with rain! This is what Belgian researcher Joseph Országh proposes on his Eautarcie website (English version at eautarcie.org/en). The site provides free information on inexpensive and environmentally friendly domestic devices for "rainwater harvesting for whole-house reuse." It also proposes environmental solutions for sanitation, greywater management, dry toilets, and water policy. All of this is accompanied by philosophical reflection enriched by over two decades of experimentation and university research on sustainable water management.

The site invites readers to shed the automatic reflex to "throw it in the garbage" and its counterpart of "pour it down the drain," both of which come at a high cost to the environment and the community. The rainwater purification solutions proposed by Eautarcie provide high-quality drinking water with no need for chemical treatment.

According to Országh, the notion of "potable" water is first and foremost a legal one: it must satisfy 50 physico-chemical and microbiological criteria to make the grade. The bacteriological standards make chemical disinfection unavoidable, especially the addition of chlorine. The researcher prefers the notion of *biocompatible* water, which ties into Louis-Claude Vincent's work on bioelectronics and bypasses all need for chemical disinfection.

Országh encourages citizens to purify their rainwater through the Pluvalor process — but don't go looking for a store-bought Pluvalor device: such a thing does not exist! You make it yourself. The Pluvalor process is a setup that can be adapted at home to your existing plumbing system. Full details can be found on the Eautarcie website. The most expensive component is the cistern.

Joseph Országh says that the objective for the purposes of health (and self-sufficiency) is to produce at least five liters of potable water per person per day: enough to drink and cook with. The simplest and most economical format is to collect water that falls on the roof in an underground reservoir made of concrete or (recovered) bricks. The concrete neutralizes the natural acidity of the rainwater and adds small amounts of mineral salts (50 milligrams/liter). The device artificially recreates the conditions of a rocky cavity; water keeps well in such an environment, where it is protected from light and temperature variations. If your budget or water usage is modest, the water can simply be extracted from the cistern with a bucket tied to a rope! For a more substantial water reserve, the cistern can be built with a decantation compartment (comprising 20 percent of the total volume) and a storage compartment (80 percent). The storage volume will depend on how large the collection roof is.

Rainwater filtration needs depend on the climate in your region; in any case, use a reverse osmosis filter with a 5-micron prefilter (to keep out sediment), a membrane, and activated carbon (to remove bacteria and chemical pollution). "Reverse osmosis is currently the only technique that corrects the chemical and electrochemical composition of water at an affordable price," says Országh.

In Belgium, over 750,000 people have been using rainwater for their personal hygiene. Of these people, over 100,000 also drink the rainwater — which benefits both their health and their wallets!

## How to filter any wild water

Bacteria can be removed from any wild water source (stream, lake, river, or water table) through a ceramic microfiltration process powered by gravity alone. The process yields high-quality drinking water. The simple filter device, which functions without electricity or complicated consumables, keeps out bacteria and other pathogenic agents while letting through the trace elements necessary for health (magnesium, calcium, etc.). As an add-on, chemical substances can be filtered out if the ceramic plug is filled with a dose of activated carbon. The device will keep out chlorine, unpleasant tastes, and pesticide residues, including any such things found in tap water. Here is an example of a ready-made filter you can buy: filtre-a-eau-ecologique-par-gravite.blogspot.com.

As a precaution, the Eautarcie website strongly advises against UV lamps, a biocidal (life-destroying) technique: observations of plants watered with UV-treated water suggest potential negative effects on human health. Meanwhile, ceramic microfiltration or reverse osmosis filters are largely sufficient to ensure high-quality potable water.

## Chapter 17

# Food from Plants

## THE URGENCY OF MAINTAINING PLANT BIODIVERSITY

FOLLOWING THE MASS DESTRUCTION of the Second World War in Europe, the euphoria of the post-war Trente Glorieuses period (1945–75) pushed agriculture into the whirlwind of the high-tech Green Revolution. This period ushered in standardized and mechanized tillage, systematic application of fertilizers and pesticides on huge parcels of deforested land, spectacularly greater yields — and, some 60 years later, soils threatened with sterility. As FAO Director-General José Graziano da Silva reminds us:

*Seven thousand species of plants have been cultivated or consumed as food throughout human history. Today, the caloric intake of most people on the planet is based today on only four crops: rice, maize, wheat and potatoes. [This represents an inestimable loss of genetic and cultural biodiversity.] We must not lose track of our agricultural and culinary roots, nor the lore and wisdom of our ancestors. If we lose these unique and irreplaceable resources, it will be more difficult for us to adapt to climate change and ensure a healthy and diversified nutrition for all... Our dependence on a few crops has negative consequences for ecosystems, food diversity and our health.* [1]

But we must not give way to pessimism! The large international organizations that establish global policies have not believed in the illusion of 100 percent industrial agriculture in years. Thanks to the trail blazed by innovative small farmers, environmentalists, and researchers, they now encourage and support family farming and biodiversity preservation. José Graziano da Silva also states that family farming helps increase productivity on small plots, contributes to food and nutrition security, and improves populations' means of subsistence. In his view, family farming preserves biodiversity from our fields to our plates, protects the Earth by using many forgotten or underutilized plant species, and safeguards our health. [2] It seems that the issues and solutions are known and proclaimed at the highest levels.

With millions of families still being dispossessed of their land and pushed into the poverty of megalopolises by the steamroller of the agrifood industry (still running full throttle), how can we reverse the trend and transition to a form of agriculture at a human scale? In practice, farmers who practice agroecology (or any other version of food production that is respectful of humans and nature) are still viewed as marginal in the eyes of many observers. It will take time for decision makers in the various jurisdictions to take notice of these new approaches, respect them, support them, and adopt them.

## AGROECOLOGY AND AGROFORESTRY CAN FEED THE WORLD[3]

The term agroecology refers to both a science and a set of practices born at the intersection of the agricultural and ecological sciences. Its purpose is to improve the resilience and sustainability of agricultural systems by imitating natural processes, i.e., by encouraging beneficial interactions and synergies among elements of the ecosystem. In other words, agroecology is the application of the permaculture principles to farming!

By recycling organic material, agroecology develops soil fertility and provides the optimal conditions for plant growth, thus avoiding the need for costly and polluting inputs. Agroecology promotes biodiversity within and around production systems by associating maximally diverse crops with livestock, trees, pollinators, insects, soil organisms, and fish farming activities. It diversifies the species and the genetic resources on farms. It improves the productivity and balance of the *whole* agricultural system rather than the productivity of a particular variety. Agroecology

EATING RAW

concentrates a huge amount of knowledge and a large number of techniques developed by farmers themselves. They become agents of development in their operations by building networks of exchange and solidarity among each other. Agroecology is a tool that breathes new life into soil and human populations while reducing poverty. The farmers maintain their soil fertility using manure, agricultural residue, and nitrogen-fixing trees and no longer depend on external fertilizer suppliers. This social dimension is key to the success of agroecology (and permaculture in general).

Many examples on different continents affirm the benefits of this process. In Zambia, for example, corn grown without fertilizer but near a variety of nitrogen-fixing acacia tree, *Faidherbia albida*, achieves average yields of 4.1 tonnes per hectare, as compared to 1.3 tonnes per hectare for corn grown outside the tree zone. You can just imagine the social impact on the affected populations.

Research and innovation form a key part of agroecology. Its practitioners have developed an original strategy for fighting weeds and insect pests: repulsion-attraction strategies, also known as push-pull. Insects are hunted by positioning "push" plants (such as *Desmodium*) among planted crops — between cornrows, for instance — while attracting or "pulling" them elsewhere, for example to plantations of Napier grass (also known as elephant grass), a sticky plant that traps them. This push-pull strategy can double corn yields! It not only fights parasites without pesticides but also confers other useful advantages: *Desmodium* may be used as forage for livestock. Over 10,000 families in East Africa have adopted this method after hearing about it in information meetings, announcements broadcast over national radio, or in farmer field schools.

Japanese farmers observed that ducks and fish were just as effective as pesticides at fighting parasites in rice paddies, while also providing extra protein for their families. Ducks eat weeds and their seeds as well as insects and other pests. This results in less weeding to be done, a task usually performed by hand by women. The duck manure also supplies nutrients to the plants. This

system has been adopted in China, India, and the Philippines. In Bangladesh, the International Rice Research Institute reports that crop yields have grown by 20 percent and net incomes by 80 percent.

International scientific studies also suggest that these practices are effective. The most systematic of these was conducted in 2008 by the team of British biologist Jules Pretty. It compares the results of 286 recent sustainable agriculture projects on a surface area of 37 million hectares in 57 poor countries, or three percent of the cultivated land in these territories. The researchers calculated an average crop increase of 79 percent and an average household income increase of 73 to 150 percent depending on the crop type. These methods are available to anyone and can be adapted anywhere, as they require little investment. They conserve water, energy, land, and work!

"Millions of people could escape poverty, hunger and environmental degradation if countries put more effort into promoting agroforestry," the FAO has announced in recent years. By mixing crops, trees, and pastures all in the same space, agroforestry offers farmers both a means of subsistence (fruits, vegetables, wood, forage, meat, dairy products, textile fibers) and export products (coconuts, coffee, tea, rubber, gum) to supplement their incomes.

Nearly half of the planet's farmland is at least 10 percent wooded. The exploitation of these woody borders offers amazing subsistence potential for millions of people in addition to greatly limiting erosion in the rainy season. Under one law in Costa Rica, subsidies are given for agroforestry activities that mix crops, trees, and livestock. In a 10-year period, 10,000 agroforestry contracts were signed, and 3.5 million trees were planted on farms. This is nothing short of a game changer for the people affected.

In arid zones, water harvesting makes it possible to grow crops on previously degraded and abandoned land. In West Africa, for example, stone fences slow runoff during the rainy season. The land's capacity to retain water thus increases by a factor of 5 to 10, biomass production increases by a factor of 10 to 15, and livestock can eat the grass that grows at the base of the stone fences after rainfall. These eminently simple structures conserve soil moisture, replenish water tables, and limit erosion — moreover, the farmers win every step of the way. These are practices that can be generalized: what are we waiting for?

Another way to increase productivity naturally is to grow perennial plants:[4] of the over 50,000 edible plants that exist on the planet, 99 percent remain in place for multiple years. However, our modern diet is primarily composed of annual plants that must be re-seeded each year. "Perpetual" varieties of many garden plants exist — including lettuce, spinach, sorrel, onions, leeks, cabbage, and rhubarb. These obviously demand much less work, cost, and energy but are just as delicious as annual varieties. Let's try a little audacity!

## Quinoa, an ally of international food security and sovereignty

**Quinoa** — "the mother of all grains" in the Quechua language — is the only plant that contains all nine essential amino acids (proteins) in addition to various trace elements and vitamins. This plant, which originated in the Bolivian highlands (4,000 meters of altitude) can also be grown on plains (in the Pays de la Loire region of France, for example). It can withstand drought, poor or salty soil characteristics, and temperatures between −8 and +38°C. In a context of climate change and food crisis, quinoa stands as an excellent alternative food source. In 2013, the United Nations invited the governments of the world to grow quinoa with a view to increasing their food sovereignty. Quinoa is not a grain but belongs to the Chenopodiaceae family (which includes spinach). It does not contain gluten and can be prepared in a variety of ways.

### PRODUCING AND EXCHANGING FARMERS' SEEDS

Seeds are life. Each one contains a millennia-old genetic identity and assures the continuity of species — both the plants themselves and the species that eat them, including humans. Historians believe that, since the dawn of agriculture over 10,000 years ago, humans have selected the most productive seeds from the most delicious plants to grow their food. Later, trade between Europe and the East and the activities of the Exploration Era transported seeds around the world. The resultant crossing of seeds helped enrich the plant heritage of different regions in the world.

## SAYING NO TO F1 HYBRIDS

The era of agro-industry is putting this rich heritage in peril. In 1933, the first F1 (*first filial generation*) hybrid corn was produced in the United States, thus opening the door to a substantial manipulation of life. An F1 hybrid is the result of crossing between two "parent" plants selected for their particular qualities: color, size, growth rate, resistance, etc. In the first generation, the combined traits of both plants are guaranteed. The only snag is that plants obtained in this manner are unstable: certain characteristics are not preserved in the next generation. This means that gardeners or farmers have to buy new seeds instead of saving and re-growing a portion of their seeds as they have done since the dawn of farming. This traps them in a situation of reliance on — and indebtedness to — seed suppliers.

Today, five major international companies control three-quarters of the world's seeds. They patent their seeds, prohibiting farmers from using them unless they pay.

## BOYCOTTING GMO PRODUCTS

Every country has its own definition of genetically modified organisms (GMOs). Generally speaking, a GMO is a plant, animal, or microorganism that has had some DNA from another organism inserted into its genome (transgenesis), typically through genetic engineering, to bestow new traits upon it. This modification can be passed on to the modified organism's descendants. GMOs are used in research, agriculture and agri-food, health, industry, and cosmetics.

The first genetically modified plant, a tobacco plant, was produced in 1983. Eleven years later, in 1994, the first edible genetically modified (GM) plant, a tomato, was brought to market. According to the International Service for the Acquisition of Agri-biotech Applications (ISAAA), GM plants were being grown in 28 countries in 2014,[5] on a worldwide total of 180 million hectares of farmland. The United States leads the pack with 73 million hectares, followed closely by China and India. These are mainly soybean and corn crops for livestock feed as well as rapeseed, cotton, and tobacco. The European Union is holding out, with only 0.1 percent of cultivable farmland being planted with GMOs. Between the two extremes, Canada has 12 million hectares of transgenic crops. Nearly everywhere, the crops are becoming more common.

The sales pitch may be a seductive one: prevent attacks from diseases and insects, increase productivity. But in reality, these GM plants pose a major hazard for unmodified plants in the same family, whose genetic heritage is at risk of being degraded. When it comes to the long-term health impacts on GMO consumers, no one at present has enough perspective to be able to judge. Therefore, it's reasonable to apply the precautionary principle.

## DEMANDING THE FREE CIRCULATION OF HEIRLOOM SEEDS!

In the face of these threats and abuses, a resistance is brewing. Activist networks are facilitating contact among people and groups wishing to exchange or purchase heirloom seeds, circumventing the monopoly held by large companies.

As an element in the ecosystem, humans have a role to play in circulating seeds, just as birds, terrestrial animals, and wind have always freely distributed them. The great seed voyage can be helped along by a sheep's wool or a hiker's shoes, as landscape architect and botanist Gilles Clément reminds us. Today, caring for seeds has become a priority in resisting the threats of the big seed companies.

If you are a permaculturist wishing to grow your own food and contribute to the food sovereignty of your family or community, find a distribution network that guarantees the origin and quality of the seeds or plants. Save your own seeds to sustain your crops into the future and exchange them with other growers. This kind of care requires commitment, patience, observation, sound botanical knowledge, and practice. Every species has its own traits and its own needs. Beginner gardeners can start with a few rustic self-fertilizing varieties, such as tomatoes, eggplants, beans, peas, lettuce, and mâche (corn salad/lamb's lettuce).

As individuals, we should get into the habit of asking our suppliers what kinds of seeds have been used to produce the fruits, vegetables, and grains they sell. If people request this information more often, suppliers will adapt. As the saying goes, the customer is always right. If you are a farmer, get in touch with activist networks to find heirloom seeds. Most legislation prohibits the sale of such seeds, but nothing can stop people from bartering them.

In most countries, citizens' networks are organizing to ensure the free circulation of farmers' seeds. Quebec artist Patrice Fortier became a seed producer to preserve rare and forgotten species of plants and to create the "heritage varieties of the future"! In his garden in the Bas-Saint-Laurent region, he grows plants and sells them all over the world, transforming his harvest into art projects along the way. This inventive farmer who dedicates his passion to serve biodiversity has been made the subject of a film.

**TO FIND OUT MORE:**
– La société des plantes, lasocietedesplantes.com.
– *The Sower*, a documentary film by Julie Perron, Les films du 3 mars, 2013 (77 minutes), vimeo.com/ondemand/thesower.

INSPIRING EXAMPLE

# An educational forest garden in the middle of the city

The Garden of the Workers Brotherhood in Mouscron, Belgium, is a modern-day Garden of Eden that produces abundant food and generously passes on its invaluable teachings. People come from far and wide to meet Gilbert Cardon and see his fabulous garden. You really must see it to believe it: 2,000 varieties of trees and 5,000 varieties of edible or medicinal plants thrive on 1,800 square meters, right in the middle of the city. For over four decades, Gilbert and his wife Josine have been tending this garden and sharing their permacultural approach with anyone and everyone who wants to hear about it. His vision of growing food is natural to him, almost innate, and one that he crafted through observation "and a touch of laziness" even before the concept of permaculture was defined. Cardon says that at age 30 he knew nothing about gardening. Then the textile crisis hit. Like many others, he was forced to find another way to feed his family. The young autodidact was connected with popular education movements and stumbled upon organic gardening, including the works of Claude Aubert. Eventually, Cardon discovered permaculture and its Australian pioneers. He was hooked and began practicing it right away.

Over the years, his vocation of gardening has evolved and become primarily pedagogical. "I wanted to prove that abundance is within our reach, as long as we leave nature alone," Cardon says. Touring the site is a dizzying experience: 800 varieties of tomatoes, 400 varieties of apple trees, 160 varieties of pear trees, 80 varieties of vines and citrus fruits, 70 varieties of plum trees, 60 varieties of cherry trees, 50 varieties of raspberries, 35 varieties of fig trees and fruit-bearing brambles, and hundreds of flower varieties. A weeping cherry tree neighbors a lemon hedge, a pepper plant, a row of brambles, edible dahlias, and mulberry trees that sag under dozens of kilograms of fruits — all without an ounce of chemical inputs, of course. Cardon summarizes the magic as follows: "The secret is the soil!" The soil is extremely rich; for over three decades it has been the direct recipient of the family's fruit and vegetable peelings and plant clippings. The soil is never turned, which leaves the microorganisms undisturbed. As a result, the soil teems with earthworms (three kilograms per square meter!) and is exceptionally high in humus (12 percent). Thanks to its blanket of organic material, there is no need to water, even during heat waves, our guide points out. Water seeps into the maze of tunnels dug by the earthworms and is stored there, as in a sponge. "We are always a bit ahead of the books," Cardon jokes. "We work less and less and produce more and more! We can't even collect everything the garden produces. People help themselves and still so much is left for the birds and the soil."

All the seeds begin life in pots (the vegetation is too dense for direct seeding); one variety per pot, marked with clear labels. These are stored under more or less waterproof shelters or along walkways. There are no high-tech solutions at the Garden of the Workers Brotherhood. The gardeners are content to use an old tarp for a greenhouse, a piece of sheet metal for a windbreak, and sewer grates for walkway stones. "Here, we cooperate with nature. Nature does the work. We just create the proper conditions," the master gardener explains. "Potted plants receive water through the dish underneath so they don't get thermal shock. When the plants are large enough, the best-looking ones are transferred to larger pots and later into the ground, with no watering," he continues. "Humus provides the necessary moisture. And the stress of potting up the plants strengthens them. This allows us to extend the season by three weeks. During that time, the soil is available for other plants. We pot up cabbages with their roots bare, carrots are four or five to a pot, and turnips with the soil still on. The squash establishes before the weeds. The land is used twice." Cardon has all the information at his fingertips! We struggle to keep up with him. "No need for bean trellises here. They climb the trees all by themselves!"

In Cardon's garden, wild plants are the only fertilizers used. "Everything that was alive rots and returns to the soil," Cardon reminds us. "Nourishing elements remain active in the dead plants. Through the use of liquid plant manure, the properties of the plants balance out and harmonize, fortifying the seeds and healing the garden — naturally and free of charge!"

Biodiversity also prevents attacks from pests or diseases, "as in Bolivia, where hundreds of different potato varieties are grown in combination. Parasites become lost in such a diversity of colors and odors.

## Liquid plant manure recipe

The recipe is easy: start with a non-metallic tank or pond that is 200 to 1,000 liters (50–250 US gallons) in volume and fed by rainwater. Toss in the leaves and roots of nettle, comfrey, horsetail, buttercup, fern, elderberry, or any other "weed" that grows in the place (before they go to seed). "The land 'knows' which plants it needs to be fertile. It allows them to develop where it needs them," Cardon confides in the style of an old sage.

Use 100 to 200 grams (¼ to ½ lb.) of fresh plants for every 10 liters (2.5 gal.) of water. Allow to ferment for two or three days, stirring occasionally. Let rest for two or three weeks. Dilute before watering: one part liquid manure to five parts water. Throw in a handful of seaweed to keep down the odor if desired.

They become food for each other; one fungus is eaten by another fungus. The land is 'vaccinated.' Everything is regulated naturally," Cardon says.

A pond fed by rainwater attracts insects, amphibians, and hedgehogs. Refuges are created for these animals, which play the crucial role of auxiliary species. Small pots suspended upside down from fruit tree branches and packed with rags provide habitats and cover for earwigs. This encourages the earwigs to feed on insect larva or eggs that would otherwise set up shop in the fruits. Here and there, piles of stones or brush serve as nests for honey gatherers that pollinate the garden.

The only remaining challenge, albeit one that wanes over time, is slugs. Cardon's team tried everything and finally settled upon "slug parking lots," which use rye bran to attract the hungry creatures. Once baited, the troublemakers are simply collected and fed to the chickens.

Indefatigable, Cardon continues his lesson to a rapt audience. "A weakened tree produces more, and more quickly, than a strong tree," he says. He recommends the Lorette pruning system (named after its inventor, Louis Lorette, and developed around the year 1900). The Lorette method involves only summer pruning — from mid-June to mid-September — which, in his opinion, provides all the advantages. "The fruits are already formed; you can see what you're doing. This style of pruning keeps the tree smaller and allows you to also grow different vegetables or small fruit plants that maintain moisture at the tree base. The pruning takes place at a time when pests (such as aphids and caterpillars) typically develop on the apical buds and cause damage. However, the pruning changes the sap composition, which the pests do not like. They starve or go elsewhere, and the branches are free to grow back. To limit the propagation of fungus, the sick branches are placed at the tree bases, where they 'vaccinate' the trees homeopathically. Nature does not burn branches that fall on the ground," Cardon exclaims. "We should follow its example! In summer, the wounds caused by the pruning cause natural scar formation thanks to the higher temperatures. Lorette pruning is easy and can be learned in two or three hours. It completely avoids the need for chemicals, even organic ones. The most simple, popular, and accessible solutions are always the best!" the teacher concludes.

As a result of all these practices, the vegetation is so dense that it creates a microclimate. In winter, the soil is 3 to 4°C warmer than the air, which is quite an achievement in a relatively cold country.

Continuing on our way, we see a passive solar (bioclimatic) greenhouse built around an old washtub fed by rainwater; the structure provides tomato, pepper, eggplant, and melon plants with a warm and sunny shelter several weeks before their regular season. Along the south wall, water pipes painted black capture heat from the sun, which is stored in the washtub water, thereby regulating external temperature variations. Goldfish make their home in the basin and feed on mosquito larvae. In summer, deciduous bushes planted outside the greenhouse prevent overheating.

Another curiosity of the Garden of the Workers Brotherhood is the seed bank (open to members only). There, meticulously stored in small envelopes handmade by volunteers, 5,500 varieties of seeds, originating from far and wide, are numbered and classified — only Cardon knows all the codes by heart. Members can buy their seeds here for just a few cents. The cash register is on the table, and it's on the honor system. Also available is the "natural gardening course," a collection of teachings delivered by Cardon in the form of a photocopied volume that can be bought for a few euros (and which may hopefully be available digitally one day). "Previously, we could mail seeds to our members who lived far away. We don't have time for that anymore. We receive so many visitors," the professor grins.

Gilbert and Josine's home is also the site of the local neighborhood food co-op. Today, the co-op has 1,500 members, including a hundred active volunteers. About 250 people regularly take the courses (offered free of charge) to learn gardening, pruning, and grafting. Group purchases have extended to include books (2,000 titles available), washing machines, and other common consumer goods. It is a happy microcosm created from scratch in a rather ordinary little Belgian city.

**TO FIND OUT MORE:**
– Garden of the Workers Brotherhood (with free online video gardening courses): fraternitesouvrieres.over-blog.com.
– Documentary film, *La jungle étroite* by Benjamin Hennot, 2013 (57 min.).
– The Good Food Portal, goodfood.brussels.

## PRODUCING LOCAL, ORGANIC FOOD IN THE CITY

One major issue to be dealt with in future is supplying cities by growing food as closely as possible to where it will be eaten. Recall that three-quarters of the world's population will live in cities by 2050. We know that supermarkets will have only three days' worth of supplies if a disturbance in the oil supply occurs (e.g., a transportation strike or a social, economic, or geopolitical crisis). Given this reality, citizens have every interest in proactively organizing local alternative supply circuits to build food sovereignty where they live.

Additionally, local food is guaranteed to be fresh; this means it can be eaten raw, which is better for human health, as we have discussed elsewhere.

Modern urban agriculture was born in the late 1960s in Detroit, Michigan, amidst an economic crisis and rising unemployment. The local population, overwhelmed and resource-deprived, gradually began using marginal land and land left vacant by the decline of the automobile industry. The primary objective was to grow edible food. Farms, gardens, orchards, greenhouses, beehives, and chicken coops began popping up in the city, setting the stage for the development of a new local economy. In the face of future uncertainty (demographic, economic, environmental), city dwellers and political figures are rethinking the relationship between the city and the areas that supply it. Today, local urban agriculture is a production model on the make in many cities around the world.[6] The objective is simply to supplement the needs of local populations. Individuals, restaurant owners, hospitals, and schools are making the leap by gardening on public lawns, private lawns, and rooftops. Land that was previously abandoned is becoming potential space for food production. All of this goes to show that helping grow food in the city is no pipe dream! In France, about 30 communities have been working towards this objective for years.[7] In Quebec, Montreal is already considered a food-growing city, with numerous urban

**INSPIRING EXAMPLE**

# Brooklyn Grange Farm, New York

Created in 2010 by Ben Flanner and Anastasia Cole Plakias, Brooklyn Grange Farm is recognized as the largest and most noteworthy of urban farms. It covers more than one hectare in New York City, spread across the rooftops of two buildings. It produces over 25 tonnes of fruits and vegetables per year, which are sold to neighboring restaurants and to customers in an on-site boutique. The experiment later grew to include chicken coops and beehives. The farm regularly opens its doors to residents in neighboring buildings and organizes all kinds of activities for school-age children as well as professional training for adults.

### A new way to grow food in the city

Brooklyn Grange Farm practices organic growing in an innovative way on flat roofs. Through the use different structures and rainwater collection, food can be grown field-style in soil 20 to 30 centimeters deep. The farm produces about 40 varieties of tomatoes, lettuce, bell peppers, kale, Swiss chard, herbs, beans, radishes, and carrots. Laying hens and about 30 beehives have allowed the farm to diversify its offering.

### Short supply chains

Brooklyn Grange Farm's products are sent to neighborhood restaurants, local markets, retailers, and the farm boutique. People who live in the two buildings can of course get their vegetables directly from the farm through a box system.

### On-site waste recycling

The farm recycles organic waste on site with compost bins and surface composting. The hens help agriculture initiatives in operation: a survey conducted in 2013 indicates that 42 percent of Montrealers grow fruits and vegetables.[8]

## GROWING PLANTS AT HOME

On a smaller scale, anyone can grow a few herbs, mushrooms, tomatoes, and sprouts — even apartment dwellers. With just a tiny bit of space, investment, effort, and mental freedom, you can

have your crops on their way in no time. These mini-crops provide welcome nutritious food and a great deal of pleasure, including for children who love making plants grow. The pioneers have broken the trail…

out by eating the vegetable peelings and scratching the soil. The material from the waste decomposition nourishes the soil, which in turn feeds the garden plants. This approach is part of a virtuous circle that maintains and renews nutrients within the rooftop substrate.

### Toward shared abundance

Growing local food in the city through the urban farming model benefits neighborhood residents and even people who live in adjacent neighborhoods. The name of the game is to create an abundance of fresh, organic, local, seasonal fruits and vegetables and to form relationships among city dwellers centered around a shared space and a common activity.

### Educational outreach

The farmers have also given themselves a pedagogical mission. In 2011, they partnered with City Growers, a not-for-profit educational program, to

give children and young adults the opportunity to discover the site and the farming activities that take place there. The farm offers tours and workshops on the topics of life, nutrition, and sustainable development. Over 10,000 young people have visited Brooklyn Grange Farm.

### Professional training

Each year, the farm issues a hundred certificates to adults who have taken its urban farming professional training program. The aim is to seed the next generation of farmers feeding cities and to expand the urban farming model. The farm recently partnered with the Refugee and Immigrant Fund in Queens, to hire refugees from Africa, Asia, and Central America. The refugees also contribute their own cultural and agricultural traditions, thereby increasing diversity on the farm. (brooklyngrangefarm.com)

INSPIRING EXAMPLE

# Windowfarms – growing food in windows!

Society is up against colossal new challenges, such as managing energy and supplying cities with food. Originally created in the US in 2009, the Windowfarms project was designed to grow plants hydroponically in one of the most unexpected locations for farming: the urban apartment. The two main objectives are to allow citizens to produce a portion of their food at home all year long and to innovate together (facilitated by the Internet) to make consumption in cities more sustainable.

### A new way to grow, soil-free

A window farm is a vertical hydroponic system. Hydroponics is a soil-free farming technique: plants are grown in a neutral and inert substance (sand, clay pebbles, rock wool) and regularly irrigated with a solution that supplies the plants with mineral salts and essential nutrients. This technique is used in greenhouse production. The innovation of Windowfarms was to adapt greenhouse techniques for apartment dwellers, creating a relatively simple and inexpensive hydroponic system that could grow spices, herbs, fruits, and vegetables in windows.

### Growing at home all year long

This installation is ideal for herbs, lettuce, kale, cherry tomatoes, strawberries, peppers, gherkins, chili peppers, peas, and medicinal plants. However, the system doesn't work for growing tubers, grains, or root vegetables. A window farm can produce up to 25 plants at a time. This method of year-round indoor growing increases food security and improves quality of life in the home: the green columns add a decorative, fresh, and living accent to the room.

### Modular design featuring recovered materials

The equipment is designed to be modular and flexible so that users can fit it to any kind of window and customize it to their personal needs. Recycled bottles or other everyday items can be used as plant containers. A small air pump adds liquid nutrients drop by drop into containers filled with clay pebbles.

### Open-source design plans

As of 2020 the most active source for information about windowfarms, along with an active and enthusiastic community, is in the Netherlands. Unfortunately, the American based project became relatively inactive after a kickstarter project initially succeeded in funding but subsequently failed in the manufacturing and delivery phase. Links for the Windowfarms Netherlands Foundation and for its Facebook page are listed below, along with a link to an archived copy of the original WindowFarms Version 3.0 DIY Instruction Book:

windowfarms.nl • facebook.com/windowfarms.nl. windowfarms.nl/wp-content/uploads/2018/03/Version-3.0-DIY-Instruction-Book.pdf

# Hélène, wild plant interpreter

Hélène lives at the edge of a wooded area. She has chosen to lead a simple life close to nature. The young woman enjoys walking in her bare feet, free from the constraints of shoes, "to experience the richness of sensations with the plants, to feel the temperature of the soil, and to avoid crushing things." We joined her on one of her wild plant discovery walks, which she organizes with the Le Val'heureux association in Côtes-d'Armor, France.

"Spring is the best time to harvest wild plants," she explains. "The buds brimming with life are so tasty. Certain plants have a stronger taste later in the season." Those who know their plants can observe flowers, berries, and other fruits any time of year. With her identification book in hand, Hélène leads us along the beaten paths she knows by heart, far from the nearest pollution source. She finds her first nettles, the "queens of the ditches, high in protein, iron, and vitamins; there's nothing better for perking yourself up when you're feeling lethargic." Farther down the path, dandelions, already in flower, attract foraging bees. You can eat the blossoms right off the plant. We also spot some plantain, which is good for calming insect bites and tastes delicious in a salad. There's yarrow, a healing plant that Hélène seems particularly fond of. And a little clump of violets, which are quite lovely as a garnish on sorbet. All along an old stone wall, we see navelwort; its fleshy leaves crunch under our teeth.

Farther still, ground ivy is in flower: it's high in vitamin C and has expectorant properties — plus it's delicious in salad. After a short detour by the shore, we stand awe-struck before a large bed of wild arugula.

Back in the kitchen, the excitement gets the better of us. A handful of rose petals from the garden and wild mallow tossed into the water pitchers transforms them into living paintings! Magnificent — and so simple. The green salad from the garden takes on new colors and flavors with the addition of a few borage, vetch, and nasturtium flowers. Hélène is struck by how nicely wild and cultivated plants pair with each other: "as good in the garden as it is on the table." Some of us prepare sautéed nettles. Meanwhile, others cook up elderflower fritters and still others infuse sparkling water with sage flowers. Pies, syrups, jams, sorbets, jellies — the ways to prepare and preserve wild plants are endless.

Of course, Hélène has a warning for us: "Never harvest plants unless you recognize them for certain. If you aren't absolutely sure, let it be! The only way to avoid toxic plants is to learn directly from experts. Books aren't enough. And, of course, only harvest what you are sure you will use. Rather than ripping up everything, pick selectively in order to preserve the resource."

Hélène learned everything she knows by honing her observation skills, reading books, and taking herbalism courses — but most of all by listening to elders whom she has accompanied on many botanical outings. She learned about "soil indicator plants" from botanist Gérard Ducerf, discovered the language of the flowers alongside mandala garden enthusiast Marc Grollimund, joined herbalist Thierry Thévenin on the herbs of life trail at the "Simpletons' Feast," and learned how trust the "the good herbs" with ethnobotanist Pierre Lieutaghi. "It's comforting to be in tune with wild plants, to know that they can feed us, pass on their strengths to us, and even heal us," Hélène says. "Little by little, you start to see that we live in the same ecosystem. We can lean on them. Nature provides for our needs without asking anything of us. It's a gift: all we have to do is say thank you!" It was in the throes of a health problem that Hélène began studying wild plants. "A doctor had diagnosed me with an infection," the young woman recalls. "I didn't want to take antibiotics, so I looked in books to see which plants corresponded to my situation. And it worked! Since then, every time I have a health problem, I look to plants first. Gradually, I stopped taking medication altogether. I consult only to get a diagnosis. For that part, doctors are irreplaceable."

Through her involvement with wild plants, Hélène has been fortunate enough to meet good people, explore places she never would have visited on her own, and get to know a secret world. It has been "a great pleasure!" It's as simple as that.

Contact: Le Val'heureux association, 22400 Hénansal, France. levalheureux.com.

**TO FIND OUT MORE:**
- Gérard Ducerf, *Encyclopédie des plantes bio-indicatrices alimentaires et médicinales* (Briant, France, Promonature,  2014).
- Marc Grollimund, *L'almanach des fleurs sauvages: Quatre saisons de découvertes végétales* (Paris, Delachaux et Niestlé, 2007).
- Thierry Thévenin, *Les plantes sauvages: Connaître, cueillir, utiliser* (La Geneytouse, France, Lucien Souny, 2012).
- Pierre Lieutaghi, *Le livre des bonnes herbes* (Arles, France, Actes Sud, 1996).
- Marie-Claude Paume, *Sauvages et comestibles: Herbes, fleurs et petites salades* (Saint-Rémy-de-Provence, France, Édisud, 2011).

**Courses:**
- Association pour le renouveau de l'herboristerie: arh-herboristerie.org
- Syndicat des Simples: syndicat-simples.org/fr/index.php
- Cap Santé: capsante.net
- Guilde des herboristes (Québec): guildedesherboristes.org.
- Herbothèque – Institut de formation en herboristerie et en médecine traditionnelle: herbotheque.com.

## HARVESTING AND COOKING FROM THE WILD

In both city and country, increasing numbers of citizens are enjoying learning how to recognize edible the wild plants they encounter on walks. Wild plants are beautiful, abundant, highly nutritious, and free.

## PRESERVING PLANTS

There is no shortage of methods to preserve plants. These techniques are designed to extend the shelf life of foods by starving any microorganisms that may form on them of resources (especially oxygen). In the home kitchen, we should capitalize on prime fruit and vegetable season by eating them raw, but also set a certain portion aside to enjoy in other seasons.

Whatever preservation method you choose, it's preferable to minimize energy consumption and reduce your dependence on fossil energy:

- Nuts, certain varieties of potatoes, and apples can simply be stored in a dry and well-ventilated place (but be careful of pests)
- Certain vegetables can be buried in sand (e.g., carrots)
- Fruits and vegetables can be dehydrated in a solar or wood oven
- Some foods can be sterilized and made into syrups or jams: this can be done on a wood stove
- Food can be cooled in a "zeer" or "desert refrigerator"

## The desert refrigerator

Consumption: zero fossil energy. And easy as pie to build. Take two terra cotta pots (flowerpot type) of different sizes. Plug the bottom holes with corks. Soak the pots, then place one inside the other, lining the in-between space with packed wet sand. Place the whole structure on a dish filled with water to keep the pots and sand moist. Place your butter or yogurt inside and cover everything with a thick damp cloth. The temperature difference between the inside and the outside produces condensation, which

DAMP CLOTH

WATER THE SAND

INNER CLAY POT

SAND

OUTER CLAY POT

WATER EVAPORATION

DESERT REFRIGERATOR

KEEP FOOD COOL WITH NO NEED FOR ELECTRICITY

generates cool temperatures in the interior. That means the hotter it is outside, the cooler it will be inside!

– Refrigeration, freezing, and deep freezing all have the major drawback of requiring sophisticated equipment and constant electricity throughout the preservation.

Certain plant preservation techniques don't require any outside energy:

– Vegetables can be preserved in oil (e.g., dried tomatoes).

– Fruits can be preserved in alcohol (although this destroys their vitamins).
– The only process that doesn't require outside energy and allows vitamins to develop is lacto-fermentation. Yeast, yogurt, sauerkraut, brined pickles, kefir, and soy sauce are all made through lacto-fermentation.

## Lacto-fermentation: the best in environmentally friendly preservation!

### How does it work?

In the absence of oxygen (anaerobic environment) and with a little salt, vegetables and citrus fruits — rather than being degraded by certain bacteria they contain — develop lactic ferments that feed on carbohydrates. Lactic ferments inhibit the development of other bacteria. When the environment is sufficiently acidic (around a pH of 4), lacto-fermentation stabilizes and the food can keep for months. It remains raw and living. Lacto-fermented foods can be considered vitamin-rich food supplements that stimulate the digestive system and strengthen the immune system. Care must be taken not to eat too much of them, however, since they are quite salty. Consider adding a tablespoon of ferments to a salad or starchy dish.

### How do you do it?

– Wash and grate (or very finely chop) organic vegetables. Mix the vegetables, spices, and aromatics to taste and add coarse salt — 30 grams per liter (1 ounce per US quart).
– Scald the glass jars and metal lids.
– Fill the jars with the vegetables up to the rim to keep out air, then fill with room-temperature water.
– Place a wooden board on the filled jars and let sit at room temperature (between 15 and 25°C / 60–77°F) in a dark place to start the fermentation process.
– After two or three days, close the lids tightly and store in a cool place (such as a cellar) for a month before eating.

Lacto-fermented preserves keep for up to a year. If the vegetables have an unpleasant color or odor when you open the jar, it means the process was unsuccessful. *Dispose of the contents.*

# Chapter 18

# Food from Animals

## A MATTER OF PUBLIC HEALTH

PRODUCING QUALITY RED MEAT requires one hectare of pasture per cow. Yet for over four decades, industrial meat production has deprived cattle of the natural nutritional richness of pasture grass. Livestock health and the nutritional quality of meat and other by-products (milk, butter, cheese) have suffered as a result. The meat diet is increasingly being fingered as a prevalent human health risk factor and a public health problem.

The meat diet, which has become traditional in modern Western societies, also happens to be devastating for the environment: it takes up large tracts of farmland — often displacing forests — and huge amounts of water. The FAO estimates that beef production doubled over a 40-year period.[1] It is estimated that by 2050, the world's population may consume 60 percent more animal protein than it did in 2012, which will increase the pressure on our planet's natural resources. Farm animal products account for nearly half the protein consumed in developed countries (48 percent on average) but less than a third (28 percent) in developing countries.

## THE NATURAL RICHNESS OF PASTURE LAND

What is the difference between milk from a cow that spends its days grazing on a meadow and milk from a cow that spends its life in industrial housing? Well, nothing you can see with your eyes. But a distinguished palate can quickly tell whether or not cream comes from a pasture-raised cow. And a biological analysis reveals the starkest differences of all.

We interviewed Dr. Bernard Schmitt, an endocrinologist and researcher and the director of the Human Nutrition Teaching and Research Centre (CERNH).[2] Schmitt and his colleagues have observed a worrying trend in the last two decades or more: a massive increase in "modern" pathologies, such as overweight, obesity, diabetes, cardiovascular diseases, and cancer. He began researching the link between food and health. "We are what we eat," the nutritional researcher reminds us. "The nutritional quality of our food has a decisive impact on our health."

Dr. Schmitt conducted studies on livestock, the environment, and humans. The results indicated that cows that spend their days on pasture have an appropriate balance of omega-6 and omega-3 fatty acids, while those fed dry fodder and mash in indoor stalls have an excess of omega-6 and a major deficit of omega-3. Similar differences were found in free-range and battery poultry and the eggs they lay. Animal health, of course, directly depends on diet and lifestyle. Imbalances in animals carry over to the bodies of the people who consume the milk, butter, or eggs of these animals, which over multiple years add up to cause human health impacts.

Dr. Schmitt's studies demonstrate the impact of different farming sectors on the health of patients suffering from obesity, diabetes, and cardiovascular disease. Groups of volunteer patients followed strict diets for three months. All of them ate the same foods, but half were given foods from a farm, produced in accordance with precise specifications, while the other half were given industrial products. After one month, the blood tests of the two patient groups were very different: the former had a desirable balance between omega-3s and omega-6s (a 1:4 ratio) while the other still had the pathogenic imbalance (a 1:12 ratio) between the two essential fatty acids. In the months following the experiment, the patients who were given the farm products were able to maintain the advantages of the diet over time — since "omega-3s inhibit the production of fat cells," Dr. Schmitt explains — while those who had eaten industrial food quickly gained weight. Dr. Schmitt found evidence to suggest that a diet high in omega-3s from meat produced by animals given a flax supplement (which is

naturally high in omega-3s) had the same protective effects against cardiovascular disease as a diet high in fish.

With this scientific demonstration of the influence of production methods on the nutritional quality of meat, milk, cheese, and eggs in mind, Dr. Schmitt decided to make it easier for people to buy healthful animal products. How? By changing part of the food chain, i.e., livestock feed. "I am convinced that most patients suffering from these modern diseases can improve their health with diet alone. They just need access to healthful foods," he says. In 2000, on his initiative, a collective created a charter of production and processing[3] that guarantees a balance between omega-6s and omega-3s known as the Blue-White-Heart charter.

In France, persuaded by the positive impact of this health-centered approach, the chef of the AURI interministerial restaurant, where the staff of the French prime minister and the staff of the agriculture minister dine, have included Blue-White-Heart and organic products on the menu since 2011. (A word to the wise.)

The knowledge gained from these studies leads Dr. Schmitt to say something you don't normally hear from doctors: "Crop rotation and polyculture are key to good health. They help us grow food with fewer inputs and preserve biodiversity and soil life!" This statement aligns with the view of the most up-to-date agricultural researchers and officers: agriculture practised on a human scale preserves livestock health — and, in

## AMAZING DATA
## Food and health

### Obesity kills more people than hunger

Around the world, obesity kills three times as many people as malnutrition: 3.4 million people in 2010. This figure has doubled over about a 30-year period. In 2014, half a billion people were obese and 1.5 billion were overweight. In 2013, 66 percent of Americans were obese or overweight (compared to 55 percent in 1990).

### Overweight children

About 42 million children under the age of five are overweight.*

### Cardiovascular disease

This is the leading cause of death in the world (9 million per year); this is the second most common cause in France after cancer.

### Cancer

Over 30 percent of deaths attributable to cancer would be preventable through healthier living practices, especially cutting back on red meat.**

### Diabetes

The number of diabetes diagnoses in the world rose from 30 million to 260 million between 1985 and 2005. About 7.3 percent of the global population is affected. In France, cases of type II diabetes have doubled in about the last 15 years. In Quebec, 80 percent of diabetics are overweight or obese at the time of their diagnosis.

### Food allergies

These have become the fourth most serious public health problem in the world, according to the World Health Organization (WHO). This potentially chronic pathology affects 25 percent of children in rich countries. In 2050, one in two people will have an allergy, according to WHO projections.

SOURCES:

\* FOOD AND AGRICULTURE ORGANIZATION OF THE UNITED NATIONS, *ROME DECLARATION ON NUTRITION*, SECOND INTERNATIONAL CONFERENCE ON NUTRITION, NOVEMBER 19–21, 2014, FAO.ORG/3/A-ML542E.PDF.

\*\*WORLD HEALTH ORGANIZATION, *CANCER PREVENTION*, WHO.INT/CANCER/PREVENTION/EN.

turn, human health. "Inuit are one-tenth as likely to have cardiovascular problems as Westerners," the doctor says. "This is because they eat fish, which feed on plankton, an excellent source of omega-3s."

## THE CRITICAL BALANCE BETWEEN OMEGA-6S AND OMEGA-3S

Omega-6 and omega-3 fatty acids are absolutely critical to human and animal health. Humans cannot manufacture them independently and

## AMAZING DATA
## Animal protein and the environment

**Meat consumption**

In the last four decades or so, worldwide poultry production has increased by 700 percent.* In the same period, pork production has tripled while beef production has doubled. Consumption appears to have peaked in rich countries and has dipped slightly in recent years.

**Milk monopoly**

83 percent of global milk is produced by the Holstein breed alone.** Not exactly the paragon of biological or economic diversity…

**Impact of beef production**

Producing one kilogram of beef protein requires an average of 10 kilograms of grain. It also requires 100 times the water that would be required to produce a kilogram of plant protein.

Beef production requires 28 times more surface area and 11 times more water than raising pork or poultry. It produces five times the greenhouse gas emissions and has ten times the overall environmental impact compared to other kinds of animal production.

**Insects**

Producing insect protein requires almost no water.

Sources:

* Food and Agriculture Organization of the United Nations, *World Livestock 2011: Livestock in Food Security* (Rome, 2012), fao.org/docrep/016/i2373e/i2373e.pdf.

** Heinrich Böll Foundation and Friends of the Earth, Meat Atlas: Facts and Figures about the Animals we Eat, 2014, foeeurope.org/meat-atlas.

must obtain them either by eating plants that naturally contain them (thanks to photosynthesis) or the products of animals that eat these plants (meat, milk, eggs). A ratio of 1 (omega-3) to 4 (omega-6) is considered a proper balance. Industrial products more often have a balance of 1 to 10 or 12, and may even be as high as 1 to 40, which is highly pathogenic.

Omega-3s (anti-inflammatory) are found in the green grass of pastures (the green comes from chlorophyll), flax, rapeseed, alfalfa, quinoa, and plankton. In winter, a cow receiving 5 percent of its diet in the form of flaxseeds will double the amount of omega-3s in its milk within one month. The human who drinks this milk will see their omega-3 levels increase by a factor of 2.5 within a month. Fatty wild fish, such as salmon, trout, sardines, and mackerel, which feed on small fish that eat lots of plankton, are excellent sources of omega-3s.

This is bad news for the pharmaceutical industry: simply adding flax meal to bread at a rate of 5 percent is enough to cover our omega-3 needs. Eating 80 grams (about two slices) per day of flax-fortified bread for a month lowers cholesterol by 10 percent, triglycerides by 36 percent, and insulin requirements by 30 percent! Note, however, that any flaxseeds used must be extruded because their seed case is cyanogenic.[4]

Saturated omega-6s (inflammatory) are found in large quantities in animal fodder, corn, soybeans, and palm oil. Milk from human mothers who eat industrial food contains about four times the proper amount of omega-6s, an imbalance that they of course pass on to their babies, along with risks of obesity, diabetes, and cardiovascular disease.

## TO EAT OR NOT TO EAT ANIMAL PRODUCTS?

Should we eat meat or not? Should adults drink milk or not? Should we eat cheese or not? These highly sensitive questions may spark controversy. They have nutritional, dietetic, economic, cultural, philosophical, religious, and emotional import. Here we offer some food for thought on the subject. It is up to each individual to eat as they see fit, and to clarify their understanding by reading and by learning from others. If needed, they can seek advice from a doctor or nutritionist and consciously decide on their personal and family transition.

In any case, permaculturists should avoid excess and refrain from endorsing industries in which animals are reduced to the status of mere consumer products and live in inappropriate conditions. The same attention should be paid to plants: they too are living and "sensitive" to whether they are treated well or poorly.

## A WIDE DIVERSITY OF PLANT-BASED PROTEINS AND VEGETABLES

Proponents of meat often point to protein requirements, and it is certainly true that meat is high in protein. Today we know that plenty of other foods also contain protein, particularly if whole grains (rye, wild rice, etc.) are paired with legumes (soybeans, beans, lentils, peas, green beans, etc.) or if buckwheat, quinoa, amaranth, oilseeds, sprouts (radish, alfalfa, sunflower, etc.), dry fruits, nuts, seaweed, and plankton are eaten. These plant proteins have benefits for human health (being high in fiber and low in fat) and to the environment: they require 10 percent as much farmland as livestock does. In addition, legumes fertilize soil (acting as green manures). Eating insects is another remarkable source of protein in the diet. Advocates of milk and cheese speak of people's requirements for calcium and vitamins B[12] and D, but we know that many other foods contain just as much (sesame seeds, dried fruit, tofu) or even more (plankton).

## COMMON-SENSE ENVIRONMENTAL ARGUMENTS

Aside from dietetic concerns (such as the acidity meat adds to our bodies), followers of the "less or no animal products" approach invoke

## To drink or not to drink milk?

More and more nutritionists and naturopaths are issuing warnings against the negative effects of cow's milk on health, while industrial lobbies praise the health assets of this animal product. *Homo sapiens* is the only mammal that drinks milk into adulthood, and the only species that drinks the milk of other species. Dairy products such as cheese, yogurt, and curds seem to present fewer disadvantages than milk itself, according to certain dieticians. You be the judge. In any case, massive consumption of milk and dairy products has the same environmental consequences as livestock farming: it uses significant farmland, water, and energy.

common-sense environmental arguments. When we consider that the planet's surface is finite and that producing 1 kilogram of meat takes 3 to 14 kilograms of plants (and the corresponding agricultural land to produce the plants), it's easy to see that with 9 billion mouths to feed in 2050, meat consumption cannot continue to rise indefinitely. The projected change in meat demand by 2050 ranges from −50 percent to +80 percent depending on which studies you look at. Our observations indicate that it is the affluent and educated classes in industrialized countries that are first to follow nutritional advice and trim their meat consumption before these attitudes trickle into the rest of society. The need to control demand is definitely on the radar of certain

countries (such as Brazil), which are implementing educational (and contraceptive) policies accordingly. If environmental arguments fail to persuade, the health costs of unbalanced diets may push certain governments to act. In China, where meat consumption has risen by a factor of four and milk consumption by a factor of 10 in approximately 30 years, nearly 25 percent of the population is overweight or obese. What government can remain passive for long in the face of such a trend?

One potential solution for addressing protein needs may be to strike a better balance between plant and animal sources, for example by gradually introducing vegetarian and insect-protein meals into the diet. This is being recommended by a number of nutritionists and environmentalists. Sweden is considering a carbon tax on red meat.

### THINKING OF RAISING YOUR OWN ANIMALS?

If you choose to eat meat, it's important to know where it comes from. What quality of life did the animals have, and what were the slaughter conditions? Inside slaughter plants, animals must await their turn. They hear the cries of those who go before them and produce toxins associated with fear. We can easily imagine that their meat becomes imprinted one way or another with this stress. Has anyone measured the subtle impact on the consumer's emotions? By contrast, free-range animals slaughtered in natural environments don't have time to become afraid, and the quality of the meat is beyond compare.

If you have land, why not raise some small animals yourself? You may wish to keep poultry, sheep, goats, etc.

### A few questions to ask yourself before raising animals

- What are my family's meat needs?
- What animal species could live together on my land (to avoid monoculture)?
- How much space does each animal need (outdoor space, pen, shelter)?
- What ecological functions could the different animals fulfill on the farm?
- How much energy would they consume and contribute?
- What could I grow on site to feed them?
- What will be my budget to care for these animals?
- Where will their water come from?
- How will I manage the manure?
- How will I limit soil damage?
- Who will slaughter them, and where?
- How much time will the animals require of me every day?
- Who will learn to care for them?
- How will I manage the animals' offspring?
- Who can I ask for advice and guidance?

Rudolph Steiner's biodynamic philosophy may provide a starting point for you to answer these questions.

### Multifunctional roving chickens

Raising a few chickens in your garden is one way to produce fresh eggs and high-quality meat for your family. This is in keeping with the permaculture principle of stacking functions (at least three functions per action). In addition to providing food, chickens mow the lawn, fertilize the soil with their droppings, and eat many insects, slugs, snails, and larvae. They represent a potential income stream. It also is a great pleasure to communicate with these highly sociable birds!

To maximize the usefulness of chickens in the garden, you can build them a light floorless mobile cage complete with roosts, water, and protection against the weather. The cage can be readily moved where you want to work. This will turn your chickens into veritable garden assistants.

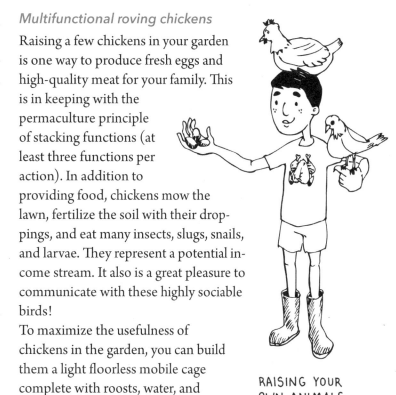

RAISING YOUR
OWN ANIMALS

### Pigeon keeping

Arborist, apiculturist, and philosopher Maurice Chaudière practices a peaceful form of animal husbandry on his land. He keeps pigeons, a protein source that requires very little work and zero budget outside of building the dovecote. The birds find food almost entirely on their own and return to the dovecote to raise their young and to sleep. By controlling the number of couples, permaculturists can produce however many squabs they wish. If too many are born, more eggs can simply be removed and eaten!

### Beekeeping

Permaculturists wishing to ensure their garden is pollinated and get some honey out of the deal can install one or more beehives depending on the space and plant life available. Bees and their honey have been part of the human adventure since its origins. Cave paintings show that our ancestors were already harvesting honey and wax from hives in the wild. The bee-human alliance is all the more necessary given that bees perform 70 to 80 percent of pollination in wild species — and one-third of our food depends directly on their pollination services. This is a relationship of dependence summarized in the well-known (but disputable) quotation: "If the bee disappeared off the face of the Earth, humans would only have a few years left to live." Bee troubles have been a growing threat since the first years of the 21st century: monoculture is starving bees, pesticides are poisoning them, and the tiny varroa mite, accidentally imported from Southeast Asia, is decimating their populations (in its region of origin, the varroa mite does not destroy the native bee on which it feeds). The result: half of the planet's colonies have disappeared in about the last quarter-century. In certain parts of the world, colony collapse disorder is affecting over 50 percent of the remaining colonies. Bees are now taking refuge in cities, which does not solve the problem of pollinating our food plants. The greater diversity of pollen sources and the warmer air temperature in cities appear more favorable to foraging bees. With this in mind, no less than 600 hives have been installed throughout Paris: they can be found on the rooftops of the Grand Palais and the Paris Opera, in the Luxembourg Gardens, and near flowery balconies and tree stands. These urban hives are three to four times more productive than their rural counterparts.

## Time is honey

A Honey Bank has been created by a group called the "Poetic Party" in the Paris area; the bank features a city pollination program, a "swarming mission," foraging zones, and "bee savings accounts." The precious urban honey is produced at a rate of 200 to 300 kilograms per year and distributed under the "Concrete Honey" label. "Honey from the Bank" is also a hot commodity at citizen-led and arts events in the French capital. In addition to supplying honey, the idea behind the project is to supply human richness and critical thinking where it is needed. Don't hesitate to become a member of the International *Honey* Fund — the FMI in French, which is a pun on the IMF! (banquedumiel.org/banque.html)

A number of apicultural collectives with a similar mission also exist in Quebec. See the Miel Montreal co-operative (mielmontreal.com/en/) and the Alvéoles company (alve ole.buzz.)

If you are ready to get started with your first hive, don't forget to design your project properly and verify that it is feasible.

The following texts are worth consulting:

– Jérôme Alphonse, U*n petit rucher bio: Tous les conseils pour bien débuter* (Paris, Rustica, 2015).
– Maurice Chaudière, *Apiculture alternative* (Suilly-la-Tour, France, Findakly, 2005).

– Alicia Munoz, "Tendance: les ruches urbaines prolifèrent," *Bio à la Une*, October 12, 2012, bioalaune. com/fr/actualite-bio/6034/ tendance-ruches-urbaines-proliferent.

The following films are worth consulting too:

– Markus Imhoof, *More than Honey*, 2012.
– Mark Daniels, *The Strange Disappearance of the Bees*, 2010.

INSPIRING EXAMPLE

# Food from animals

### Michel Jarry, farmer, forager, hunter, partner of nature

Michel Jarry has been practising "agro-sylvo-hunting" in Dordogne, France, for over two decades. He maintains a dynamic equilibrium between semi-wild animals that he hunts (mainly fallow deer) and intelligently controlled woodland and agricultural biodiversity. It is a multi-pronged activity that enables him to provide his own food, water, and wood — and to make a good living.

Jarry is a happy man. He lives "in communion with nature" and feels that he enjoys an "idyllic quality of life." The former head of a large industrial butchery grew weary of the too-busy life he led in Paris. One day chose to move with his family to the heart of France's Périgord region. In 1970 he acquired 80 hectares of land with poor soils, but forested and at 500 meters altitude. Initially, Jarry practised conventional agriculture, "like everyone in this area." He bought a herd of Limousin cattle (100 head). "We had a dream; we wanted to succeed." But after four or five years, Jarry found that it was not viable. "I didn't want to become a low-income person with a limited future." He sold his herd and turned to crops, devoting 30 hectares to irrigated corn and over 20 hectares to rye and oats. "The prices were good; we were master harvesters. We sold to anybody who would take it; we were making a good living." Then along came the Common Agricultural Policy (CAP) of the European Union, which would have forced him to sell through a farm co-operative. Jarry flatly refused, preferring to "maintain his liberty and not feel led by others." With

RED
DEER

ROE
DEER

FALLOW
DEER

BOAR

PHEASANT

PARTRIDGE

HARE

RABBIT

*Animals of the French forest.*

higher prices for seed, fertilizer, and fuel, outside financing became necessary. Sale prices fell by 40 percent. "They promised us assistance, but we could see the system was floundering." Jarry jumped ship from the CAP "out of pride and common sense." He liquidated everything, including his tractors and his irrigation system. He realized that high-end, quality products were coming into vogue. Very quickly he saw a new path before him: he liked forests, game, freedom, and innovation.

Hunting activities were still unregulated in 1986, there was no need for heavy equipment or fertilizer, and there was potential for good profit. "I wanted to present my proposal to the Chamber of Agriculture. They took me for a crackpot and refused to give me a hearing! The Crédit Agricole rejected my requests for financing. I was a contrarian, a disgrace to the farming world, a utopian." So, he decided to go it alone. Fronting the money himself, Jarry built a two-meter-high fence around 40 hectares of land. He bought fallow deer and red deer (though he soon got rid of the red deer, which were "too big and too violent"). He established for the animals "a life of semi-freedom, as close as possible to the natural context." His dream of autonomy was now within reach. He could provide all the food his family needed on his own land: meat (game, poultry), vegetables, and fruits. He had firewood and a source of drinking water on site (a gravity-fed system that supplied the house). Jarry planted 350 fruit trees, put in a garden, and managed his game herd in accordance with the available space.

He refined his plan by making observations, consulting with professionals, and reading. "In the wild, you find one or two animals per 100 hectares, which allows nature the time to regenerate," Jarry explains. "I opted for controlled management, which is more concentrated: three or four animals per hectare, or about 40 kilograms of meat. At €12 per kilogram, that gives me a very nice profit. Even counting the maintenance on 5 kilometers of fencing." Today, his herd numbers about 80 head.

Looking at the animals' alimentary bolus revealed the secret of their favorite foods. He discovered that the deer gravitated to the foods of the forest — chestnuts, acorns, roots, brooms, brambles, quackgrass, lichen, and wild mushrooms — rather than the beautiful meadows that Jarry had originally planned. Humans adapt. He organized the terrain to give the game animals one-third woods, one-third semi-wood, and one-third grasses. He also put in a few hectares of crops (turnips, kohlrabi, buckwheat, rye) in rotation, as a food reserve in the event of climate variations. Jarry knows the meaning of diversity. In the woods he prunes only what's necessary to maintain and encourage mushrooms. "People like porcini mushrooms. Two hundred kilograms per year at €15 per kilogram is profitable! No work other than picking." Working with an association, he set up a chestnut preserving shop to capitalize on the best nuts; the rejects go to the deer. He is starting to produce triticale, a wheat-rye cross, to feed his chickens. Forty tonnes per year! It's all about autonomy.

Jarry is a salesman, a businessman who diversifies his income streams. But first and foremost he's a tree lover. He could talk about trees for hours. He planted two hectares of red oak, acacia, Douglas fir, willow, and alder. But the storm of 1999 ravaged the resource that was supposed to fund his retirement. "I am conjoined to nature. Nature makes the decisions," the old sage humbly admits. "All humans do is protect themselves from the water, sun, and wind." Since that time, Jarry replanted 10 hectares of fruit trees, many of which have proven quite appetizing to the deer.

Jarry's primary tool is observation. Every day, he can be found driving through his forest on a 4 x 4, with his binoculars in hand. He spots does about to give birth, follows fawns, identifies young does (females aged one to two years — the most delicious), and monitors young bucks (males aged six months to one year) and prickets (bucks aged one to two years) ready to be hunted. "My goal is to have a top-quality herd! If pressure from the herd becomes too great and threatens the health of the forest, I regulate. I play predator. Customers place orders and tell me their preferences." When the time comes, he kills the animal on site in the forest, in its natural environment." There is no undue stress on the animal, which makes for better meat. He bleeds, guts, and skins the animal before taking it to the veterinary inspection. Then, in the workshop he built on the farm, he cuts the meat — properly processed and vacuum-packed — which he stores in a cold room (his butchery skills are exemplary). Through word of mouth, he has built up a loyal base of customers who love to buy his top-notch products, all within a 50-kilometer radius. The taste of this meat is something to remember! The customers (200 to 300 families) can shop at the on-site boutique. Jarry also delivers his delicious grain-fed poultry by truck in his immediate vicinity (€20 per bird on average). And of course, he grows the grain on site too.

The woodsman is "happy with this quality of life, happy to sell well and to sell good quality products." How many hours per week does he work? "Planting and grafting a tree — you call that work?" he exclaims. "It's a pleasure. And there is so much satisfaction in leaving behind a good legacy. This forest represents 50 years' worth of energy!"

From time to time the farm plays host to sport hunting events, inspired by practices used in Quebec. Enthusiasts, often from abroad, come to hunt one or two animals chosen from a catalogue (no dogs or horses are allowed). They stay for a day and leave with their trophies (the antlers). It's a lucrative activity that demands little time.

Since 2007, Jarry's son, a former civil servant, has taken over the operation, though of course his father continues to work with him. Only recently did Jarry discover that his holistic approach, based on making detailed observations and seeking balance between the different ecosystem elements, was connected to a growing movement; it goes by the name of permaculture.

***Contact information:*** <michel.jarry36@sfr.fr>

# Chapter 19

# Food from the Ocean

## THE OCEAN, A VAST FOOD SOURCE

THE EARTH'S OCEANS cover three-quarters of its surface and contain incalculable resources for supplying food. Fishing, aquaculture, and crustacean and shellfish farming are only the visible part of this gigantic food store. Science is beginning to discover the nutritional virtues of plankton and algae, organisms that abound in the sea and already figure into many of the world's cuisines, especially in Asia. Today, a few fringe actors in the West are inviting us to cook with them too.

## ARTISANAL FISHING: A WINDFALL FOR MILLIONS OF FAMILIES WORLDWIDE

Fish provide the same amount of protein as meat from land creatures. Most species are rich in omega-3s and contain all kinds of vitamins (A, B, D), trace elements (zinc, copper, iodine, selenium, and fluorine), mineral salts (phosphorus), and iodine — all of which greatly benefit health.

According to a UN report, fishing and aquaculture directly employ 55 million people in the world, mostly (87%) in Asia.[1] When you add in the associated sectors upstream and downstream of this activity, this figure triples. Around the world, the activity is for the most part an artisanal pursuit, and half of those who practice it are women.

Artisanal fishing accounts for 30 million tonnes per year of fish caught exclusively for human consumption. With its much more developed technical and financial resources, industrial fishing captures roughly the same amount, over 35 million tonnes per year; most of this is made into fish meals and oils fed to farmed fish and livestock.

Fish farming, which represents nearly 50 percent of fish-related economic activity, is the most dynamic food sector in terms of jobs. In Asia, where 90 percent of the activity is concentrated, assets have quadrupled in about the last decade. Industrial fish farming is exploding, and its products are mainly for export. While it is supposed to prevent the pillaging of the oceans, aquaculture poses other problems:

CATCHING YOUR OWN FISH

it mainly deals in carnivorous fish (salmon, red porgy, and sea bass) and therefore consumes enormous quantities of small "forage fish." Producing one kilogram of farmed salmon, red porgy, or sea bass requires 4 to 5 kilograms of wild fish (herring, sardines, or mackerel). This means farms remove four to five times as much volume from the ocean as they produce. Furthermore, these operations generate a lot of pollution and use large amounts of hormones and antibiotics. And farming herbivorous fish appears to be a long way off.

Per-capita world fish consumption ranges from 10 kilograms per year in poor countries to 29 kilograms in rich countries. Fish's share of the global food supply climbs by three percent per year. Thus, fish consumption greatly contributes to improving the diet of many fragile populations.

## A RESOURCE UNDER MAJOR THREAT

Significant threats weigh upon the world's fishing resources: overfishing, increasingly destructive capture techniques, large quantities of dead fish thrown back into the sea each year because of their low market value, illegal fishing (which is measured in millions of tonnes), certain equipment (such as nets, trawls, and bottom longlines, which damage the seabed), chronic or accidental ocean pollution, and development in coastal areas (which destroys marine habitats).

A third of the world's mangroves, seagrass beds, and coral reefs have disappeared in about the last 50 years, along with a quarter of its salt marshes. There is added pressure from increased population growth to consider, and climate change is aggravating the situation further. The rising atmospheric $CO_2$ concentration causes temperature increases and ocean acidification, two factors that lead to the sporadic proliferation of toxic algae, which cause certain species to die or migrate. The accidental displacement of animal and plant species is also accelerated by oceangoing ships, which constantly spill tonnes of ballast water from one ocean to another, thus disturbing biodiversity by threatening food chains.

The world's fishing fleet has become twice as powerful as it would be under a sustainable model of ocean harvesting: more ships, more fishing capacity per ship, more technology (aerial tracking, sonar, radar, underwater maps, refrigeration). And government subsidies to the sector are no help. Countries with industrial fleets have so thoroughly depleted their original fishing zones that they are now sending their oversized vessels all over the world. Artisan fishers in turn suffer the effects of overfishing and must travel farther afield to catch the fish they need, using more fuel in the process.

According to the FAO, 90 percent of large marine predators have disappeared from certain parts of the ocean since the 1950s.[2] This is because their food — smaller fish — has disappeared as a result of overfishing or plankton shortage, which ruptures the food chain. Will the international community take the actions needed to balance human needs with those of the resource?

## THE SOMETIMES-ABUSED UNIVERSAL RIGHT OF GLOBALIZED FISHING, AND LOCAL SOLUTIONS

Today, 40 percent of products of the world's fisheries are sold internationally (compare this with 20 percent for wheat production and 5 percent for rice production). Of course, this outflow of wealth fails to benefit many small fishers and weakens local economies.

The FAO negotiated the Code of Conduct for Responsible Fisheries with the actors concerned, which came into effect in 1995. This document has inspired many others. In recent years, on the initiative of Olivier De Schutter, former UN Special Rapporteur on the Right to Food, the international community has become involved in establishing a series of obligations under the umbrella of respecting human rights. These obligations are intended to protect artisanal fishing and local populations. They include, for example, reducing fishing volumes and creating marine protected areas (MPAs), which in principle guarantee food security for coastal populations. While these international legal measures are full of good intentions, some observers feel that they pose the risk of privatizing the oceans. Indeed, these MPAs, often financed by private investors working through NGOs, primarily favor the interests of the investors themselves (not the fishers' interests); most of the time these investors have

nothing to do with the world of fishing yet impose their own criteria of "sustainable fishing." Under the new criteria, many small fishers discover that they are prohibited from working in traditional and productive fishing zones[3] while private operators are permitted to engage in lucrative activities such as the purchase of fishing quota[4] and "nature" tourism. "Coastal fishing isn't what threatens the oceans; chemical pollution does that," ranted marine biologist Pierre Mollo when we interviewed him in 2015.

Nevertheless, bit by bit, the collective imagination is tending in the direction of protecting fish stocks and defending small fishers. In the Maldives, for example, the only authorized tuna fishing is line fishing from local boats. In the Brazilian state of Ceará, lobster fishers have organized themselves into co-operatives to sell their products directly to American retailers. The result has been a 70-percent increase in profits for small fishers! In Peru, which supplies nearly half the world's production of fishmeals and fish oil, the government instated a voluntary policy several years ago to encourage local fishing and consumption and to limit the production of industrial by-products.

In many countries, zones set aside for artisanal fishing have been negotiated under pressure from small fishers. In Cambodia, for example, fishers were successful in securing local user rights. The violations continue, of course, but the tables have turned in a legal sense at least. Successes such as these open the door to change in other countries.

In Europe too, governments have undertaken measures to further the transition to sustainable fishing, protect the resource, and develop aquaculture. It goes without saying that the difficulty lies in monitoring the enforcement of commitments and avoiding adverse consequences.

## AMAZING DATA
## Artisanal vs. industrial fishing

– In Europe, 80 percent of fish schools in the Mediterranean Sea and 47 percent of those in the Atlantic Ocean are overfished.

– In France, artisanal fishing accounts for 80 percent of the fleet and 50 percent of the jobs.

### Comparison between the performance of artisanal and industrial fishing

|  | Artisanal Fishing | Industrial Fishing |
|---|---|---|
| Amount of fish for human consumption per year | 30 million tonnes | 35 million tonnes |
| % of boats / % of the resource | 99% of boats / 50% of the resource | 1% of boats / 50% of the resource |
| Jobs | 12 million fishers | 500,000 employees |
| Amount of catch reduced to fishmeal and fish oil for livestock consumption | Almost none | 35 million tonnes |
| Fuel consumption | 5 million tonnes | 35 million tonnes |
| Catch per tonne of fuel consumed | 4 to 8 tonnes | 1 to 2 tonnes |
| Subsidies | $6 billion US | $26 billion US |
| Amount of fish thrown back into the ocean (non-surviving) | Almost none | 25% to 30% of catch |

SOURCE: FOOD AND AGRICULTURE ORGANIZATION OF THE UNITED NATIONS, FISHERIES AND AQUACULTURE DEPARTMENT, *THE STATE OF WORLD FISHERIES AND AQUACULTURE 2012*, ROME, FAO.ORG/DOCREP/016/I2727E/I2727E.PDF.

*How do permaculturists choose "sustainable" ocean products?*

All these statistical realities are cause for vigilance. Unless you're able to buy your fish straight off the wharf when the boats come in, you'll need to have a few questions at the ready and read labels closely at the fish market or grocery store:

- Is the fish in season? Where was it caught? Is the species overfished or threatened? How was it caught (by selective fishing or otherwise)? If it was raised through aquaculture, how was it fed? Does it have a label? If the package is not explicit enough, ask! Consumers have the right to make informed food choices.
- Find out about the fish seasons in your own area.
- To help you know which species to favor or steer clear of, the WWF has prepared Seafood Guides for many regions around the world: wwf.panda.org/get_involved/ live_green/out_shopping/seafood_guides.

On the international scene, the ecolabel of the Marine Stewardship Council (MSC), a not-for-profit organization created in 1997 by the WWF and Unilever, certifies that wild, fresh, or processed fish products bearing the label have been caught in a "sustainable" manner.[5] While the MSC presents itself as an independent organization, this is disputed by certain fishers' organizations who think it serves other

## Health precautions

In the last fifteen years or so, parasites that are potentially dangerous to humans have been observed in 15–100 percent of wild fish species. *Anisakis* begin as parasitic nematodes that live in the digestive tract of cetaceans and marine birds. Their larvae enter the food chain and develop in fish guts and flesh. These larvae are particularly pernicious because they are invisible to the naked eye. The adult worms are barely more visible: they take the form of a small, translucent, tightly coiled spiral. In humans, the larvae or worms may trigger allergies and digestive problems that can be violent; the disease is known as anisakiasis.

To prevent this infection, the fish must be gutted as soon as it is caught or purchased and kept cold. Before being eaten, it must be cooked at a temperature over 60°C or otherwise frozen at –20°C for at least 24 hours to destroy the parasites it may contain. Sushi and any marinated, smoked, or salted fish should be consumed only *after* freezing.

 **TO FIND OUT MORE:** French Agency for Food, Environmental and Occupational Health & Safety, anses.fr.

(economic) interests than their own. They prefer the approach employed by Blue Fish, an association founded in Europe.[6] Blue Fish includes all kind of stakeholders — professionals, scientists, public institutions, and citizens living in coastal communities — and defends a social model founded on the diversity of occupations in the sector to "protect both the marine environment and the fishers' communities." Other labels exist on a local scale, such as France's "Bar de ligne de la pointe de Bretagne" brand, which assures consumers they are buying very high-quality wild fish caught in an environmentally respectful manner.

### MICRO- AND MACROALGAE: RESOURCES OF THE FUTURE

"In 2050, we will have 9 billion humans to feed. The protein from land organisms won't be enough. Plankton can play a decisive role in food chains," Pierre Mollo says

*Pierre Mollo*

OHHH...

WHEN YOU STOP TO THINK THAT THESE TINY ALGAE WERE HERE 3,500,000,000 YEARS BEFORE US ...

emphatically in his talks. Mollo has been a marine biology researcher and plankton champion for over 40 years.

In both their micro and macro forms, algae distill the benefits of seawater. "In their tissues, they store all the basic elements that constitute our planet and our bodies: every kind of marine algae contains all known mineral salts and trace elements. These veritable vitamin bombs have tonic properties, form a protective shield, and stimulate our natural defences. They are a better dietary source of $B_{12}$ than milk. The fact that this nutritional richness is available in a natural organic form makes it especially assimilable."[7]

Today, algae represent a viable nutritional resource for the future of humanity. This is especially true for compromised eaters (undernourished children and adults, people convalescing from illness, refugees) and those with special circumstances (expeditioners who can carry only small volumes of food).

### THE IMMENSE NUTRITIONAL AND THERAPEUTIC POTENTIAL OF PLANKTON

High in protein (50 to 60 percent), fat (omega-3 fatty acids), and vitamins C and $B_{12}$, the known species of plant plankton represent a substantial nutritional resource. And the adventure is just getting started! So far, we know how to grow only about ten of the hundreds of thousands of species that exist in nature (though not all are edible by humans). Edible microalgae can go well with pasta; they are already used in candy, drinks, breakfast cereals, nutrition bars, and cookies. "One day, every table will have a plankton grinder right next to the pepper grinder, and we will sprinkle our meals with dried spirulina," Pierre Mollo says prophetically in his talks.

Microalgae-based food supplements are already popular in organic and online stores in the form of tablets, capsules, powders, soluble extracts, and drinkable phials. Sold at prices that are sometimes in the hundreds of euros per kilogram (and sold in quantities of tens of grams), they are slowly winning the hearts (and stomachs) of consumers. Plankton's active ingredients also represent immense therapeutic potential. This represents a market of €1 to 2 billion (€1 is equiv. to 1.1$US in early 2020).[8]

## BIODIVERSITY UNDER THREAT

Certain factors threaten these precious marine resources. Certain plant and animal plankton species are disappearing because the food and conditions they need to live can no longer be found in their usual environment. Global warming, pesticides, and exotic species that arrive by boat are upsetting the food chain (and, in turn, the fisheries).

Global warming is causing certain animal and plant species to migrate northward at a rate of 23 kilometers per year. This represents a distance of over 1,000 kilometers since the 1950s! The result is that the less motile species — shellfish, attached larvae — aren't getting their food and are disappearing.

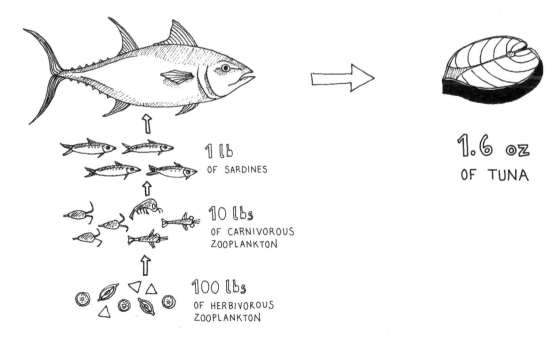

1 lb
OF SARDINES

10 lbs
OF CARNIVOROUS
ZOOPLANKTON

100 lbs
OF HERBIVOROUS
ZOOPLANKTON

1.6 oz
OF TUNA

In the presence of pesticides, toxic plankton species are displacing native species, rendering certain shellfish inedible and suppressing the appetite of fish. "Cutting pesticide use by 50 percent is not enough. We urgently need to get to zero pesticides," Mollo states.

Commercial fishing vessels, which carry 60 percent of cargo worldwide, also carry seawater in their ballasts containing up to 7,000 different plant and animal species. This they eventually release into other oceans. Lacking natural predators, certain species, introduced in this way, become invasive and destroy ecosystems. The situation is particularly critical in enclosed waters, such as the Black Sea and the Baltic Sea.

Also threatened is maerl (or *Lithothamnion*), a marine substrate composed of the debris of algae and shellfish. Very high in mineral salts (calcium, magnesium, iron), this reservoir of biodiversity was widely used as a fertilizer in the organic sector, as a remineralizing agent for drinking water, as a food supplement, and more. A ban on extracting the material was instituted in 2010 to prevent it from disappearing. But the damage is serious. "It is the fishes' pantry and habitat. We must no longer touch it," Mollo pleads.

## PLANKTON AND POLAR BEARS: PART OF THE SAME STRUGGLE

"Plankton is the source of life, and humans don't know it," Mollo laments. "It is invisible, so we don't believe it! The polar bear is much more popular. And yet, they both belong to the same food chain: one at the bottom, the other at the top. If the former disappears, the latter follows, along with all the species in between."

The researcher regrets that neither governments nor citizens think about defending "this population of little marine creatures which are, in fact, the masters of the seas, accounting for 98 percent of marine biomass and producing over 50 percent of the oxygen we breathe.... Plankton should be considered part of the world heritage of humans," the scientist argues. "It can provide simple and sustainable answers to the problem of nutrition. It is up to cooks, community leaders, NGOs, and consumers to lead the way."

## THE "WANDERERS" THAT SHAPED OUR LANDSCAPES

The word "plankton" — from the Greek *planktos*, meaning "wanderer" — refers to aquatic beings that are unable to locomote by themselves and move only with the currents. A great diversity of planktonic species can be found in saltwater, freshwater, and brackish environments.

Depending on the species, their size ranges from a fraction of a micron to several millimeters, with some even measuring tens of centimeters. The smallest planktons are classified as viruses and bacteria. Next come those in the fungus family. The most well-known are the plant planktons (phytoplanktons) and animal planktons (zooplanktons). A few species live permanently in planktonic form (e.g., phytoplanktons and certain zooplanktons) while for others this form is temporary: most marine animals, molluscs, and crustaceans begin their lives in a zooplanktonic stage as larvae or fry. Jellyfish, which generally drift with the ocean currents, are among the largest planktons.

Microalgal sedimentation from 3.5 billion years ago sculpted the contours of our landscapes. In France, for example, calcite-rich coccoliths and other organisms helped form the chalky cliffs of the Pays de Caux in France's Haute-Normandie region. Similarly, the silicate rocks of Auvergne and Ardèche were formed through sedimentation and fossilization of diatom skeletons.

In order to produce 100 grams of tuna meat, the carnivorous fish must eat one kilogram of small blue fish (sardines), which themselves have swallowed 10 kilograms of carnivorous zooplankton, which ate 100 kilograms of herbivorous zooplankton, which in turn had swallowed a whole tonne of phytoplankton! Tuna is an absolute plankton concentrate!

The discovery of plankton came about with advances in microscopy. The first classifications date from the 19th century. Researchers continue to discover new species.

## Two major plankton families: phytoplankton and zooplankton

| | Phytoplankton or plant plankton | Zooplankton or animal plankton |
|---|---|---|
| **Characteristics** | Produces over 50 percent of our oxygen. Fixes as much $CO_2$ as forests do. | Mass greater than total human mass |
| **Type** | Permanent | Temporary or permanent |
| **Form** | Unicellular microalgae | Uni- or multicellular |
| **Feeding method** | Autotrophic * Performs photosynthesis | Heterotrophic ** Herbivorous, carnivorous, or omnivorous |
| **Place in the food chain** | Food for all aquatic herbivores | Food for fry, fish, and crustaceans |
| **Most common forms** | Diatoms: 66 percent of phytoplankton | Copepods (permanent plankton): 80 percent of zooplankton |

SOURCE: CAP VERS LA NATURE, *LE PETIT GUIDE DU PLANCTON*, CAP-VERS-LA-NATURE.ORG

* *Autotroph:* produces its own organic matter from sunlight, minerals, and water.
** *Heterotroph:* unable to produce its own organic matter; must get it through food.

## The curious case of copepods

The copepod, a small crustacean, is the most common animal on the planet. The world's copepod population turns over every two months and represents 40 billion tonnes of food — that's 150 times more than global meat production!

Krill, which are permanent zooplanktons ancestral to shrimp, contain especially high amounts of omega-3s and chitin (calcium). They are eaten by jellyfish, shrimp, sea birds, fish, and whales. Humans can take advantage of krill's benefits by eating crustaceans and fish. This resource is also used in aquaculture and in the pharmaceutical industry. Through many complex and subtle interactions that are still largely not understood, krill are also the key to balance in other ecosystems. They should be protected from being pillaged.

### OF NUTRITIONAL AND EDUCATIONAL INTEREST

Currently, three kinds of phytoplankton, among the highest in both protein (up to 70 percent) and fat (omega-3 fatty acids), are currently approved for human consumption in Europe. Other species may follow. Phytoplankton tend to neutralize the acidity created in our bodies by our industrial diet. These microalgae, already recognized as a food supplement, are slowly making an entrance into the world of fine dining. The only deterrents to them being eaten as food are people's lack of familiarity with them, their blue-green color, and a slight sea taste that is not to everyone's liking.

1 *Chlorella:* This unicellular microalga lives in both fresh water and salt water. Exceptionally high in plant protein (60 percent), chlorophyll (4 percent), essential fatty acids, vitamins (A, beta-carotene, $B_{12}$, C, E, and K), mineral salts (calcium, iron, phosphorus, manganese, and zinc), and amino acids, it has highly beneficial health effects. According to the science website *Plancton du monde* — an authority on plankton —

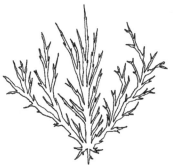

*Edible algae and plankton.*

SPIRULINA    CHLORELLA    KLAMATH    ODONTELLA AURITA

it provides 40 times as much protein as soybeans, rice, or wheat and 10 times more vitamin A than beef liver. It contains more chlorophyll than any other plant (four times more than spirulina). Known for its cleansing and purifying properties, chlorella helps repair damage resulting from pollution. It is reported to have curative properties: it fights gastric and duodenal ulcers, heals wounds, regenerates cells, protects against respiratory diseases, and fights constipation.

**TO FIND OUT MORE:** "Module de formation du plankton," *Plancton du monde*, plancton-du-monde.org/module-formation.

**2** *Odontella aurita:* A diatom high in omega-3s, mineral salts, trace elements, and vitamins. Scientists from the French Research Institute for Exploitation of the Sea (IFREMER) say two to three grams per day is enough to cover our needs and make up for any deficiencies from eating unbalanced industrial food.

**3** *Spirulina:* This cyanobacterium is one of the oldest forms of plants to have appeared on Earth. It is found naturally in the fresh water of Lake Chad and the salt waters of Lake Texcoco in Mexico. It is increasingly grown in basins. High in protein (65 percent), iron, vitamins A and $B_{12}$, trace elements, antioxidants, and omega-3s, it comes recommended by the FAO for reducing infant malnutrition. Eating 15 grams of spirulina is like eating 100 grams of beef. It is one of the only non-animal protein sources (along with soybeans) to contain all the essential amino acids. It can be produced cheaply and easily. Its dark blue-green color and slight fishy odor remain a barrier to its inclusion in fine dining for the time being, especially in France.

"Spirulina is a good food supplement for people who suffer from food deficiencies or who are healing," says Geneviève Arzul, a former IFREMER biologist. "You don't need to use it regularly if you are properly fed and healthy."[9] For his part, biologist Pierre Mollo sees spirulina as a full-fledged food: "It is true that it is ideal for athletes, elderly people, and sick people who need an especially rich diet. But spirulina is good for everyone. Experimental school menus include three grams of spirulina per meal. It is used in early childhood development programs to teach children about environmental balances between land and ocean. At home, we can have spirulina shakers on the table, as we do for salt and pepper, to enjoy with food. Soon, people will be producing fresh spirulina in their own homes."

**TO FIND OUT MORE:** French Federation of Spirulina Producers, spiruliniersdefrance.fr.

## AN ECO-FRIENDLY AND ECONOMICAL MICRO-CROP

There are many advantages to growing microalgae. The crop requires little space — it can even be produced in an apartment or on a sailboat! It is grown in closed loops, which means it doesn't consume much water or generate much waste. It does require light, heat, and plenty of patience and rigor. In the optimal temperature conditions (around 35°C), microalgae develop very quickly: their biomass can increase by 25 percent per day. Unheated greenhouse crops of the stuff yield very good results, even in cool parts of the world, for six months of the year. Spirulina goes dormant and rests for the other half of the year.

Spirulina farms are popping up in the French countryside at a rate of about 30 per year! Two hundred farms are already producing 30 tonnes per year of the precious blue-green alga.

*For those wanting to produce traditional artisanal spirulina:*

- Maria Fuentes and Gilles Planchon, *La spiruline pour tous. Culture familiale* (La Chapelle-sous-Huchon, France, Passerelle Éco, 2014). A basin of seven square meters is enough for a family of six.
- Jean-Pierre Jourdan, *Manuel de culture artisanale*, 220 pages, free download, includes 32 page summary in English. spirulinefrance.free.fr/Resources/Manuel%20du%202%20fevrier%202018.pdf

Klamath Lake plankton (also known as *Aphanizomenon flos-aquae* or AFA) is another interesting find. Identified by Cortés in the 16th century, this blue-green microalga, naturally found in Upper Klamath Lake in Oregon, is among the most complete and balanced foods: 60 percent protein (3.5 times more than beef or eggs); over 115 micronutrients including vitamins $B_1$, $B_{12}$, and K; minerals; trace elements; amino acids; and omega-3s. It is recognized for many qualities, especially its anti-inflammatory and antioxidant properties. However, certain studies warn against the possible presence of toxins associated with this microalga.

**TO FIND OUT MORE ABOUT PLANKTON BIODIVERSITY:**
- Pierre Mollo and Anne Noury, *Le manuel du plancton* (Paris, Charles Léopold Mayer, 2013).
- Maëlle Thomas-Bourgneuf and Pierre Mollo, *L'enjeu plancton* (Paris, Charles Léopold Mayer, 2009).

## HOW DO YOU COOK WITH PLANKTON?

Plankton is the "in thing" right now! Chefs are beginning to try their hand at cooking it, as are aficionados who see a culinary future for these precious marine plants. Tastings featuring the ingredient are becoming more common in fine dining circles. Open your eyes and prepare your taste buds!

One chef at a Paris restaurant has taken Pierre Mollo's talks to heart and plans to treat his guests with a caviar substitute made of balled spirulina in the near future. "Why should vegetarians be deprived of this delicious appetizer?" the gourmet scientist asks.

*For those wishing to cook with plankton at home:*

– *La Cuisine au plancton*, a film by Jean-Yves Collet (26 minutes, 2010). Chef Marc Foucher tries out different plankton dishes with nutritionist Dr. Bernard Schmitt and researcher Pierre Mollo.

### SEAWEED ON OUR PLATES!

While a microscope is needed to observe microalgae (plankton), macroalgae (seaweed) are quite visible on our ocean coasts, nestled among rocks, and under our feet. In addition to giving us shifting landscapes between low and high tide, the 25,000 species of seaweed also offer excellent nutritional potential. The 850 species found in France are all edible — though some taste better than others. Since February 2014, the French government has authorized 24 varieties for human consumption.

Seaweed types include blue (the oldest kind), brown, red, and green. In actual fact, they are all green under their colored pigments because they all contain chlorophyll. Dip a piece of brown or red seaweed into boiling water and you'll see. All depend on photosynthesis to live. Green seaweed slowly colonized dry land by diversifying and

## Tips for harvesting seaweed to eat

The best time to collect seaweed is in the spring: like all plants, the youngest shoots are the most tender and delicious. Visit the lowest point of the foreshore during low tide (especially during periods of high tidal coefficients)[10] to access varieties that are otherwise inaccessible. The farther away from the shore you go, the lower the risk of pollution in the seaweed. Only harvest seaweed that is attached to rocks. Never eat seaweed strewn on the beach: it is likely dead.

Don't rip out seaweed when you collect it! Using a knife or scissors, cut the stem above the base so that it has a chance to regrow. And, contrary to the popular saying, leave every stone unturned: moving stones will cause the plants and animals that live there (sunny side, shady side) to be disturbed for several years.

Since common or commercial names for seaweed vary by region, using the unambiguous Latin names is recommended. You will be able to tell them apart fairly quickly!

When removed from the water, seaweed degrades rapidly. Only collect what you can consume within 24 hours; after this point, it is too late. French law permits individuals to harvest as much seaweed as they can fit in one hand. There is no point in filling baskets that you will have to throw out after two days.

branching into mosses, lichens, and later all the terrestrial plants we are familiar with, including trees!

## THE NUTRITIONAL PROPERTIES OF SEAWEED

In countries such as Japan, seaweed is a part of the culinary tradition and is enjoyed raw or cooked. Its use as a vegetable is a recent phenomenon in the West, though different kinds of seaweed have long been used as additives in the agri-food industry (gelling agents, stabilizers, and thickeners). In coastal parts of France, some seaweeds were also historically used for livestock feed.

Seaweed is high in protein, omega-3s, vitamins, trace elements, antioxidants, and fibers. It is an excellent substitute for animal milk in terms of calcium content. Different forms of the stuff can be found in organic stores or in the specialty aisle: dehydrated, or canned soups and sauces, or as seaweed pasta.

If you are fortunate enough to live near the ocean, there is nothing easier than collecting seaweed while you're out for a stroll on the rocks.

## HOW DO YOU PRESERVE SEAWEED?

If eaten fresh, seaweed must be prepared immediately after harvesting. Some kinds of seaweed can be preserved: the plant matter can be sun-dried on fishing line or on a drying rack (or, in a pinch, in an oven at a very low temperature on

---

## AMAZING DATA
## Facts about seaweed...

- 90 percent of French seaweed is produced in Brittany.
- France's edible seaweed sector has been active in France only for about three decades.
- About 1,000 tonnes per year are consumed in France.
- There are about thirty companies operating in the sector, supplying the food, cosmetics, and pharmaceutical industries.
- About 3,000 hectares of coast in Brittany are available for growing macroalgae.

- Each year, France produces 70,000 tonnes of seaweed, only 50 tonnes of which is cultivated; the rest is wild.
- France imports 140,000 tonnes of algae every year.
- Total world production of seaweed is 15 million tonnes (mostly in Asia), three-quarters of which is meant for human consumption.
- China is the world's leading seaweed producer with 10 million tonnes per year.
- Japan consumes 2 million tonnes of edible seaweed per year.

parchment paper to prevent it from sticking) and then flaked (*Porphyra, Palmaria palmata, Ulva*).

Some kinds of seaweed can be frozen by rolling them into small freezer bags (*Palmaria palmata, Himanthalia*). They can be thawed under cold water and cooked immediately. They can also be lightly salted and stored in the crisper.

Only the delicious *Laurencia pinnatifida*, with its light peppery taste, cannot be preserved. It can be eaten in moderate quantities "on the rocks" (i.e., immediately after harvesting) or within the day. This makes it an excellent appetizer!

## WILD OR FARMED?

France's seaweed sector is developing rapidly, especially in Brittany. The plants are either harvested from the ocean or grown in marine farms. Aqua B Marinoë in Lesconil, France, produces 300 tonnes of kelp per year, with processing done on site. Dried kelp reduces to one-seventh the original volume. The company, which has been developing steadily since it launched in 1992, offers a wide variety of delicious seaweed-based products: fresh in salads; dehydrated in flakes, tartares, tapas, and pasta.

On the farmed side, there are 1,000 hectares of seabed that could potentially be turned over to seaweed farming in Brittany. Existing shellfish farmers (Brittany boasts 700) — especially oyster farmers — are well poised for this activity: they already have the marine "land" base (which is hard to access) and ocean-ready equipment. Peak season is winter for oysters and summer for seaweed, meaning the two activities could pair well. The first company, Algolesko, launched in 2013 on the tip of Brittany growing *Saccharina latissima*, a long form of sweet kelp (it grows 2 to 7 meters in length). The company plans to eventually farm 200 hectares and produce about 6,000 tonnes per year to supply national and international markets (including China, Russia, the United States, etc.). Opportunities exist not only in food but also in cosmetics and pharmaceuticals, which would create jobs. We just need to make sure seaweed farming does not fall into the trap of monocultured megafarms.

## THE DIFFERENT GROUPS OF SEAWEED

Here we describe the different kinds of seaweed as they appear, from the bottom to the top of the foreshore (the portion of the shore that is uncovered during low tide).

### Red seaweed

- **Porphyra tenera** (or nori): high in protein, eaten in sushi or maki roll or flaked.
- Palmaria palmata (or dulse): eaten dried, flaked, or in chips; also used for animal feed.
- **Chondrus crispus** (or Irish moss): used as a gelling agent, and as a setting agent in jams, jellies, and flans; must be exposed to sun and rain until it turns white to neutralize the traces of arsenic it naturally contains.
- **Laurencia pinnatifida** (or pepper dulse): has a slight peppery taste and is delicious raw, served as an appetizer.

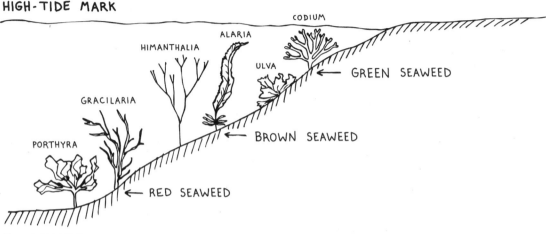

*Foreshore cross section.*

– ***Gracilaria verrucosa:*** can be extracted to produce the plant-based gelling agent agar-agar.

*Brown seaweed*

– ***Saccorhiza polyschides*** (or furbellow), ***Undaria pinnatifida*** (or wakame), ***Himanthalia elongata*** (or sea spaghetti): these keep well in the freezer uncooked and can be enjoyed as a vegetable or appetizer.
– ***Saccharina latissima*** (or sugar kelp): farmed in Brittany.
– ***Laminaria digitata*** (or oarweed)
– ***Alaria esculenta*** (or badderlocks)

This seaweed of the kelp family makes a good replacement for aluminum foil! You can wrap meat or fish in it before cooking it in the oven. The seaweed tenderizes the meat and makes it cook faster; it can also be used for legumes and potatoes. It also reduces the acidity of tomato in sauces.

*Green seaweed*

– ***Ulva lactuca*** (or sea lettuce): proliferates in water containing too much nitrogen; can be eaten dried, flaked, or *en papillote* — as a wrap for baking.
– ***Ulva intestinalis*** (or gutweed): shaped like small tubes; high in calcium; eaten flaked or in sushi.
– ***Codium:*** rare; mostly used in cosmetics.

**SOME EASY RECIPES TO TRY AT HOME**

Even if you don't live near the ocean, you will find most of these seaweeds in organic stores either dehydrated, canned, or fresh in the produce aisle.

### Seaweed salt

Sun-dry *Palmaria palmata, Porphyra, Ulva lactuca,* or enteromorphs harvested in spring. Grind into a powder and mix with sea salt. The resulting colored mix is beautiful. An easy way to eat seaweed often and in small doses.

### Seaweed butter

Combine freshly harvested and finely chopped *Laurencia, Porphyra, Ulva,* and/or *Palmaria palmata* with soft (room-temperature) butter. Mix with a fork. Serve on toast as an appetizer or simply use it to flavor potatoes, pasta, or green beans. Add chopped garlic if desired.

### Seaweed mayonnaise

Immediately before serving, combine dried seaweed and mayonnaise. Goes very nicely with crustaceans. The seaweed can be replaced with sea fennel gathered at the upper foreshore.

### Seaweed toasted seeds

Combine seeds of carrot, celery, poppy, squash/pumpkin, sunflower, and sesame. Toast in a skillet. Add seaweed flakes (see "Seaweed salt" above).

### Seaweed appetizers

Dry freshly harvested *Himanthalia elongata.* Fry in a pan with a little oil, stirring constantly. The seaweed will turn green, then brown, then black. Remove from heat and season with tamari and sesame. Cut with scissors and serve as an appetizer.

### Ocean potatoes

Cook organic potatoes in their skin either by steaming or, better yet, in a fish soup or a crab court bouillon. Let cool to room temperature, coat with oil, and wrap in *Porphyra.* Roast in oven. Serve piping hot. Eat all parts. A lovely treat.

## OCEAN POTATOES

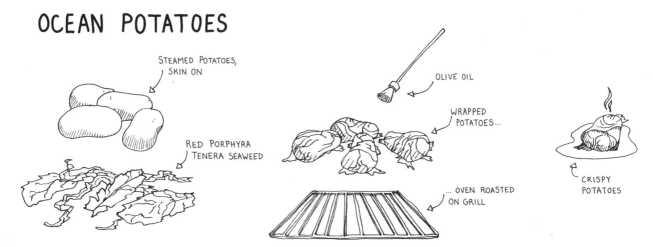

STEAMED POTATOES, SKIN ON

RED PORPHYRA TENERA SEAWEED

OLIVE OIL

WRAPPED POTATOES...

... OVEN ROASTED ON GRILL

CRISPY POTATOES

### Surf and turf salad

Cook and shell a crab or spider crab. Combine with the following ingredients, finely chopped: a green cabbage, a few radishes, fennel (stalks and fronds), onion, aromatic herbs, sea fennel, *Laurencia* and other fresh seaweed, the juice and zest of a lemon, olive oil, and the crab's eggs. Serve with seaweed mayonnaise.

### Seafood platter

To impress your guests, present your seafood on a bed of wrack that has been boiled and (of course) cooled. Guaranteed to amaze!

### Elderberry flan

(can also be made with orange, cardamom, verbena, rosé wine, or champagne)

Dilute 4 to 5 grams of agar-agar in one liter of milk and bring to a boil. Add sugar, spices,

flavors, and crème fraîche to taste. Chill and serve.

**TO FIND OUT MORE IN THE KITCHEN:**
- Danièle Mischlich (ed.), *Savez-vous goûter... les algues?* (Rennes, France, Presses de l'EHESP, 2016).

**SEAWEED IS GOOD FOR THE GARDEN, TOO**

While it is officially unadvisable for people to eat seaweed strewn on the beach after storms (it's dead), this wreckage will do wonders in your garden if you are lucky enough to live near the ocean. Kelp in particular contributes mineral salts that stimulate the soil life. Coastal gardeners know this and spread wheelbarrows full of the stuff in the fall. Be sure to collect it after a good rain so it won't be too salty!

**INSPIRING EXAMPLE**

# Seaweed harvest and feast on France's Point of Finistère

The Breton association Cap vers la nature hosts seaweed discovery weekends on Île de Sein and on Île-Molène in France's Finistère region. Foodies flock to these events in ever greater numbers to learn how to identify, cook, and enjoy seaweed. All aboard for a completely exotic weekend!

Simone Grass is an activist. Through Cap vers la nature, she devotes her energy to spreading the word about the ecological and nutritional treasures of plankton and seaweed on the coast of Brittany. Her partner, Dany Caderon, is a culinary artist. The excursion schedule is closely tied to the rhythms of the almanac: in the spring to get the seaweed shoots while they are as young as possible; at low tide with a high tidal coefficient to get at otherwise inaccessible seaweed.

Ankle-deep in the ocean, Simone reads the wonders of the microcosm contained within this small pool like a book. It's a bustling agglomeration of life rare in beauty: shellfish, larvae, shoots of seaweed of every color. Her practised eye catches details many would miss. The specialist talks about the symbiosis between this alga and that shellfish. She explains how to harvest the precious marine plants (using scissors) to avoid destroying the base and to allow them to grow back. One misstep (turning a rock without replacing it) and this miniature world can be destroyed.

Suddenly, someone comes across a clump of *Laurencia pinnatifida*. The tasting centers around this small red seaweed with a crunchy texture and strong flavor. Our guide warns the foodies: "Careful: if you're not used to eating wild plants, start slowly! If you don't, you may regret it [and develop a stomach ache]."

Simone speaks lovingly of plankton, which regulates the climate through photosynthesis, capturing $CO_2$ from the atmosphere and producing oxygen. She explains how, from one year to the next, fields of seaweed develop according to how warm or sunny it is. Before we leave the rocks, we taste the sea fennel, a plant from the upper foreshore, which is very flavorful and high in vitamin C — not to mention capable of transforming a whole salad.

Back on land, we spread our harvest out on a table and sort our finds by family: red, brown, and green seaweed. Captivated, we listen to our expert tell the story of how the world began, with the first plants appearing in the ocean 3.5 billion years ago, and how the forests were born thanks to the green algae that colonized dry land. Eventually we manage to wrap our heads around the long Latin names she uses!

Before long, Dany takes over. In the blink of an eye, she scans the spread of resources and sends for the fish that has been set aside for our group by one of the island's fishers. And so begin the preparations. Hours of chopping, skinning, massaging, grinding, browning, baking, and combining the fruits of the land and sea. Everyone pitches in: some hang the seaweed to dry on a line as others prepare the appetizers (a chance to be the first to taste the spreads), get the fish soup started, jot down notes, and snap photos.

Hours later, the feast is finally ready. The menu came right out of the sea (and Dany's unbridled creativity), out of our baskets, and out of the nets of the island fishers who join us in celebration. Our beachside strolls will never be the same again.

**TO FIND OUT MORE:** Cap vers la nature, cap-vers-la-nature.org

# Chapter 20

# Food from Insects

THESE DAYS, any self-respecting gourmet food fair will have a booth of insects for guests to try: they are a magnet for the curious and the brave (and their cameras). At trendy restaurants in the capitals of Europe and America, insect menus are all the rage: they may be grilled or griddled, roasted or sautéed, dehydrated or powdered, tex-mex or dusted with fleur de sel, served as an appetizer, pickled, or flambéed in rum. This ingredient, which is perplexing (to say the least) to contemporary Westerners, has nevertheless been familiar to Western tongues since Antiquity, especially in the Mediterranean Basin. Four centuries before the Common Era, Aristotle made reference to the Greeks' taste for cicada larvae and grilled grasshoppers. The Romans dined on beetle larvae (grubs). Later, the gospel reports that in the desert, the ascetic John the Baptist ate "locusts and wild honey." In the 18th century, certain insects were believed to have medicinal properties. In the industrial era, dried and powdered insects have made their way to the food supplement aisle — discretely, in the form of bars, drinks, and protein powders, or even more discretely in the form of additives. There's not even a chance to lose your appetite!

## A BIODIVERSITY BONANZA

Insects make up 80 percent of known animal species. They were the first to colonize dry land. Between 1,000 and 1,500 species of bugs — adult insects, larvae, and edible worms — make regular appearances in the meals of two billion of the Earth's inhabitants, mainly in Africa and Asia: ants, water bugs, locusts, crickets, termites, grasshoppers, caterpillars, silkworms, maggots, etc. Insects are prepared differently depending on the region and the tradition in question: they may be served alone or paired with other foods, alive, plain or fried, boiled, candied, or macerated in alcohol, with or without sauce, as a condiment, as an appetizer, as a main dish, or as a dessert.

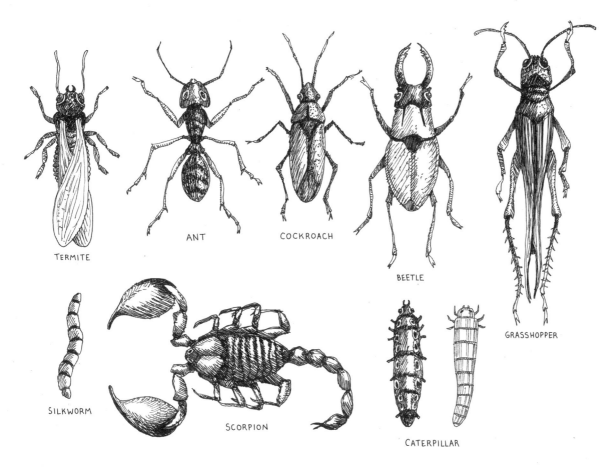

TERMITE

ANT

COCKROACH

BEETLE

GRASSHOPPER

SILKWORM

SCORPION

CATERPILLAR

## SMALL CREATURES, BIG NUTRITION

The immense biodiversity of insects represents a serious protein source for the times that are coming our way! Edible bugs have many nutritional advantages — to say nothing of the molecules that can be extracted for medical purposes. The United Nations recommends including them in animal feed as an interim measure until the culture shock dies down and insectivory (also known as entomophagy) becomes culturally acceptable in countries where people are not yet accustomed to them.

Edible insects are very high in protein: on average, they can be over 50 percent protein by dry weight. These proteins are present regardless of the insects' age, season of capture, and diet. The functional peptides in edible insects build muscle (beneficial for undernourished people and athletes), strengthen the immune system, and fight hypertension, type II diabetes, and osteoporosis.

Larvae and maggots, which feast upon spring leaves, are rich in omega-3s, as are snails, which are bigtime plant eaters. The shells of locusts, crickets, and grasshoppers, which are rich in calcium and magnesium, have antirheumatic, antimicrobial, and antioxidant properties. Like dietary fiber, the shell acts as a probiotic, regulating the digestive flora and the absorption of fat, making it a slimming agent! Finally, the vitamins and trace elements these invertebrates contain give them antioxidant and immune-stimulating properties.

Because insects are very distant cousins of humans on the evolutionary tree, they do not act as disease vectors for humans, unlike traditional livestock species in certain epidemics (mad cow disease, avian influenza). Their nutritional value makes them a viable poultry feed alternative, being both cheaper and more environmentally friendly than grains.

### HIGH PROTEIN CONTENT, LOW ENVIRONMENTAL IMPACT

Bruno Parmentier[1], an economist specializing in food, calculates that insects are the factor that will supply the protein we will need to feed the 9 billion humans expected by the year 2050. Parmentier points out that it takes 10 kilograms of plants to produce one kilogram of beef, while the same 10 kilograms of plants can yield 9 kilograms of insects. Warm-blooded animals such as beef cattle eat primarily to maintain their body heat, while cold-blooded animals are much more efficient, using small amounts of food to manufacture much more protein.

Insect harvesting as traditionally practiced in Southern countries provides precious nutrition and a potential means of subsistence for the poorest people (through trade). It can also help regulate invasive pest species (e.g., grasshoppers) and protect farms.

Edible insect farms are just beginning to emerge in northern countries. In Frelighsburg, Quebec, the Co-Entreprise Paysanne d'Armandie, has launched production.[2] Insect farming carries many environmental and economic benefits. Because so little feed is required, its yield is 70 times higher than that of cattle and other animals. It requires little in the way of investment, space, water, energy, or work. The insects are swift to reproduce, making them a profitable product that can even be grown in cities — precisely where food demand is growing. Finally, insect farming avoids the risk of removing too many resources from the natural environment.

**PERMACULTURE PRINCIPLE 6:**
Produce no waste

**TO FIND OUT MORE ABOUT INSECT FARMING:**
- Montreal Insectarium, espacepourlavie.ca.
- "Comment faire son élevage d'insectes comestibles?", *Des insectes dans l'assiette*, restaurantdinsectes.fr/elevagesinsectes.php.

So, are you ready to become an insectivore? As with anything new, it takes a little time to get used to the idea. Circumstances may require this of us regardless. We already eat other arthropods in the form of crabs and shrimp! It's all in how you look at it — and in the presentation!

## Protein from city streetlamps

Claire Lemarchand, a French designer, has come up with urban devices for raising insects in the city. The "urban microlivestock" model provides a local food product, creates jobs, and beautifies the lives of urbanites. Crickets can be raised in a kind of streetlamp located near markets, where they can eat fruit and vegetable scraps. When night falls, the LED lights switch on as the urban space pleasantly fills with cricket calls. In this model, a farmer is responsible for caring for and selling the insects. Mealworms can be raised in adjacent offices, fed with paper (made of cellulose and grain bran) discarded by the employees. By shredding their paper in an *ad hoc* digester, they would help feed animals, recycle waste, and supply the company restaurant. Willing partners are all that's needed! Until that time, Lemarchand thinks the proposal stands as "a tool for dialogue and awareness, as well as a call for people to act." Let's hope that her project also motivates citizens to request this type of planning from their politicians and employers!

Contact: claire.lemarchand@citedudesign.com

## Simple and original recipes for an insectivore meal

### Cricket appetizers
Spread fromage blanc mixed with crushed garlic and herbs on cucumber slices. Top with a black olive, a small piece of tomato, a basil leaf, and a few dehydrated crickets. Serve chilled.

### Main course: insect pizza
On a pizza crust, spread tomato sauce, button mushrooms (thinly sliced), 10 grams of dehydrated crickets, a few black olives, and grated gruyère cheese. Bake in a hot oven for 15 minutes.

### Dessert: grasshopper apple crisp in verrines
Prepare apple crisp filling and topping separately, adding 10 grams of dehydrated and ground grasshoppers to the topping. Bake in oven for 8 minutes. Spoon apples and salt caramel into the verrines (a verrine is a small glass) and add topping. Set aside one whole grasshopper per verrine for garnish!

Source: Recipes inspired by *Mangeons des insectes*, mangeons-des-insectes.com/recettes.

# I farm insects in my living room

Chanel lives in a small Canadian village. When she first sampled insects, the young woman enjoyed the taste so much that she decided to raise some herself — mainly for pleasure, but also for protein. She gave us a peek at her insectivorous world.

"Fabulous! Better than good! It's a bit like the skin of a roast chicken or really crunchy chips." This is how Chanel describes her delight in eating insects. It all began in 1995, when she was a student volunteer for the "Croque-Insectes" event at the Montreal Insectarium. Her first taste of chocolate-covered scorpion, a Thai specialty, has been with her ever since.

Failing to find any insects for sale in stores, the permaculturist knew that the only solution would be to start her own farm, which she did in May 2013. She ordered mealworms intended for animal feed off the Internet. She bought two thousand mealworms (technically a beetle), or 200 grams, for $20 Canadian. "I am poor; I couldn't do more than that." Having had "excellent training in major restaurants," Chanel had no doubts about her tastes, and no fear about her ability to prepare delicious dishes from insects! When she heard from the WHO that insects were the protein of the future, her decision was cemented.

Why mealworms rather than crickets or grasshoppers? "Worms don't jump!" explains the young woman with a laugh. "They don't fly or climb either. They are the easiest insects to raise." The worm bins are stored in a bakery rack in her living room, which doesn't take up much space. What do they eat? Bran, oatmeal, and a few vegetable peels for hydration (the larvae don't drink). One kilogram of food gives her one kilogram of insects. They can live very crowded together in small spaces (200,000 individuals per bin) and produce no odor or waste. All pros, no cons. The only wrinkle in Chanel's entomological venture is the creatures' relatively long life cycle. At room temperature, it takes six months for one generation to grow and reproduce, a period that could be shortened to three months if the temperature were a few degrees higher. Still, Chanel's stock increased from 200 grams to 6 kilograms in a year and a half.

While waiting for her stock to reach a sustainable threshold (i.e., equal amounts harvested and regenerated), Chanel harvests only a few individuals for her family and friends to taste. Her partner is now a fan, as are her nine-year-old son and his friends. Chanel is already dreaming about the insect quiches, burgers, chilis, and sausages she will be soon be able to cook up. She is surprised that no one can tell her when she will be able to harvest enough larvae each week to feed her family. "Even the breeder at the Montreal Insectarium doesn't know," she chuckles.

Once she has gained enough experience with mealworms, Chanel plans to diversify her production.

She is considering crickets (which have a six-week cycle), walking sticks, and locusts. Why not kickstart the whole industry? "The Montreal Botanical Garden is considering opening a restaurant where insects will be served. They'll need to find suppliers," the young woman suggests. Yes indeed, insectivory is on the upswing in the West!

## THE OMNIVORE'S FUTURE?

Humans are constitutionally omnivorous. Nature offers a wide variety of things to eat. It follows that we should appreciate this diversity and marshal our inventiveness to develop production methods geared towards today's issues.

Whether on city streets, suburban lawns, village squares, or building rooftops, we should be using the available surfaces to produce high-quality local food. We should consider establishing microfarms as described by Perrine and Charles Hervé-Gruyer in their book *Permaculture*.[3] "It is possible to produce the equivalent of 12 weekly fruit and vegetable baskets year-round on two hundred square meters (approx. 2000 sq.ft.) if the land is worked properly," the authors assert. And they know what they're talking about: on their farm in Bec Hellouin, they produce 60 to 80 baskets on 1,000 square meters (¼ acre). These microfarms can combine berries, medicinal plants, mushrooms, small animals, apiculture, and aquaculture. "The smaller the farm, the more productive it is," the couple insists. This view is shared by the Quebec market gardener Jean-Martin Fortier, author of *The Market Gardener: A Successful Grower's Handbook for Small-Scale Organic Farming*:[4] in it, he shows how to provide food for 200 families on one hectare.

In the countryside, we should be fostering plant and animal biodiversity on many human-scale operations and restoring soil. Perrine and Charles Hervé-Gruyer's concept of "farm systems in solidarity" provides inspiration here too: the value of these innovative prototypes — treasure troves of agricultural knowledge and productive manual techniques — is clear. It's all about "bringing a large number of complementary farming activities together on one piece of land," to feed local populations. Land already grown in monoculture (grain crops, for example) could be *renatured* through massive tree plantations and converted to polyculture. These models would feature biodiversity reserves, an edible forest, grain production, a beef farm, aquaculture, and as many microfarms as needed. Such an organizational structure would allow for all kinds of associated activities to develop: artisanship, processing and sales, energy production, green tourism, education, etc. The outcome would be positive, not just ecologically but also economically and socially.

In city and country, let's dare to eat insects, one of the most environmentally friendly proteins in existence. Let's learn how to produce plankton at home. In coastal areas, let's include seaweed in our wild foraging. No matter what we do, it is urgent that we bring production spaces and consumption spaces closer together and overcome our addiction to oil. By increasing food sovereignty in local areas, these practices can help create social ties and jobs.

## Novel foods and nanoparticles: the unknown

In the last few years, so-called "novel foods" have begun appearing on the market. Novel foods are those that were not recognized as part of the human diet in a given region before a given date. Health authorities assess the risks and benefits of such innovations and decide whether or not to authorize them for sale in their jurisdictions. In Europe, a novel food is considered a food or ingredient not recognized as such before May 15, 1997. Generally speaking, these are either the products of scientific and technological research or traditional foods from other countries. Algae, insects, and certain plants fall under this category.

The category also includes "nanofoods," high-tech products that use nanoparticles (particles on the order of one millionth of a millimeter in size) to "improve" the color, taste, consistency, and shelf life of food. Nanoemulsions, nanocapsules, and nanosensors: there are some 300 nanoingredients and nanoadditives already on the market. The big agri-food companies (Nestlé, Kraft, Heinz, and Unilever) take advantage of legal loopholes to avoid displaying the presence of these nanoingredients on food labels. These particles are small enough to cross the cell membrane. Their toxicity and long-term effects are not understood. This is experimental territory that lies even beyond the reach of most scientists. Nanotechnologies are also used upstream of food in agriculture (nanochips, nanosensors for detecting diseases, nanopesticides, and nanovaccines) and downstream of food in packaging. What of their effects on health and the environment? They are certainly a far cry from the models of nature and simple solutions. In the name of the precautionary principle, we'd rather have the daily special: a plate of grilled grasshoppers. It's a safer choice.

# Food pioneers

**Hildegard von Bingen,** German mystic (1098–1179): "Spelt … makes man's spirit cheerful and serene."

This nun's teaching on the "total man" (total in his physical, mental, and spiritual dimensions) were confirmed over eight centuries later by modern science (and by the Catholic Church, which declared her Doctor of the Church in 2012). When it comes to food, von Bingen highlighted the connection between our diet and our inner state. The Benedictine abbess recommended certain foods and recipes which "give joy and clarity to the spirit." These happen to be alkaline foods, which balance the pH in our bodies. This is the case with spelt, a grain that contains all the essential amino acids and is rich in calcium, phosphorus, and magnesium. Von Bingen wrote that the grain was "warming and purifying for man" (wheat, which is lower in nutritional value, has gradually supplanted this ancient grain). Fennel, chestnuts, almonds, and galangal are also among these precious "foods of joy." Von Bingen also recommended using medicinal plants and a "day of unloading" (fasting or eating lightly) once a week.

**TO FIND OUT MORE:**
- Jany Fournier-Rosset, *Les "recettes de la joie" avec sainte Hildegarde* (Saint-Cénéré, France, Pierre Téqui, 2005).
- Gottfried Hertzka and Wighard Strehlow, *À la table de sainte Hildegarde* (Montsûrs, France, Résiac, 2011).
- Wighard Strehlow, *L'art de guérir par l'alimentation selon Hildegarde de Bingen: Recettes, traitements et regimes* (Paris, François-Xavier de Guibert, 2007).

**Deepika Kundaji,** seed saver from Tamil Nadu, India: "Family seeds are the key to food autonomy."

The primary vocation of the "Universal Garden," located near Auroville in southern India, is to preserve and disseminate a hundred traditional Indian seed varieties of garden plants. The objective is that anyone who so desires can take back control over their own food production, no matter the quality of their land, even if they have no money. Kundaji's adventure began some two decades ago at Pebble Garden, on three hectares of land that had been completely sterilized by uncontrolled deforestation. She and her partner Bernard Declerq, a Belgian agricultural engineer, patiently restored the soil — with no imported organic material, external labor, or mechanization. Today, a forest of native species and a 2,000-square-meter garden have replaced the desert that was once red with laterite! And Kundaji devotes her energy to promoting the development of family seed banks, even in Western countries.

**TO FIND OUT MORE:**
Adeny, "Les leçons de Deepika," *Défendre l'environnement*, July 20, 2013, adeny.overblog.com/les-leçons-de-deepika-1.

**Renée Frappier,** Quebec nutritionist: "Choose the foods you want to look like!"

Dealing in awareness, education, and prevention, Frappier was originally a chemistry professor and later a vegetarian nutrition trainer before co-founding the Quebec-based association Healthy Organic Eating and spearheading the Healthy Eating and Green Living expo. Frappier has devoted over four decades of her life to food education. A thinker who is both scientifically minded and intuitive, she has come up with a multitude of simple and concrete solutions that marry food, pleasure, health, and the environment. "It's important to learn how to choose foods that look like us or that we would like to look like," she explains. "The objective is to gradually adopt a diet that is healthful, vegetarian, organic, local, seasonal, and ethical!" This ardent defender of fruits and vegetables recommends eating raw foods as much as possible. Her website brims with original how-to information for better cooking, gardening, and understanding. The ideas are proposed by an array of specialists who work with her.

**TO FIND OUT MORE:**
- Healthy Organic Eating association, mangersantebio.org.
- Renée Frappier, *Le guide de l'alimentation saine et naturelle* (Montreal, Asclépiade, 2 volumes, 1987–1990).

## Chapter 21

# A Design to Feed Your Family

Now that you appreciate the complexity of the links between our lifestyles and the health of the planet, you will no doubt be even more motivated to make the first of your changes. Food is one of the prime areas for experimentation. We propose that you create a healthy and balanced food design for yourself, your family, and/or your group.

**PERMACULTURE PRINCIPLE 1:**
Observe and interact

Humans have a daily need for a variety of food that they can produce on site, forage, harvest, glean, hunt, fish, barter, or purchase. They also need quality water. No single way of eating is right for everyone. It's up to each person to

use observation and reflection to create the diet that's appropriate for them, according to their geographic situation, age, activities, surroundings, etc. And don't forget to listen to the voice of your intuition — the right brain! An appropriate diet is one that brings joy and health.

**GOOD QUESTIONS TO ASK YOURSELF**

It helps to refer to the detailed description of the nine design steps.

**❶ Observe**

– What types of foods do I consume most often?
– Which foods do me the most good?
– Where do the products I eat most often come from?
– Do I buy processed foods or prepare them myself?
– Where does the water I drink come from?
– Do I produce some of my food myself?
– How much time do I spend producing or preparing my food?
– Do I enjoy preparing and eating my own meals?
– What motivates me to eat? Is it to feed myself, to socialize, to find pleasure, to fill emotions, to fill a void, or to feed a habit?
– Do I have food reserves on hand? What kind? For how long?
– If my health requires a particular diet, how do I handle this? Am I connected with people in the same situation? Do I get enjoyment out of my meals? Do I understand the properties of the foods I can and cannot eat?

**❷ Identify the border effect**

– Do I most often eat alone or with others?
– Do I eat at home or outside my home?
– What role do my culture, my education, my religion, and my health play in my food choices?
– Who are the organic fruit, vegetable, and meat producers located near me? What are the alternative distribution circuits, farmers' markets, organic restaurants, etc.?
– Who could I join forces with to buy local and organic foods?
– How could I arrange food bartering among my neighbors (trading leeks for apples, for example)?

**❸ Determine resources and needs**

– How much of my budget can I spend on food?
– What foods (including herbs) can I grow at home?
– What are my caloric needs (depending on my activity level)?

**❹ Evaluate and sort the data**

Link my needs to the available resources:

– Can I produce some of my food?
– Which of my current food habits align with permaculture principles? Which of them are out of alignment? What changes would be beneficial?

– In the event of a disruption in the energy supply, which products — of the ones I use regularly — are likely to become unavailable? In North America or northern Europe, this may include tea, coffee, chocolate, olive oil, oranges, bananas, lemons, etc.

### 5 Consider dietary niches

If you engage in particular food practices, try to clarify your motivations: are you vegetarian because you care about animals, because you don't enjoy meat, or because you have trouble digesting it? Take an honest look and see whether your diet suits you energetically and whether it satisfies you, especially philosophically or ideologically. In any case, your food design is something you tailor to your needs and decisions. No one will force you to change.

### 6 Dream and brainstorm *(to be done with family and friends)*

What would my ideal diet be? Where would it come from? Where, how, and by whom would it be produced, distributed, and cooked? Would I produce some of my herbs, fruits, vegetables, or eggs myself? How would I preserve these foods?

### 7 Conceive the design

Determine any possible relationships you could form with local producers and distributors, neighbors who garden, friends, and family members. These allies are your team. See what solutions you can implement where you live (e.g., in a garden, on a balcony), including for water. Don't try to change everything at once! Give yourself time to make your transition a gentle one.

### 8 Install and implement the design in space and time

Establish a calendar of actions with concrete steps for each season. Account for your needs, your tastes, your suppliers, and potential allies and limitations. Don't eliminate any food you like unless you replace it with something that fully suits you. The main ingredient in health is joy!

### 9 Maintain the sustainability of the system

Verify that the system you have created is coherent (re-read passages from this chapter as needed). Can it function sustainably? Does your garden provide a baseline amount of vegetables, fruits, and medicinal plants? Are your suppliers located close to your home? Do you like cooking with local and seasonal products? Does your diet give you satisfaction in terms of nutrition and sharing with your friends and family? All these conditions must be met if good resolutions are to last!

**PERMACULTURE PRINCIPLE 9:** Use small and slow solutions

**KEY TO SUCCESS:** Understand that the best time to start your transition, including your dietary one, is now! What are you waiting for?

**Conclusion**

# Becoming Artisans of Change

NOW THAT YOU HAVE READ THIS BOOK, you are ready to become an artisan of change. You will join the multitudes of anonymous citizens everywhere who are quietly helping to build the world of tomorrow: a world we all dream of, with more beauty, fairness, and community than ever before.

Armed with the tools proposed in this book, you'll be able to chart your personal path of transition and support those around you — your family, association, movement, neighborhood, or village — in their own transition. Working in their own way and at their own speed and motivated by their own needs and desires, each person will develop their life design and project designs, determine a strategy, and build an action plan to attain their objectives.

Beginners will find motivation: why is it necessary to undertake all these changes? Where do you begin? Those already engaged in the adventure will find reasons to augment their practices and expand them to other fields. But, of course, the human permaculture approach is beneficial in all of life's dimensions: it's there in how we relate to one another, to ourselves, to our inner nature; it's there in how we grow food, work, share, live, travel, and dress. This book offers pathways to lessening the planetary impact of all our activities.

Wherever you are on the path, you can take one step further:

1 Verify that you are indeed in your "niche." If not, make the effort to discover what it is.

2 Train yourself to activate the right hemisphere of your brain. Its agility is precious when it comes to developing your intuition and paying conscious attention to the here and now.

3 Remember to frame your life design within a project that is larger than yourself, collective in nature, and of benefit to the common good.

4 Lean on your team and increase the number of border effects.

5 Celebrate your small victories! Be positive and patient. The progress you make will stimulate those around you and vice-versa!

Soon you'll be able to retry the tests we suggested at the start of this book to see how far you've come, and to encourage yourself to keep going. Your personal ecological footprint will probably have improved; bravo, keep up the good work! If not, reread Part 1, The Keys to Human Permaculture! Also verify that your team's footprint is also improving, without wearing anyone out! It is up to you to delicately and subtly create the conditions for those around you to make progress.

**Afterword**

# Next Steps in Human Permaculture

SUCCESSFULLY PRACTISING PERMACULTURE opens up all kinds of pathways to making changes and stimulating creativity. That's a good thing! Perhaps the approach has won you over and you have decided to commit to your personal transition. Perhaps you want to learn more about permaculture. If so, you'll want to choose a quality training environment. Be advised that some people claim to be permaculturists, designers, or teachers after taking just a few days of training and tossing some mulch over a garden bed — that's nowhere near enough! Clearly, there can be no substitute for years of research and practice. More than a diploma, what makes a good teacher is concrete life experience, especially in permaculture.

However you decide to learn, pay close attention to your potential teacher's career trajectory and years of practice. Where were they trained? What concrete projects have they completed by applying the permaculture principles? Over what period? What have the outcomes been? In what networks are they recognized?

## THE HERITAGE OF ANGLOPHONE PERMACULTURISTS

The first permaculture training in the Francophone world took place some thirty years ago.[i] In France, Spanish farmer Emilia Hazelip was the first to organize intensive 72-hour training courses by inviting Anglophone teachers (American, Australian, English) who communicated through simultaneous interpretation. These included Sego Jackson, director of the Permaculture Institute of North America, in 1985, and Lea Harrison, an Australian who learned directly from Bill Mollison, in 1986. Marc Bonfils of France delivered the course in 1987.

Since that time, more training courses have become available in France. Living on their farm in Aude (in southern France), Andrew and Jessie Darlington, who provided the interpretation for the first Anglophone teachers, have become important figures. The first permaculture festivals, which began in 2009, inspired other Francophone teachers such as Steve Page (who no longer practises), Steve Read, and Bernard Alonso, co-author of this book. In 2010, the Australian Robin Francis delivered her first course in France (with simultaneous interpretation by the Darlingtons). She returns from time to time to deliver "social permaculture" training.

## PERMACULTURE DESIGN COURSES

Permaculture design courses (PDCs) are inevitably the first port of call for training in the field. These are organized into 72-hour modules that cover 14 topics involved in achieving good design. Once you have completed a PDC course and earned your Permaculture Design Certificate, you can ask an instructor — yours or someone else — to let you help deliver their training. This is one way to solidify your foundations in permaculture, to familiarize yourself with different ways of teaching and practising permaculture, to expand your network in the permaculture world — and to travel! In general, assistants are exempt from training fees, paying only for food and lodging.

After a PDC, it is a good idea to practice permaculture for two or more years (according to Bill Mollison), focusing on one or more concrete projects before advertising yourself as a professional. This allows you time to tweak your decisions ("design and re-design"), to apply permaculture in your daily life, and to refine your approach.

Next, it's time to find a coach to guide you until you become certified. This is the person who will assess whether you are ready to teach. You have the rest of your life to become a good teacher by gaining experience over years of practice!

Meanwhile, students of permaculture can organize "Introduction to Permaculture" workshops (often two days in length) with their coach's permission.

## WANT TO MAKE YOUR LIVING THROUGH PERMACULTURE?

If you are considering becoming a professional, the first thing is to determine your motivations and needs. Why do you want to become a professional? To create your own job? To pass on what you have learned (i.e., "pay it forward")? To teach the principles and practice of permaculture? To conduct or share concrete experiments for the transition? To become a "professional designer"? What part of permaculture interests you the most?

You can pursue your training in the field by seeking out experienced people to guide you in your chosen interests; the main thing is that your mentors draw inspiration from the model nature provides. You can always barter: offer them something in exchange for sharing their knowledge and experience. Later, it will be easier to validate what you've learned with trainers who are recognized in permaculture networks.

When a cohort of candidates is ready, their coaches gather to organize a public presentation, usually jointly. This is not an exam; rather, it's an opportunity to share experience, followed by a discussion allowing them to ensure that the candidate has fully understood the overall approach, namely that of design. Such events can be quite inspiring!

## TRAINING THROUGHOUT THE WORLD

Training opportunities are popping up all over the world, highlighting permaculture and its principles as ways we can support the changes our society faces.

What's the best way to choose a training opportunity? Start off on the right foot; begin with your needs and delve into topics that correspond to your niche. Don't pull yourself in all directions and rush to become a farmer unless gardening truly is part of your profile or passion. Assess your life's priorities. In general, they are the same for all of us: in this era of change, we need reassurance on how we will feed ourselves, house ourselves, and socialize.

## TRAINING ONLINE

Bernard Alonso offers online training, currently available in French and soon in English. The online courses are faster and cheaper, but of course the precious person-to-person dimension is missing. Bernard and his team are also developing a human permaculture curriculum and training people who wish to include this approach in their professional practice — in business, human resources, education, social work, career shifts, etc.

The curriculum, which will soon be available online, will also be of interest to young people struggling to find their path.

To meet the growing demand, Bernard Alonso offers three- to five-day training sessions to learn how to discover or affirm your niche and build your own "life design."

Visit www.permaculturehumaineinternation ale.org or www.internationalhumanpermacul ture.org for more information.

*Web links are notoriously unstable. Often the quickest way to find a journal article, for example, is to simply search the author's name and the article's title. That information is more stable than any one web link and the search is more tolerant of spelling and keystroke errors than entering a precise link.*

*Many links to sources for this book and to material for further study will take you to articles and websites that are mostly or only in French. Happily, we have arrived at a time when web browser translation is now able to do a respectable job of translation. So if you are doing research make computing power your friend and do not let French intimidate you!*

 **PERMACULTURE PRINCIPLE 9:**
Use small and slow solutions

# Endnotes

## Chapter 1

1. *Permaculture One: A Perennial Agriculture for Human Settlements* (London, Transworld, 1978) and *Permaculture Two: Practical Design for Town and Country in Permanent Agriculture* (Sisters Creek, Australia, Tagari, 1979).
2. *Introduction to Permaculture* (Sisters Creek, Australia, Tagari, 1991).
3. *Permaculture: Principles and Pathways Beyond Sustainability* (Holmgren Design Services, 2002).

## Chapter 4

1. Edward Teddy Goldsmith, *The Way: An Ecological World View* (London, Rider, 1992; Revised Edition, Cambridge, UK, Green Books, 1996).

## Chapter 5

1. Pope Francis, Encyclical Letter Laudato si' on Care for Our Common Home (Rome, Vatican, 2015), w2.vatican.va/content/francesco/en/encyclicals/documents/papa-francesco_20150524_enciclica-laudato-si.html.
2. biomimicry.org.

## Chapter 7

1. Rita Levi-Montalcini, *L'atout gagnant: À un âge avancé, notre cerveau garde des capacités exceptionnelles que chacun peut utiliser* (Paris, Robert Laffont, 1999).
2. Jill Bolte Taylor, *My Stroke of Insight: A Brain Scientist's Personal Journey* (New York, Penguin, 2006).

## Chapter 8

1. "Les Inuits," *L'encyclopédie polaire,* jeanlouise tienne.com/poleairship/encyclo_histoire_05.htm
2. Rob Hopkins, *The Transition Handbook: From Oil Dependency to Local Resilience* (White River Junction, Vermont, Chelsea Green, 2008).

## Chapter 10

1. Rob Hopkins, *op. cit.*, p. 166.

## Chapter 12

1. Vincent E. A. Post *et al.*, "Offshore Fresh Groundwater Reserves as a Global Phenomenon," *Nature*, no. 504, December 5, 2013, pp. 71–78.

## Chapter 14

1. "Eau et forêt, une association naturelle," French National Office of Forests, onf.fr/gestion_durable/++oid++91e/@@display_advise.html.

2. Francis Hallé, *Plaidoyer pour la forêt tropicale* (Arles, France, Actes Sud, 2014).

3. Paul Falkowski *et al.*, "The Global Carbon Cycle: A Test of Our Knowledge of Earth as a System," *Science*, vol. 290, no. 5490, October, 13, 2000.

4. scribd.com/document/126709536/RRAlogging-english-scr-pdf

5. fao.org/3/a-i3710e.pdf

6. awsassets.panda.org/downloads/lfr_chapter_5_executive_summary_final.pdf

7. Aymeric Lazarin, *Mon potager de vivaces: 60 légumes perpétuels à découvrir* (Mens, France, Terre vivante, 2016).

8. Laure Waridel, *Acheter, c'est voter: Le cas du café* (Montréal, Écosociété, 2005).

### CHAPTER 15

1. Jane Goodall, Gary McAvoy, and Gail Hudson, *Harvest for Hope: A Guide to Mindful Eating* (New York, Grand Central, 2006).

2. See Deni Ellis Béchard, *Of Bonobos and Men: A Journey to the Heart of the Congo* (Minneapolis, Milkweed Editions, 2015).

3. Équiterre, "Kilométrage alimentaire," equiterre.org/fiche/kilometrage-alimentaire.

4. Olivier De Schutter, Special Rapporteur on the right to food, The transformative potential of the right to food, March 10, 2014, srfood.org/images/stories/pdf/officialreports/20140310_finalreport_en.pdf.

5. Catherine Esnouf, Marie Russel, and Nicolas Bricas (eds.), *duALIn – Durabilité de l'alimentation face à de nouveaux enjeux: Questions à la recherche,* Inra-Cira report, France, 2011.

6. Water Footprint Network, Product Water footprint waterfootprint.org/en/water-footprint/product-water-footprint.

7. Kousmine Association of France, kousmine.fr.

### CHAPTER 16

1. French National Centre for Scientific Research, "L'eau dans l'organisme", sagascience.cnrs.fr/doseau/decouv/usages/eauOrga.html.

2. An excess of these nutrients can be detrimental.

3. Food and Agriculture Organization of the United Nations, *Le droit à une alimentation suffisante et le droit à l'eau,* fao.org/docrep/007/y4683f/y4683f0d.htm.

4. World Wildlife Fund, *L'eau de boisson: Analyses comparées de l'eau du robinet et l'eau en bouteille,* 2011.

5. Joseph Jenkins, *The Humanure Handbook,* 4th Edition (self-published, 2019).

### CHAPTER 17

1. International seminar, *Crops for the 21st Century*, Food and Agriculture Organization of the United Nations, *Cordóba, December 2012,* fao.org/news/story/en/item/166370/icode.

2. Ibid.

3. Report of the Special Rapporteur on the right to food, presented to the United Nations General Assembly under the Human Rights Council, December 20, 2010.

4. Aymeric Lazarin, *op. cit.*

5. James Clive, *Global Status of Commercialized Biotech/GM Crops: 2014,* International Service for the Acquisition of Agri-biotech Applications (ISAAA), *Brief* no. 49, 2014.

6. See especially Jennifer Cockrall-King, *Food and the City: Urban Agriculture and the New Food Revolution* (Amherst, New York, Prometheus, 2012).

7. Terres en villes, terresenvilles.org.

8. City of Montreal, "Agriculture urbaine: sondage auprès de la population de l'île de Montréal," donnees.ville.montreal.qc.ca/dataset/agriculture-urbaine-sondage.

## CHAPTER 18

1. Food and Agriculture Organization of the United Nations, *World Livestock 2011: Livestock in Food Security* (Rome, 2012), fao.org/docrep/016/i2373e/i2373e.pdf.

2. The CERNH is based in the hospital of Lorient, France.

3. The Blue-White-Heart charter was established in 2000 by a group of scientists, farmers, agrologists, doctors, and consumers. It guarantees balance between omega-3s and omega-6s. As of 2014, some 5,000 farmers and 750 products had the Blue-White-Heart label, a symbol controlled by the health authorities. Similar initiatives have been developed elsewhere, including in Switzerland (2001), Quebec (2008), and Belgium (2014).

4. See the Blue-White-Heart charter, bleu-blanc-coeur.org.

## CHAPTER 19

1. Olivier De Schutter, Interim report of the Special Rapporteur on the right to food, presented to the United Nations General Assembly, New York, August 8, 2012, srfood.org/images/stories/pdf/officialreports/20121030_fish_en.pdf.

2. Food and Agriculture Organization of the United Nations, *The State of World Fisheries and Aquaculture (SOFIA)*, 2014, fao.org/fishery/sofia/en.

3. See the documentary film by Mathilde Jounot, *Oceans, The Voice of the Invisibles,* Portfolio Production, 2016.

4. Alain Le Sann, "Qui veut des millions? Les pêcheurs entre les mains des fondations, des lobbies environnementalistes et des fonds d'investissements," *Bulletin Pêche et développement, no. 129,* Centre de réflexion, d'information et de solidarité avec les peuples d'Afrique, d'Asie et d'Amérique latine, June 1, 2016.

5. Marine Stewardship Council, msc.org.

6. Blue Fish, European Association for the promotion of sustainable and responsible fisheries, bluefisheurope.org/en.

7. "Les algues," *Biocontact,* no. 210, February 2011, biocontact.fr/magazines-numeriques-au-format-pdf/19-b.html.

8. TecKnowMetrix, *État de l'art: Projet Algasud,* July 2009, algasud.fr/getlibrarypublicfile.php/100/algasud/collection_library/2009 00074/0001/LivrableDraft_AlgaSud_300 709.pdf.

9. Interview with Cécile Guiochon.

10. The tidal coefficient is associated with the amplitude of the oscillation of the semi-diurnal tide. See marees.free.fr/coefficients.html.

### CHAPTER 20

1. Bruno Parmentier, *Faim zero: En finir avec la faim dans le monde* (Paris, La Découverte, 2014).

2. See cepdarmandie.com.

3. Perrine and Charles Hervé-Gruyer, *Permaculture: Guérir la Terre, nourrir les hommes* (Arles, France, Actes Sud, 2014).

4. Jean-Martin Fortier, *The Market Gardener: A Successful Grower's Handbook for Small-Scale Organic Farming* (Gabriola Island, British Columbia, New Society, 2014).

### NEXT STEPS IN HUMAN PERMACULTURE

i. Two links on the history of permaculture in France: Passerelle Éco, passerelleco.info/auteur.php?id_auteur=11261, and Le paysage comestible, lepaysagecomestible.com/andy-et-jessie-darlington.

# Index

# About the Authors

**BERNARD ALONSO** has been a permaculture practitioner since 1993, and he is the co-founder of the Collaborative International University of Transition (UCIT). Increasingly in demand as a facilitator, speaker, coach/project designer, Alonso makes himself available around the world to promote the application of his effective human permaculture tools. His reputation as a coach attracts businesses, associations, schools, and groups in search of change who wish to make sense of their actions to rebuild or build their own life design. He currently resides in Quebec, Canada. permaculturehumaneinternationale.org

**CÉCILE GUIOCHON** is a French journalist and works on topics related to the ecological transition. Holder of a Permaculture Design Certificate, she co-created in Brittany, France, the association E-Kêr, Where We Live — in the Breton language, which is raising awareness on climate issues. She is co-founder of the company KerWatt, which develops citizen renewable energy projects in Brittany, France. e-ker.org

**MARIE QUILVIN** is a French illustrator and designer. After working in Parisian creative agencies, she created Ecotopie, a studio that gives shape to new ideas and ecosystems centered on humans with high social and environmental values.

"Utopia is not the unrealizable but the unrealized" — Théodore Monod (French biologist, scientist and humanist [1902–2000]).

mariequilvin.com

## A Note about the Publisher

NEW SOCIETY PUBLISHERS is an activist, solutions-oriented publisher focused on publishing books for a world of change. Our books offer tips, tools, and insights from leading experts in sustainable building, homesteading, climate change, environment, conscientious commerce, renewable energy, and more — positive solutions for troubled times.

We're proud to hold to the highest environmental and social standards of any publisher in North America. When you buy New Society books, you are part of the solution!

- We print all our books in North America, never overseas
- All our books are printed on **100% post-consumer recycled paper,** processed chlorine free, with low-VOC vegetable-based inks (since 2002)
- Our corporate structure is an innovative employee shareholder agreement, so we're one-third employee-owned (since 2015)
- We're carbon-neutral (since 2006)
- We're certified as a B Corporation (since 2016)

At New Society Publishers, we care deeply about *what* we publish — but also about *how* we do business.

Download our catalogue at https://newsociety.com/Our-Catalog, or for a printed copy please email info@newsocietypub.com or call 1-800-567-6772 ext 111.

### ENVIRONMENTAL BENEFITS STATEMENT

**New Society Publishers** saved the following resources by printing the pages of this book on chlorine free paper made with 100% post-consumer waste.

| TREES | WATER | ENERGY | SOLID WASTE | GREENHOUSE GASES |
|-------|-------|--------|-------------|-------------------|
| 39 | 3,200 | 16 | 130 | 17,000 |
| FULLY GROWN | GALLONS | MILLION BTUs | POUNDS | POUNDS |

Environmental impact estimates were made using the Environmental Paper Network Paper Calculator 4.0. For more information visit www.papercalculator.org.

MIX
Paper from
responsible sources
FSC® C016245

new society
PUBLISHERS
www.newsociety.com